VANCOUVER

THE UNKNOWN CITY

VANCOUVER

THE UNKNOWN CITY

John Mackie
and
Sarah Reeder

ARSENAL PULP PRESS

VANCOUVER

ARSENAL PULP PRESS
103 - 1014 Homer Street
Vancouver, B.C.
Canada V6B 2W9
arsenalpulp.com

The publisher gratefully acknowledges the support of the Canada Council for the Arts and the
British Columbia Arts Council for its publishing program, and the Government of Canada
through the Book Publishing Industry Development Program for its publishing activities.

Design by Lisa Eng-Lodge
Production assistance by Judy Yeung
Cover photography by Joseph Devenney/Getty Images

Printed and bound in Canada

National Library of Canada
Cataloguing in Publication Data

Mackie, John, 1956-
  Vancouver : the unknown city / John Mackie & Sarah Reeder.

  (Unknown city)
  Includes index.
  ISBN 1-55152-147-4

  1. Vancouver (B.C.) ñ Guidebooks. I. Reeder, Sarah, 1971- II. Title.
III. Series.

FC3847.18.M32 2003   917.11'33044   C2003-911200-4

c o n t e n t s

acknowledgments

Thanks to all the Vancouver experts whose brains I have picked over the years for information about the city, particularly John Atkin, Don Luxton, Carol Haber, Joan Seidl, Verne Bethel, Dal Richards, Hugh Pickett, Archie MacDonald, Jim Kearney, Red Robinson, and the late greats, Jack Cullen and Al Principe (who could remember the pre-First World War streetcar routes, for God's sake). If I didn't thank my good friend Kerry Gold she'd probably kill me, so thanks, Kerry, and thanks also to fellow writers Tom Hawthorn, Greg Potter, Doug Ward, Tom Barrett, Lee Bacchus, and Nadia Moharib. I suppose I should also thank inspirational music buddies like Pete Bourne and the Copyright/Slow crew, Kurt Dahle, Corrine Culbertson, Randy Bachman, k.d. lang, Jeff Hatcher, Billy Cowsill, Wimpy, Gerry Useless, Joey Shithead, and Art Bergmann. And, of course, I would like to thank my family, my friends, my dog Junior, and my cat Rocky.
– John W. Mackie Jr

Many thanks to the sharp-eyed researchers who worked on sections of this book: Elizabeth Bachinsky, Karen Munnis, Marguerite Pigeon, and Emily Urquhart. My gratitude to the many talented *Vancouver FASHION Magazine* interns, writers, and staff whose work for the magazine informed several of this book's chapters, including: Murray Bancroft, Tanya Bielas, Deborah Campbell, Gelareh Dahrabi, Kate Maclennan, Sarah Murray, Jenni Nelson, and Lisa Sherman. And thanks to our many informants and co-conspirators, who shall remain faceless and nameless. We could not have done it without you.
– Sarah Reeder

introduction

As cities go, Vancouver is just a toddler. Founded in 1886, the city is still forging its identity and discovering its place in the world, like a two-year-old finding its feet. It's a city of youthful vigour, optimism, and pioneerism: a staggering forty-eight percent of Vancouver residents were born outside Canada. There is a constantly morphing civic landscape to explore (with a few bumps and scrapes along the way) and a quickly disappearing heritage to document and preserve. Vancouver is one of those places that's hard to draw a bead on, because it's a constantly moving target. It gets torn down and rebuilt anew every few decades, subcultures (like the hippies) come and go, and so do whole industries (not so long ago, False Creek was filled with lumber mills and bears roamed Kits Beach).

The city also has two distinct personalities: there is the official picture postcard Vancouver – safe, clean, and somewhat bland – and the *real* one – a little wild, a little underground, and much more fun. This book deals with the latter. It attempts to shed some light on secret parts of the city even lifelong residents might not be aware of, to gather stories and anecdotes and lists and fashion them into some sort of alternative guidebook for people looking to dig a little deeper into Canada's Terminal City.

For this book, we've walked the back alleys, rattled on locked doors, tickled the city's underbelly, and muddled over manuscripts. We've made new friends – perhaps new enemies – along the way. All in the interest of what we hope will be both a subversive and seductive account of the unknown city.

Did we miss something? Have you got an unknown story about Vancouver? Let us know at *arsenalpulp.com* and you could win a free copy of the next edition of this book.

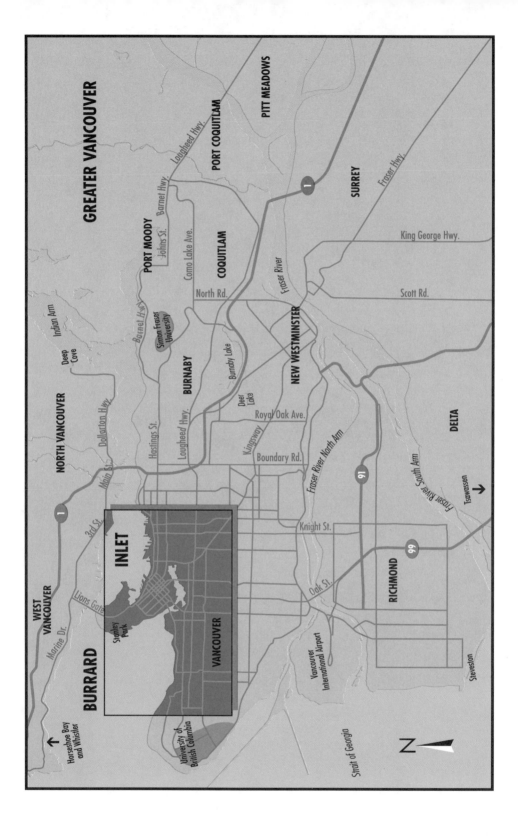

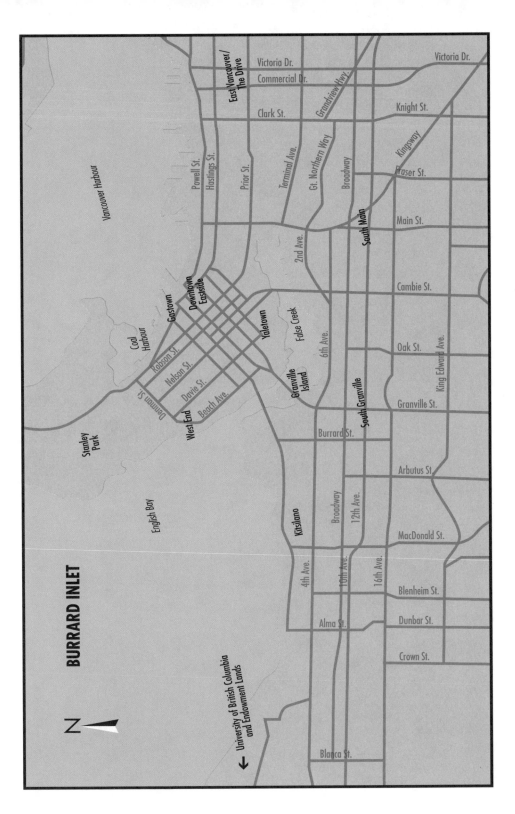

Landmarks & Destinations

I once sat on a plane beside a Trotskyite chainsaw salesman from Ottawa who noted that while Vancouver had a beautiful setting, it was blandsville as a city. Now, Ottawa, that was a city, he proclaimed.

I beg to differ. Vancouver may be young, as cities go, but it has a wild history and plenty of fantastic cultural attributes. Ottawa may have the Parliament Buildings, but we have the neon seahorse of the Only Sea Food restaurant. Toronto has the CN Tower, but we've got a high-rise with a tree on the roof. Paris may have the Louvre, but we've got the Marine Building, the finest art deco structure in Canada. This is a city, dammit, not just a great location.

Tall Tree

One of the oddest landmarks in Vancouver is the high-rise apartment building with the tree on the roof in the West End. The tree isn't just there for novelty's sake; it's there to symbolize the height of the 250-foot-tall Douglas fir trees that dominated the area before Europeans arrived to cut them all down. Just in case you don't get the message, there are also faux-fossilized tree stumps in front of the building.

Located at 1919 Beach Avenue and designed by architect Richard Henriquez, **Eugenia Place**'s interior is quite luxurious. All apartments in the building take up an entire floor,

Photo: Solo

and one family apparently owns five. Many of the 3,000-sq-ft apartments are *pied à terres* for wealthy people who live elsewhere: if you pass by at night and most of the building is dark, it's 'cause nobody's there.

One of the most interesting features of old buildings downtown is their exterior walls, which were often painted as giant ads for long-dead companies. Sadly, time takes its toll on the old ads, as the rain, sun, and wind chip away at the paint. But a fully intact and incredibly bright ad wall recently appeared from the dead when a 1907 building was knocked down at 537 Main Street. The largest ad was for G.A. Barrett and Co., a real estate company that went out of business around the time of the First World War. There was also a big sign for F.E. Hose Co. Wines and Liquors, a company that folded shortly after B.C. introduced prohibition in 1917. A third ad was for Murray Brothers plumbing, which lasted until 1952, after moving shop to West Vancouver.

The Barrett and Hose companies pop up in city directories in 1902-1903, which is probably when the signs were made; the Murray Brothers sign was probably completed in 1906. The Barrett ad features a giant orange flag waving in front of a black backdrop. Beneath the flag is a painted globe topped by the legend, "We cover the earth." There is also a giant white finger pointing across the street, because the Barrett store was actually located on the other side of Main. Except it wasn't called Main Street in those days: the sign reads "G.A. Barrett and Co., 538 Westminster Avenue." Westminster became Main in 1910, when several street names were changed.

The Hose sign is more straight-forward – simple lettering on a wall. F.E. Hose was also located across the street, at 514 and 504 Westminster. It appears to have been a retail and wholesale booze outlet – in Vancouver's infancy, liquor was sold in private stores. Hose may also have been a co-owner of the Stanley Park Brewery in the West End.

The signs date to a very early period. Vancouver was only 16 years old in 1902, and had a population of only 24,342. The early 1900s were a boom period and the population doubled to 50,379 by 1906, only four years later. During this time, Westminster Avenue was a major thoroughfare: the Carnegie Library was on the corner of Hastings, City Hall was next door, and retail merchant Charles Woodward had his first Vancouver store at 624 Westminster.

START OVER STRATHCONA

The city's oldest neighbourhood has become its trendiest, after a century of being considered the poor side of town. **Strathcona** residents include artist Stan Douglas, CBC radio host Bill Richardson, photographer Lincoln Clarkes, Railway Club booker Janet Forsythe, heritage advocate/author John Atkin, movie writers/directors John and Tony Pantages and David Hauka, and musicians Kurt Dahle (New Pornographers), Dan Bejar (Destroyer, New Pornographers), Corrine Culbertson (The Gay), among others. k.d. lang used to have a place there before she left Vancouver for L.A., and photographer Jeff Wall has a studio there.

Unfortunately, the old ad wall was covered up again only a couple of months after it was unearthed when a new building was erected.

Hycroft isn't just one of Vancouver's grand old mansions, it's also one of its most haunted. There are apparently seven ghosts stalking the 30-room house (*1489 McRae Ave.*), which was built for General Alexander Duncan McRae in 1909. McRae and his wife Blanche are presumed to be still in residence at the house, six decades after they passed into the hereafter. Three ghosts are supposed to be soldiers who died in the mansion when it was used as a hospital/convalescent home from 1943 to 1960. The head nurse of the convalescent home is also there, looking after them.

And there is a crying ghost on the upper floors who might be the spectral remains of Janet Smith, a young Scottish nursemaid who was murdered in 1924 at 3851 Osler, which was owned by one of McRae's daughters. There is a long-standing high society rumour that Smith was really killed at Hycroft, and spirited away to the Osler house. This doesn't make much sense – if you going to move a murder victim, would you move her to your daughter's house? But the rumour persists, nonetheless.

It seems the ghosts aren't particularly fond of film crews who use the house for shoots, and often try to scare them silly (admittedly, something many Vancouverites would also like to do to film crews). One carpenter swears a ghost threw a chair at him, and a director claims to have seen Mrs. McRae walking down the grand staircase during shooting. The big hot-spot for apparitions is by the bar in the basement, where a morgue was located during the hospital years.

Whether or not there are ghosts, the house does harbour secrets. McRae had a secret door to his personal library. He also had secret stairways at the back of the house for the servants, a secret passageway from the bar to the wine room (maybe used to sneak away booze during prohibition), and a secret tunnel under the house to his vegetable garden across 16th Avenue.

For most of its life, Strathcona has been called the East End, and was home to successive waves of working class immigrants: English, Italian, Ukrainian, Japanese, and Chinese. Most of the modest homes in the neighbourhood, which runs from Gore to Clark and Alexander to Atlantic, were built before the First World War, and until recently were in a fairly bad state. In the '50s and '60s, the 'hood was declared a ghetto and a blight by politicians, do-gooders, and the media, and many houses were knocked down to make way for social housing. Now the Victorian and Edwardian houses are considered *très chic*, and fetch prices between $300,000 to $400,000. But there are still bargains to be had. Some homeowners and realtors feel the old homes are just tear-downs, and several have been listed for under $200,000 in the last couple of years.

A remake of the movie classic *The Mummy* unleashed a world-wide wave of hysteria (or laughter) among horror fans around the globe in 1999. But if you want to see the real thing, you can head down to the **Vancouver Museum** (*1100 Chestnut St., 604-736-4431*), and see Panechates, who met his maker 2,000 years ago.

"It looks like he might have been murdered," says Venetia Nelson of the Museum. "He had a lot of broken bones and a fractured skull. He was probably 10 years old, but was very tiny – people were a lot smaller back then."

Panechates hails from the Valley of the Kings in Egypt, and was donated to the museum by a collector named Kidd in 1922. "When it was donated to the museum they thought it was a girl, because he was small," relates Nelson. "When X-rays came about they realized he was a boy. I think his name used to be Diana."

The mummy was a big favourite at the old Vancouver Museum in the Carnegie Library (now the Carnegie Centre) at Hastings and Main. Because he's fairly fragile and can't be exposed to light, he was out of circulation for several years. But old-timers kept asking where he was, so the Museum decided to make him part of its Orientation Room.

The Orientation Room is brimming with cool objects. The mummy isn't nearly as scary-looking as a homemade bicycle that was made in Barkerville in 1869 – your bones rattle just looking at the iron and wire frame. But for kids, especially naughty ones, the most sinister object is probably the strap from the old Boys Industrial School. It may have been made in 1910, but it still looks like it could inflict a lot of pain today. On a cheerier note, there are also some marvellous turn-of-the-century toys, like a windup horse racing toy and a toy racing car.

The Museum's permanent display gives visitors a capsule history of Vancouver. The displays are excellent, including a reconstruction of a 19th-century trading post, a reconstruction of the cramped steerage quarters that brought thousands of immigrants to B.C. in the 19th century, and a reconstruction of a typical parlour, bedroom, and kitchen in Vancouver circa 1910. Take special note of the model of the Vancouver area in 1881, which is fascinating – virtually all the city was forest and the shoreline was totally different.

Photo: VPL 22035A

OFF-LIMIT RESORT

The **Wigwam Inn** is one of Vancouver's most out-of-the-way landmarks. Located at the head of Indian Arm and accessible only by water, the inn was the brainchild of a former *Vancouver Province* advertising salesman, Benny Dickens, who envisioned a luxury resort with a Native theme that could cater to the upper crust. He brought in a German financier who was living in Vancouver, Gustavo Constantin Alvo von Alvensleben, who talked champagne heiress Emma V. Mumm (and maybe Kaiser Wilhelm) into investing in the venture. The inn was opened in 1910, and in 1911 attracted guests like John D.

Photo: Solo

Rockefeller and John Jacob Astor. But when the First World War broke out in 1914, von Alvensleben was accused of being a German spy (something he denied to his death), and moved to Seattle.

In any event, the rich and famous soon stopped coming. Still, it flourished as a local resort until the 1950s, when it entered a somewhat seedy period. In 1962, owner Fats Robertson was charged with operating an illegal gambling club on the premises. It fell into disrepair until 1986, when it was bought and refurbished by the Royal Vancouver Yacht Club. Alas, it's now off-limits to the public.

At 48 storeys and 450 feet high, the **Sheraton Wall Centre** was the tallest building in Vancouver on the highest point of land downtown when it was opened in 2001. Its striking elliptical form and two-tone blend of light and dark glass make it a natural landmark, and one that will be generating controversy for years to come, because it was originally supposed to look a lot different.

Developer Peter Wall saw the Wall Centre as the crowning achievement of his life's work, and looked at a staggering 800 different colours before settling on a cool dark silver-blue. He also made sure there were no aluminum mullions visible on the exterior to clutter the smooth, reflective effect he wanted to get with the glass. "I had a '79 Aston Martin Lagonda and it had no chrome," he says. "I said [to the architects] 'Visualize this car: that's what I want [the building] to look like.' Elegant, but simple."

City of Vancouver planners were wowed by architect Peter Busby's design, and Wall got the go-ahead. But when Wall started to install his glass, the city freaked, insisting he had agreed to use lighter glass. The city sued Wall, Wall counter-sued the city, and a compromise was reached in which the bottom 30 floors are dark glass and the top 18 are lighter (which is the reason why the Wall Centre is a two-tone building).

Wall is a flamboyant fellow, known for wearing huge wraparound shades and a scarf and for smoking big stogies. He had offered the city $2 million to $3 million to let him keep his dark glass on the building, but it declined, so he changed it, at a cost of about $5 million.

But he had one final trick up his sleeve. Take a close look at the building in the afternoon, and you'll notice that the lighter part of the building is riddled with dark patches. That's because Peter Wall outfitted each unit with dark blinds which mimic the original dark glass when closed.

Incidentally, the dark part of the tower is a hotel, and the lighter half is made up of 74 luxury condos that sold for $575,000 to $4 million. One couple combined four units on the 47th and 48th floors into a 6,800-sq-ft mansion in the sky. Movie star Jean-Claude Van Damme combined another three units to live in when he's in town. And about 40 percent of the condos were purchased by wealthy Americans.

The Promise of Gold Mountain

The modern, cosmopolitan, ethnically diverse Vancouver didn't develop without a lot of struggle. The first Chinese arrived in B.C. during the Fraser River gold rush in 1858; unable to stake a claim on virgin ground because of racism, they worked the discarded tailings from white miners. But the back-breaking work paid off for some miners, who were able to return to their impoverished homeland and purchase property with a few gold coins. In China, British Columbia became known as Gold Mountain.

The next big wave of Chinese came in the 1880s, when 17,000 were imported to build the Canadian Pacific Railway. They were paid $1 per day – half what Caucasians earned – and were usually given the most dangerous work. An estimated 600 died.

GASTOWN CODE BREAKER

Gastown looks pretty cool on the outside, but its interiors can also be pretty wild. Or scary. The 1907 **Winters Hotel** (*Water and Abbott*) is one of the few buildings in Vancouver with enclosed interior courtyards. Rooms in the middle of the structure have windows onto a hallway, rather than the outside; the hallways are partly illuminated by skylights. This arrangement is so against the modern building code it's ridiculous, but is allowed because the building was built long before the code came in. Many of the rooms in the Winters Hotel also feature original antique furnishings that date to when the hotel opened, or at least did before the current owner started selling the furnishings off in favour of more modern decor.

When the railway was finished, Vancouver's Chinatown was established on the shores of False Creek, which then came up to Pender Street. Chinatown thrived, but some Caucasians were alarmed at the growing Chinese population. Chinatown was portrayed as a centre of vice, opium dens, gambling dens, and secret passageways under the streets.

The federal government tried to stem the flow of Chinese immigrants with the Chinese Immigration Act of 1885, which imposed a head tax of $50 on Chinese immigrants. When Chinese kept coming, the head tax was raised to $100 in 1902, and $500 in 1903. In 1907, simmering racism exploded in a two-day riot by Caucasians against the Chinese and Japanese populations.

From 1923 to 1947, Chinese immigration was officially blocked by the Chinese Exclusion Act. Only 25 Chinese were allowed to immigrate to Canada during that time. Even after it was repealed, immigration was restricted to 200 per year.

Chinese were given the right to vote in 1949, but the immigration restrictions weren't lifted until 1967. The first wave of immigrants came in the late '60s from Hong Kong, where the Cultural Revolution in China had spawned riots. Hong Kong emmigration surged in the 1990s in the political uncertainty over the 1997 handover of Hong Kong to China. In 1994 alone, 16,159 Chinese moved from Hong Kong to B.C.

But Chinese immigration to the Lower Mainland has not been restricted to those from Hong Kong. In fact, mainland China is now the biggest source of Chinese immigrants, followed by Taiwan, and then Hong Kong. The population with Chinese ancestry in 1961 was approximately 15,000. In the 2001 census, it was 342,665.

HARDWIRED SPEED SPINE

Have you ever wondered why so many Internet and high tech companies are located downtown? No, it's not just because young people don't like to work in the burbs. The main Internet cable for Vancouver runs underneath Hastings street to Simon Fraser University's Harbour Centre campus. Which means you get the absolute fastest Internet service downtown.

Photo: Solo

The oldest building is Chinatown is also one of the oddest. The **Wing Sang building** (*51 E. Pender St.*) was built in 1889, just three years after Vancouver was born. It was the residence and headquarters for Yip Sang, who once owned much of early Chinatown.

The main floor of the building is a few steps below the street, because it was built before the street was paved. The second floor has a door to nowhere; in the old days, workers would open it and hoist goods up and into a warehouse upstairs.

The original two-storey brick building was extended in both 1901 and 1912, so that it now covers four lots and includes a three-storey building in the front, a six-storey building in the back, and 40,000 square feet of space.

One enters the rear building via an alley just to the west of it, or through an elevated walkway that connects the third floor of the front building to the fourth floor of the rear one. (Got that?) But you can't see the rear building from the front, because there is a small wooden facade blocking off the alley.

In the back, a whole other side of Chinatown emerges: a labyrinth of brick buildings, courtyards, and alleys that housed Chinatown's residents for decades. Essentially, the front buildings on Pender were commercial, while residents lived in back.

FALSE LAND ON FALSE CREEK

The next time you're passing the Pacific Central train station on Main Street, consider this: you're driving on what used to be water, or at least mud. In Vancouver's early days, False Creek came up to the bluff at Clark Drive. To get across Main — which was then called Westminster Avenue — you had to cross a bridge from the present-day Ivanhoe Hotel to 2nd Avenue.

Most of the time, the area was mud flats. When civic leaders were looking for land for railway yards so that there would be some competition for the Canadian Pacific Railway, which owned much of Vancouver, they decided to create some by filling in the False Creek flats. Sixty-one acres (25 hectares) of marshland and mud flats were drained and filled in between 1916 and 1920. The dirt for the infill came from the Grandview cut, which then became a short-cut from the railways to the flats.

Yip Sang built the six-storey structure in the rear to house his family. He had four wives and 23 children, one of the perks of being a wealthy Chinese merchant in the late 19th and early 20th centuries. His life was a classic rags-to-riches story: he was born in China in 1845, and left, in 1864, to seek a better life in San Francisco. In 1881, he moved to Vancouver and went to work for the Canadian Pacific Railway, which was then building the western portion of its transcontinental line, largely with Chinese labourers.

Yip held several positions with the CPR: bookkeeper, timekeeper, and paymaster. He also became superintendent for the Kwong On Wo company, which imported 6,000 to 7,000 Chinese labourers to work on the railway. When the railway was completed in 1885, Yip returned to China. But he moved back to the then-two-year-old city of Vancouver in 1888 and started an import-export business called the Wing Sang Company. He also became the CPR's Chinese passenger agent for its steamship line.

Yip's building was a centre for commerce. The main floor was the unofficial bank of Chinatown where workers could send money to relatives in China. It was also where Chinese Vancouverites booked passage on steamships to the homeland.

Yip Sang became a wealthy man, but he never forgot his humble beginnings. He co-founded the Chinese Benevolent Association, and built a seven-storey building in Shanghai Alley to house new immigrants until they found work in Canada.

Shanghai Alley was a gated community, with an 11 p.m. curfew. There was a reason Shanghai Alley was locked off: during the infamous Chinatown riot of 1907, members of the all-white Asiatic Exclusion League went on a rampage, destroying every store window in Chinatown. As a result, Yip Sang put up gates to keep undesirables out.

When members of the Chinese community told Yip Sang his largesse would make him go broke, he responded by building an eight-storey building for even more immigrants. The Shanghai Alley building is gone, but the eight-storey building is now the West Hotel on Carrall between Hastings and Pender.

Two stations were built on the land, for the Canadian Northern and Union Pacific railways. Unfortunately, the railroad boom ended just as the stations were completed. Canadian Northern went out of business, and its assets were taken over by the government-owned Canadian National Railway. The Burlington-Northern eventually took over the smaller Union Pacific station, which was knocked down in the mid-1960s.

False Creek hasn't entirely vanished from the area. During high tide, the ground becomes saturated with water, making work below ground impossible, and sometimes resulting in some minor flooding in the Pacific Central station basement.

The front portion of the Wing Sang building is in remarkable shape, with upper floors that could be straight out of 1889: floor-to-ceiling wainscotting, century-old linoleum, and even a blackboard where Yip Sang's children studied their lessons. Sadly, somebody stole the original fir floor a couple of years ago: old-growth fir is worth a small fortune.

The back building has been vacant since 1975 when the city brought in bylaws that would have required the Yip family to spend a prohibitive amount of money on upgrades. It will likely be torn down and rebuilt in a redevelopment scheme if and when the oft-talked about rejuvenation of Chinatown takes place.

Yip Sang died in 1927, and his family lost many of the buildings in his empire during the Depression. But his descendants have had a big impact on Canada: his 17th son, Dock Yip, became the first Chinese lawyer in Canada in 1945, and two years later was a key figure in the repeal of the Chinese Exclusion Act of 1923, which barred Chinese immigration into Canada.

FAUX GASTOWN

Gastown is the oldest part of Vancouver, and is rightly designated a historic district. But much of what passes for heritage isn't. Thousands upon thousands of tourists gather by the Steam Clock at Water and Abbott to see its famous whistle blow. But the Steam Clock is actually powered by electricity, and dates to 1977, not the 1880s.

The cobblestone streets and sidewalks are also faux, a 1970s idea of heritage. The original streets would have looked more like the grey granite stones on Hamilton Street by Victory Square, or even been made out of wood and then covered by

Photo: Solo

asphalt. Walk down Alexander Street and you can see old wooden "cobblestones" peeking up where the asphalt has worn through. The sidewalks were originally made of wooden planks, which got quite slippery in the winter months.

Water Street is now Gastown's main commercial thoroughfare, but it was originally a warehouse district. Vancouver's first big shopping street was nearby on Cordova. There are several remnants of Cordova's glory days, such as the 1890 Boulder Hotel at the northwest corner of Cordova and Carrall and the 1889 Dunn-Miller block across the street, now the home of the Army & Navy department store. But many of the early Cordova stores were knocked down during the many expansions of the Woodwards building and the construction of its parkade.

Nice Deal If You Can Get It

Have you ever wondered why Vancouver is in Vancouver, rather than New Westminster or Port Moody? It's because the B.C. government gave much of the city to the **Canadian Pacific Railway**.

Back in 1885, the CPR was looking for a location for its western terminus. Many observers, and land speculators, felt the CPR would choose Port Moody, because it lay at the head of Burrard Inlet. New Westminster would also have been a logical location, because it was already established (it was founded in 1858).

But the CPR chose to move the line 20 kilometres up the inlet to the shore of Coal Harbour. Coal Harbour did have some natural advantages, such as deep water for a port. But it was later revealed that the railway had cut a deal with British Columbia Premier William Smithe giving it 6,000 acres of free land on what would become the west side (roughly from Macdonald to Main, and from English Bay to West 57th Avenue). Landowners also gave the CPR a ton of land in the West End.

Where Not to Be When the Big One Hits

Coal Harbour gets its name from the discovery of coal there in the 1850s; the first white settler in Vancouver, John Morton, built a house in the area in 1862. The natural shoreline of the area is at the foot of the bluff overlooking the harbour, where the Marine Building is located. Most of the land now being developed was originally tidal flats that were filled in; pictures of the first train to arrive at the CPR station in May 1887 show railway tracks on piles. As a result, you might not want to be walking along the new Coal Harbour development during an earthquake, because many areas might liquify.

Photo: VPL 6771

Charles Woodward opened his first **Woodwards** department store in Vancouver on March 1, 1892 at the northeast corner of Westminster and Harris (now Main and Georgia). The population of Vancouver at the time was 13,000. Woodward's store prospered, so he decided to expand. He gambled that the downtown would move west up Hastings, and purchased a lot at the northwest corner of Abbott and Hastings, a site described as "swampland" and a "frog pond."

The Hastings street store was a four-storey wood frame structure with a brick façade. It had a "soft opening" on November 4, 1903 – newspaper ads still listed the store at Westminster and Harris. But nine days later, on Friday, November 13, the Westminster store was closed and Hastings became the sole Woodwards outlet.

Sale items on opening day included men's suits for $6, "Catholic tooth powder" for 15 cents, and Woodwards "headache wafers" for 20 cents. "Fine quality storm rubbers" could be had for 55 cents, "$2 Bibles" were selling for $1.50, and four packets of Atlas toilet paper cost 25 cents. The new store was such a success that two floors were added in 1908, the first of 11 additions. The original 1903 store is still there, on the corner of Abbott and Hastings.

For most of the 20th century, Woodwards was *the* Vancouver department store. It was known for its one-price sales (which started off as 25-cent day, went to 98-cent day, and finally $1.49 day), its elaborate

BOOM BOOM, SPLASH SPLASH

The waters of **Coal Harbour** used to teem with halibut, herring, and octopus. But then in 1882, Sprott's Oilery, a floating fish oil and cannery plant, came along. Sprott's developed an ingenious way of bringing the fish to the surface – throwing dynamite in the water. It apparently worked like gangbusters, but within two years the fish stopped coming. Wonder why ... ?

When Captain George Vancouver sailed into Coal Harbour in 1792, he thought **Stanley Park** was an island. So did the Spanish explorers Narvaez and Galiano, who arrived about the same time.

Why? Because **Lost Lagoon** was originally part of Coal Harbour, and at high tide, the tidal marsh filled with water almost to Second Beach — there was only a thin strip of land connecting the park to the West End. At low tide, the lagoon would virtually vanish, which led Pauline Johnson to write the poem, "The Lost Lagoon," that gave the body of water its name.

When the park was first opened, visitors on the Georgia Street side came in over a bridge, or paid 25 cents to be ferried over to a pier near the Nine O'Clock Gun. In the early 1900s, the park board thought about filling in Lost Lagoon for a playground, but didn't have the cash. So it erected the causeway in 1916, and Lost Lagoon became a fresh water lake, with water pumped in from the city supply.

Christmas window displays, and a miniature Eiffel Tower that was installed on the roof in 1929. It was said that you could see the searchlight on top of the mini-Eiffel from Vancouver Island. Originally there was a Big W at the bottom of the Eiffel Tower, but this changed in 1956, when Woodwards decided to replace the searchlight with a red neon W — the same one that is there today.

At its height in the 1970s, Woodwards had 51 stores in B.C. and Alberta, and $500 million in annual sales. But like many of the big old department store chains, it experienced financial problems in the 1980s. Woodwards stores went bankrupt in 1993, and on January 31 that year, the Hastings street store closed its doors. The building and parking lot were then put up for sale for $30 million. In 1995, the department store was sold to Fama Holdings for $5 million, while the city of Vancouver spent $11 million to buy the Woodwards parking garage. Situated in what is now known as the Downtown Eastside, the store remains controversially empty as business and social housing groups debate its future.

Photo: Sofo

Photo: Solo

There are a lot of luxury hotel rooms in Vancouver, but the classiest might be the Royal Suite at the **Fairmont Hotel Vancouver**. The suite was built for the 1939 royal visit of King George VI and Queen Elizabeth (the Queen Mother), who were dispatched to the colonies to drum up support for the forthcoming war with Hitler's Germany.

In fact, the hotel owes its completion to the royal visit. Work on the hotel had begun in 1929, but was halted because of the Great Depression, with the steel skeleton of the building looming over downtown. When the royal visit was announced, the hotel was rushed to completion, opening on May 25, 1939.

The suite was indeed fit for a king and queen, designed in the latest art deco style. It originally took up an entire floor, with eight bedrooms, a sitting room, a living room, and dining room. Today, it is divided into three suites.

The north side of the floor holds what is now referred to as the Royal Suite, which contains a massive 972-square-foot parlour and four bedrooms. But it's the Lieutenant-Governor's Suite on the south side that's truly remarkable, because it is virtually unchanged since 1939 – the teak walls, teak fireplace, and curved furniture are

RAINY DAYS ARE HERE AGAIN

On a sunny day **Deep Cove** is one of the most beautiful spots on earth. Framed by the North Shore Mountains, the placid waters of the Cove and Indian Arm are a real-life postcard, with an ever-changing seascape of boats, kayaks, and marine life.

But it's also the rainiest place in the Lower Mainland. The rain is estimated at 2,200 mm per year, compared to 1,600 mm in Vancouver, and 1,100 mm in White Rock. And while the mountains are picturesque, they also block out the sun, so it gets dark about an hour earlier than other parts of Vancouver.

all classic art deco. It has doubled as a presidential suite in several movies.

The irony is, the royals never stayed in the royal suite. King George and Queen Elizabeth arrived by train at the Canadian Pacific Railway station on the Royal Hudson at 10 a.m. on Monday, May 29, and left for Victoria aboard the Princess Marguerite at 4:45 p.m. the same day.

The suites are available to the public, but at a price: the Royal Suite goes for $1,500 per day.

The Hotel Vancouver is an interesting building, filled with all sorts of weird quirks. Visitors to the 14th floor seem to have the option of using eight elevators, but it's an illusion — two were never finished because of financial constraints. But there is apparently a ghostly woman in a red dress who uses the non-elevators from time to time. The top floor has an old CBC studio which used to broadcast big band leader Dal Richards from the hotel's Panorama Roof Ballroom, where he played from 1940 to 1965. The green hotel roof contains eight storeys of spooky-looking water tanks, air ducts, and a giant chimney that looks right out of the *Titanic*.

The current Hotel Vancouver is actually the third building to use the name. The second Hotel Vancouver (built in 1912, demolished in 1949) was the grandest and best one, with a renowned rooftop garden and restaurant.

City Halls That Never Were

There were numerous alternative plans for City Hall. The Pender and Cambie location was first proposed in the 1910s, but floundered in the economic slump that accompanied the First World War.

In 1928, the American guru of city planning, Harland Bartholemew, drew up plans for a grand civic complex at Burrard and Pacific, which included a monumental deco City Hall, tiered gardens rising up from the water, and the Burrard Bridge. The bridge was the only part of the plan that was ever built.

The city was also offered Vancouver's best deco structure, the Marine Building, as a location for its government. The Marine Building proved to be a financial disaster for its builders, bankrupting them after it was completed in 1930. The receivers offered to sell the building to the city for $1 million, less than half the $2.5 million construction cost. But the city said no.

If you can take the wet stuff, Deep Cove is the epitome of the "Super, Natural British Columbia" tourist slogan. Residents have some of the best hiking, skiing, snowboarding, kayaking, and boating in Canada in their backyard. There's a bit of everything in the area: tiny cottages from the days when the Cove was a summer resort, lots of spacious suburban specials from the '70s and '80s, and some multi-million-dollar waterfront palaces.

Author Malcolm Lowry (of *Under the Volcano* fame) was one of many early residents who lived in squatters' cabins along the shoreline in the 1940s and '50s. Lowry was evicted from his cabin in 1954, and it was torn down. A few blocks away, a street has been named Lowry Lane in his honour. A few years ago, a 6,000-sq-ft house there sold for $2 million.

One of Vancouver's many quirks is that **City Hall** is located at Cambie and West 12th Avenue, far away from the action downtown. This is Gerry McGeer's doing. The art deco city hall was built in the middle of the Depression as a make-work project. McGeer was running for mayor in 1934, and one of his big campaign planks was building a new city hall – which the city's movers and shakers had been talking about since 1910.

A McGeer campaign ad from the *Vancouver Sun* on December 6, 1934 screams, "Put Idle Money To Work! Build The New City Hall NOW! Start Things Going in Vancouver – The MONEY Is In The BANK – It Should Be Put To Work Creating JOBS and PAYROLLS." The ad features an artist's conception of "how the new city hall will look." It's pretty much as it is now – an elegant structure with graceful wings that rise up in symmetrical tiers to a central tower. There is one big difference, however: McGeer's City Hall was to be located just south of Victory Square at Pender and Cambie, in the old downtown core.

Everything was set for the building's construction on Pender, which was then the site of a school that eventually became Vancouver Community College downtown. But a protest by about 2,000 unemployed demanding food and shelter led McGeer to proclaim the Riot Act in Victory Square in 1935. McGeer then decided to move the proposed City Hall out of the downtown core; a place where it would be harder to mount such a protest. The new location was 12th and Cambie, on the site of the original Strathcona Park. There was also supposed to be a complementary building across Cambie, but in the end there wasn't enough money to get it built.

The first City Hall of note, by the way, was located beside the Carnegie Library on Westminster Avenue (now Main Street). It moved to the Holden Building (near Hastings and Carrall) from 1928 to 1936, when the new City Hall was opened.

CHURCH ALMIGHTY

Downtown Vancouver has several incredible old churches, but the most historic is arguably **Christ Church Cathedral** (*690 Burrard St. at Georgia*). The church was built in the Gothic revival style popular at the end of the 19th century. The first Anglican services on the site were held in a basement dubbed the Root Cellar in 1889; the actual church building was opened on February 17, 1895. Originally a parish church, it became the cathedral for the New Westminster diocese in 1929.

Photo: Solo

The Best Damn Map in Canada

It has long been a centre of Vancouver religious life, and is the church where members of the Royal Family worship when they're in Vancouver. It was very busy during the First and Second World Wars, and many of its stunning stained glass windows were donated by families to remember loved ones killed in battle.

In 1970, a plan to raze the church and build a highrise office tower on the site prompted a public outcry that saved it. The diocese was able to sell the "air rights" to the site to a developer, which then built the Park Place highrise tower down the street. Park Place's address, believe it or not, is 666 Burrard Street.

The **Challenger Relief Map** is one of B.C.'s enduring symbols. Since it was unveiled to the public at the British Empire Games in Vancouver in 1954, hundreds of thousands of visitors to the Pacific National Exhibition gazed in awe at the scale map of every mountain, valley, and lake in the province.

The map took George Challenger and his family seven years to build, is 76 by 80 feet, and is constructed from 989,842 pieces of quarter-inch fir plywood cut, painted and assembled on 1.1 x 2.7 meter plywood panels. The vertical scale, exaggerated six times, is one inch to 1,000 feet.

Challenger started making relief maps in the 1920s as a way of figuring the most efficient route to remove timber from remote areas. He constructed a relief map of southwestern B.C. for military and evacuation purposes during the Second World War and started the Challenger Map in 1946.

The B.C. Pavilion was built to house the map in 1954, and Challenger, so proud of the map that bears his name, asked the PNE Board if his ashes could lie beneath it. They gave their approval in 1959, and after his death in 1964, his ashes were stored in an urn beneath it.

But where the hell is it now?

Since 1997, the map has been kept at a Beekin's Storage warehouse in Richmond, awaiting a new home. The map became homeless after the Vancouver Park Board tore down the B.C. Pavillion, where it was housed, in the first phase of the return of the PNE grounds to parkland. His relatives mounted a legal challenge to keep the map at the PNE, but it failed. Challenger's ashes are now with his family.

LANDMARKS & DESTINATIONS 29

Photo: Solo

To really get a sense of the age of the **Carnegie Centre** (*20 W. Hastings St, 604-689-0397*) take a walk up its marvellous circular staircase. On the inner section, a century's worth of visitors have worn down the marble stairs, so it feels as if you're walking in someone's footsteps.

The stairs are worn because the Carnegie is one of Vancouver's most well-used and beloved institutions. The handsome neo-classical building at Hastings and Main was the main branch of the Vancouver Public Library from 1903 to 1958, was taken over by the Vancouver Museum for a few years, and is now a community centre and refuge for people in the impoverished Downtown Eastside.

FOR DARK AND STORMY NIGHTS

If Dr. Frankenstein had done his mad scientist thing in Vancouver, there is only one building that would have been suitable for his experiments — the **Buntzen Lake Powerhouse**.

There are actually two Buntzen Lake powerhouses — one built in 1903, the other in 1914 — and they were Vancouver's first source of hydroeclectic power. They are best seen from the water as you travel up Indian Arm.

The 1914 powerhouse looks like a cross between Frankenstein's castle and a medieval ruin. Many of the windows on the three-storey structure are broken, and it looks like it was last painted when Mackenzie King was prime minister. But the dilapidated look gives it a faded grandeur that's unique in the Lower Mainland. It would make a wicked loft conversion, except for the fact that it is still part of B.C. Hydro's power grid — every once in a while, water will come streaming out of the gates at the bottom, so don't go too close.

The 1903 powerhouse is also magnificent, cut from grey stone that gives it a real McGill University look. Cut into the side is its name — Lake Buntzen Power House, Vancouver Power Co. Ltd.

The Carnegie was one of 2,509 libraries paid for by the Scottish-American industrialist-turned-philanthropist, Andrew Carnegie, who amassed a fortune of $400 million in steel and railroads, then gave away $333 million before his death, including $50,000 for a Vancouver library.

When it was built, Hastings and Main (then called Westminster) was the heart of the city, surrounded by Vancouver's best nightlife, restaurants, and hotels. Situated beside Vancouver's old city hall, the new library was the intellectual centre of the young city, which was less than 20 years old and had a population of about 25,000.

Architect George W. Grant's design blended neo-classical and Romanesque themes. Outside, the most prominent features are a pair of two-storey-high columns, a sculpture of a lion's head above the entrance, and a mansard-like copper roof. But the most renowned feature is its exceptional collection of stained glass windows, depicting literary giants like Shakespeare, Milton, Spenser, Burns, Scott, and Moore.

The library moved in 1958, and the museum (which had been on the third floor before taking over the entire building) left for Vanier Park in 1967. The Carnegie building was left vacant for a decade, until Downtown Eastside activists like the late Bruce Eriksen and Libby Davies (now a federal MP) persuaded the city to turn it into a community centre. After a $2-million renovation, including an addition, the Carnegie Centre was opened in 1980.

Today the Carnegie Centre is used by 2,000 people a day, 365 days a year. It offers a little bit of everything: a library, a learning centre, classrooms, a cafeteria, a coffee shop, a gym, a fitness centre, pool tables, a seniors' centre, and even a couple of computer labs.

Secret Rooms
(and Room for Cyclists)

Photo: Solo

Photo: VPL 8401

The graceful art deco lines of the **Burrard Bridge** have made it one of Vancouver's most beloved structures. It was a monumental project when it was built in 1932, the first bridge over False Creek that was high enough for ships to pass under. (Prior to its construction, the old Granville and Cambie bridges had swing spans, which impeded traffic.) It is also the site of one of the city's great mysteries: just what is inside the rooms in the bridge's arches?

These days, not much: they're currently just ornamental. But a former B.C. Electric worker named Joe McPherson says there was a time when the north arch did have a function. Joe used to work in the trouble-shooting department of B.C. Electric, which provided electricity before W.A.C. Bennett created B.C. Hydro in 1961. In the 1950s, Joe went up into the room, which contained the controls for the lights on the bridge. He was then lifted up by a coworker to a trap-door entrance. Poking his head into the room was one of the spookiest things he's ever done.

BANK GOES BUST

Before 1935, anyone who had a bank in Canada could print their own money. These old non-Bank of Canada bank notes are quite rare, few more so than notes for the **Bank of Vancouver**.

The Bank of Vancouver was launched in the midst of a real estate and industrial boom in 1910 by some of B.C.'s most prominent capitalists, including Lieutenant-Governor James Paterson and future Vancouver mayor William Malkin. The bank's headquarters were at 167 West Hastings at Cambie, and it had several branches around the province. But the financial good times ended, and the bank went out of business on December 14, 1914. At the time, $325,000 worth of Bank of Vancouver notes were in circulation. Almost all the notes were then taken in to be redeemed at other banks. Today, less than 10 Bank of Vancouver banknotes that were in circulation are known to still exist, and almost never come on the market. A handful of proofs — unissued one-sided notes — have come to light in recent years, and sell for about $5,000 apiece.

They're handsome notes. The front of the $10 bill features a vintage turn-of-the-century forestry scene, with a couple of loggers perched on planks that have been notched into a giant fir tree. One logger is about to swing an axe, the other has a saw. The back of the note features a view of the legislative buildings in Victoria.

Unfortunately, the Bank of Vancouver's timing was bad. An anticipated boom in the north from a Grand Trunk Pacific rail line to Prince Rupert collapsed in 1912, when company president Charles Hays went down on the Titanic.

In 1914, the Dominion Trust company in Vancouver also went under. It left behind a Vancouver landmark — the big orange building at 207 West Hastings at Cambie — but its collapse was disastrous for investor confidence in small institutions like the Bank of Vancouver.

Photo: Judy Yeung

"It was an experience," he says. "Holy God. It was like an old monster film." The only light in the room was provided by Joe and the coworker, and the shadows seemed very dark indeed. Moreover, the cold, quiet room seemed to have been deserted for years and years, save for some nasty pigeons who weren't pleased to have visitors. "Oh jeez, the pigeons," he says, still recoiling at the memory. "They'd hammer ya."

An alternate theory is that the bridge was designed so that a swinging railway bridge could later be added underneath the main structure. The rooms in the arches were supposed to be the control towers for the railway span, but it was never built.

Vancouver architects Rob Grant and Peter Reese have a plan to build a new walking/bicycle bridge in the space where the railway trestle would have gone. It's one of several proposals the city is looking at to make room for cyclists on the bridge.

Boom! Bust. Boom! Bust. Boom!

Vancouver is a boom and bust city: when things are going well, optimism is boundless, and people fork out insane amounts of cash to buy and build real estate. When recession hits, doom and gloom sets in, and yesterday's business heroes often go belly up. As proof, look at the record of many of the city's landmark buildings. A good number drove their builders to the poorhouses.

The 1910 **Dominion Building** (*Hastings and Cambie*) owes its name to the Dominion Trust company, which built it and then went bankrupt in 1914, causing a crisis in local financial circles that helped do in the Bank of Vancouver. Depending on who's telling the story, the manager of the Dominion Trust company either committed suicide or was murdered.

Louis D. Taylor built the **World Tower** (*Pender and Beatty*) in 1912, when he was mayor of Vancouver and owner of a very successful newspaper. He lost the mayoralty a year later and then had to sell the paper, and building, when he ran into financial problems.

Abraham Goldstein lost the **Sylvia Hotel** (*1154 Gilford St., 604-681-9321*), built in 1913, because he couldn't keep up the mortgage payments during the depression that hit Vancouver during the First World War.

Construction on Vancouver's most distinctive structure, the art deco **Marine Building** (*Burrard and Hastings*), began in

PENTHOUSE LUXURIES

Prices for penthouse apartments downtown have risen into the stratosphere: $5 million and up for the super-luxurious pads on the waterfront. Developers throw in all sorts of snazzy features to lure buyers: private elevators, swimming pools, marble floors, you name it. Still, none of the zillion-dollar condos will ever have the cachet of Vancouver's original luxury penthouse: a two-storey apartment at the top of the city's most beautiful art deco structure, the **Marine Building** (*Burrard and Hastings*).

The Marine Building was supposed to be Vancouver's signature skyscraper, the West Coast equivalent to New York's Chrysler and Empire State buildings (albeit a lot smaller). Unfortunately it was completed just as the Great Depression hit, and the $2.5 million cost bankrupted its owners. An observation deck had been planned for the top floor, but

1929. Midway through construction, the Great Depression hit; the builders decided to finish the building, but it was a financial disaster, and they offered to sell it to the city of Vancouver for $1 million, less than half the $2.5 million construction cost. But the city declined, so the Marine Building was sold to the company that developed the British Properties.

Work on the current **Fairmont Hotel Vancouver** (*900 W. Georgia St., 604-684-3131*) also began in 1929, but the Canadian Pacific Railway decided to put a halt on construction during the Depression. This left the half-completed steel skeleton of the hotel looming over the skyline, a visible reminder of the economic hard times. It was finally completed in 1939, in time for a Royal Visit by King Edward and Queen Elizabeth (the Queen Mother).

In more recent times, the **Ford Theatre for the Performing Arts** (*777 Homer St.*) and **General Motors Place** were built during the mid-'90s development frenzy that accompanied a population boom fueled by people fleeing Hong Kong before it was repatriated to China. After a couple of years, the Ford went down with Torontonian Garth Drabinsky's Livent empire (it's since been resurrected by Colorado millionaires as **The Centre in Vancouver for Performing Arts**). Meanwhile, GM Place builder Arthur Griffiths wound up selling off his family's arena and sports franchises (the Canucks and Grizzlies) to pay off the debt he incurred by Thinking Big.

nobody had the spare cash to waste on taking in a breathtaking view of the harbour, and it was closed after a few months.

Fred Taylor of the British Pacific Properties would up buying the building for about $1 million in 1933. He installed his company offices on the top floor, then decided to convert the old observation deck to his downtown crash pad. Photos show an art deco masterpiece, with a soaring 17-foot ceiling, a *très chic* black marble fireplace, and wood-panelled walls. Two bedrooms were installed on a mezzanine level, and a giant chandelier copied from Rockefeller Centre in New York illuminated the living area.

Taylor's wife apparently preferred houses, however, and the main family residence remained in West Vancouver. The penthouse has been used as offices since the 1940s.

Photo: Solo

Spinning (With) Class

At the height of the carousel's popularity, there were 6,000 in operation throughout North America. Today, there are only 250 left – and the **Burnaby Village Museum** (*6501 Deer Lake at Canada Way, 604-293-6514*) has one of the best. It was made in 1912 by renowned carousel manufacturer C.W. Parker at his factory in Leavenworth, Kansas, and bounced around Texas and California before it found a home at the Pacific National Exhibition's Happyland amusement park in 1936.

The PNE donated it to the Museum in 1989, and it has been lovingly restored to its full glory. If it were to come on the market, it would probably fetch about US$1 million, but kids can ride it at the museum for a dollar.

The carousel is one of about 30 heritage attractions at the Burnaby Village Museum, which is located on a 10-acre site in Burnaby. The buildings are arranged in a village atmosphere, simulating Burnaby circa 1925. It's an interactive attraction, with a live blacksmith, tinsmith, and printer on hand to give demonstrations of their craft.

The original building on the site is Elsworth, a home built by Canadian Pacific Railway official Edwin Bateman when he retired to "the country" in 1922. It's furnished with period antiques, including an ancient toaster with electric coils straight out of a mad scientist's laboratory.

Burnaby Wallpaper

The Jesse Love Farmhouse is one of the oldest buildings in Burnaby. Built in 1893 for one of Burnaby's pioneer families, it was moved to its present location about 10 years ago and restored. It has the latest in 1920s ornamentation – pressed tin ceilings and linoleum carpets – and has a long harvest table in the kitchen that can be converted to a ping pong table on rainy afternoons. The living room walls feature a beautiful art deco wallpaper design. When the Museum showed it to wallpaper maker Bradbury and Bradbury of San Francisco, the manufacturer was stunned – it was the first existing example of the design Bradbury and Bradbury had ever seen. It is now being sold in their catalogue as "Burnaby Wallpaper."

ROCK HERITAGE

Local-boy-made-good Bryan Adams loves old buildings – he was one of Vancouver's most prominent critics of the decision to tear down the art deco Georgia Medical Building in the 1980s. He also puts his money where his mouth is: in the early 1990s, Adams bought and refurbished the former **Oppenheimer Brothers Warehouse** at 100 Powell at Columbia in Gastown, one of Vancouver's oldest and most important structures (David Oppenheimer was Vancouver's second mayor, from 1888 to 1891). He spent several years restoring the handsome red brick building to the way it looked when it was built in 1891 (albeit

Photo: Solo

Abooooooooout Face!

The new main branch of the **Vancouver Public Library** (*350 W. Georgia St., 604-331-3600*) has been a great success since it opened in 1995. People especially love the round, Colosseum-style building designed by architect Moshe Safdie. But here's a secret for you: it was originally supposed to face the other way.

Early drawings of the library show the main entrance and plaza on West Georgia, and the federal government office tower behind it on Robson. This makes sense on paper, because then the front entrance would face the neighbourhood's other big civic structures, the Post Office, the Queen Elizabeth Theatre, and the CBC building.

After the design was approved, however, somebody noticed the path of the sun. If the building were constructed as planned, the plaza would be in the shadow of the library and tower virtually all day, which would make it a cold and uninviting place to hang out. So they flipped it, and the main entrance became Robson Street (even though its official address remains West Georgia). Now the sunny plaza is a popular gathering spot.

with a third storey that was added in 1916). And he was a stickler for details – he went through several architects, and a rumoured $6 million, before it was completed.

Adams now operates a recording studio (*warehousestudio.ca*) on the site where an A-list of international recording stars have worked. A partial roster of clients includes R.E.M., AC/DC, Metallica, Elton John, Nickelback, Sarah McLachlan, Stevie Nicks, Bon Jovi, Nine Inch Nails, and Chris Isaak. The facility is tricked out with the all the latest in high tech equipment, as well as a custom-made 1979 mixing board called a Neve Consol that is one of the best in the world. There's even a video games room and kitchens with private macrobiotic chefs (Adams' preference) and a hidden putting green where the rockers can calm their nerves after a session of heavy thrashing.

The Library's Past Lives

The first library in what would become the city of Vancouver opened at Hastings Mill in 1869. In 1887, the Vancouver Reading Room opened on the second floor of 136 West Cordova. In 1893, the library moved to 169 West Hastings and in 1901, industrialist Andrew Carnegie donated $50,000 to build the Carnegie Library at Main and Westminster (now Main). It opened in 1903 with 8,000 volumes on its shelves.

In 1957, the main branch moved to a sleek modernist glass-and-concrete structure at Burrard and Robson, designed by architects H.N. Semmens and D.C. Simpson; it won a Massey Medal (Canada's highest architectural honour) that same year. But as the city grew, it became inadequate, so a new library was built, at a cost of $30 million. The old library is now home to the Virgin Megastore, with CTV's local station on top.

Walk down the street in the old downtown core and odds are you'll come across some some small squares of purple glass set into the sidewalk. Under the glass is an "areaway," a room under the sidewalk that merchants in the late 19th and early 20th centuries used to expand their premises.

Most areaways were simple spaces used for storage, but some were spectacular. There used to be an areaway with gorgeous antique tiling and glass French doors under the sidewalk at Hastings and Main, near the former Bank of Montreal (now the Four Corners Bank), but it was filled in by the city engineering department in the 1990s. The city, worried the areaways could collapse if a car or truck ventured onto the sidewalk, has been filling them in, one by one.

Photo: Solo

Vancouver's most prominent areaway is beside the **Sam Kee Building** (*8 W. Pender St.*) in Chinatown. The building is more popularly known as the skinniest building in the world; it is only 1.6 metres wide. It was built in 1913 by Chinatown businessman Chang Toy, who was incensed when the city expropriated half his lot but refused to pay him for the other half. The areaway gave him about twice as much basement space, which he rented out to a steambath and a barber shop.

The areaway was refurbished in the 1980s when Jack Chow bought the building and spent $250,000 renovating the entire structure. The underground space is currently empty, but is quite remarkable from inside: light streams in from above, interrupted by blurry shadows of feet walking down the street.

The other prominent areaway is beside the Hotel Europe at Carrall and Powell. The building's basement was originally a bar or restaurant, with lovely white and teal green tiles that stretched to the end of the areaway. The tiles are in fine shape, but the areaway is being sealed by the city, in preparation for being filled in with

SLENDER 'SCRAPERS

One of the big differences between Vancouver and other cities is that Vancouver skyscrapers tend to be tall, slender "point towers." This is because of a huge kerfuffle that arose after the construction of the 18-storey **Ocean Towers** near the corner of Beach and Denman in 1957.

Ocean Towers was the first "modern" residential high-rise built along English Bay. It's pretty nifty, in a so-bland-it's-beautiful '50s sense. But the block-long building outraged West End residents because it obstructed the view of the water, so the city decided to kibosh view-blocking buildings in favour of view-friendly-point towers.

gravel. City heritage planner Jeannette Hlavach says that filling it in is a temporary solution because the cost of bringing the areaway to current codes is prohibitive, about $500,000 before any tile work is done.

Heritage expert John Atkin says the purple glass was originally clear – the colour changed after decades of exposure to sunlight. The glass is a prism, which magnifies the amount of light that gets into the space. He says there once were areaways beside virtually every building in Gastown, Chinatown, and the old downtown, but they have been disappearing at a rapid clip. He also says areaways may be responsible for one of Vancouver's enduring legends: that there were secret tunnels under the streets of Chinatown. "People walk over the sidewalks, which are hollow, and they think it's like Seattle and its underground city in Pioneer Square, but it's just the basement," he says.

NEON EULOGY

When you think of neon, you think of Las Vegas, the land of the multi-storey neon spectacular. But during neon's heyday in the late 1940s and early 1950s, the place to be was Vancouver. At the height of neon's popularity in 1953, Vancouver had some 18,000 neon signs – one for every 19 residents. Only Shanghai had a greater concentration.

Longtime Vancouverites wistfully recall the twirling neon coffee cup at the White Lunch Cafe, the giant toast that popped out of a McGavin's neon toaster, or the lightning bolts that zapped out of the neon Sun sign on the roof of the Sun Tower. There were so many neon signs downtown on Granville Street, it was dubbed "the Great White Way."

Where the Bluebloods Roamed

Forget Shaughnessy or the British Properties. Vancouver's original elite area was **Blueblood Alley**, located on the bluff just off Coal Harbour downtown. The alley more or less stretched from Hastings Street (then called Seaton) in the north to Georgia in the south, Burrard to the east and Bute to the west.

Sadly, all traces of Blueblood Alley have been erased save one: the **Abbott House** at Georgia and Jervis. The house is named after Henry Abbott, the Canadian Pacific Railway's western superintendent during the construction of the CPR in the 1880s. Abbott helped drive the Last Spike in November 1885, was responsible for the subdivision of the original Vancouver townsite, and gave his name to Abbott Street, one of the first four streets in the city.

When he retired from the CPR in 1897, Abbott set about building a retirement home suitable to his standing in the community. He chose a lot on a hill that offered a stunning vista of Coal Harbour, Stanley Park, and the North Shore Mountains.

Abbott's house was huge – three storeys high and 6,000 square feet – and featured a two-storey entrance hall off Jervis. Sunlight filtered in through a magnificent nine-pane art-glass window, and the Georgia Street side featured an elegant two-storey curved bay wall. Abbott lived in the house until he died in 1915. By then, Blueblood Alley was in decline, as the well-to-do had moved on to English Bay and then Shaughnessy. The Abbott mansion became a rooming house, then was converted to apartments in 1942.

Somehow the old mansion survived the various highs and lows of downtown real estate, and in 1998, was restored, somewhat, as part of the Residences on Georgia, a $115-million project that included two 37-storey towers and 17 townhouses. Because Abbott House was designated a Heritage A structure – the city's highest ranking – the developer was able to add two storeys and 20 feet to the highrises, in return for restoring the building's exterior and converting the interior to condos.

From the outside, it looks exactly the same as it did when it was built a century ago. If the colour looks familiar, that's because it's "CPR red" – the same as old CPR boxcars, and a suitable colour for one of the CPR's big-wigs.

Orpheum Dreams

The next time you're in the **Orpheum Theatre** (*Smithe and Seymour, 604-665-3050*), take a minute to appreciate its beautiful ceiling. The gorgeous Spanish renaissance design, the elaborate detailing, the wonderful mural in the dome – it's a true marvel of 1920s movie palace architecture.

Then try to wrap your mind around the fact that, in a classic case of Hollywood smoke and mirrors, it's not the real ceiling, but a false one made of plaster, suspended by thousands of thin strands of wire from the roof. "They dropped the wires, tied metal rods back and forth, put metal mesh on, and forced plaster through it," explains local theatre historian Norman Young. "When it's forced through the screen, it bubbles at the back. That keys it and holds it in place, and you would get a really thin, resonant ceiling for sound."

The Orpheum has many secrets. Lying beneath the main auditorium are catacombs, the remnants of a primitive air conditioning system from when it was built in 1927. "They brought the air in [through massive intake vents], which passed through falling water, then space, then through ice," says Young. "This cooled it to 54 degrees Fahrenheit. That was air conditioning in 1927."

Alas, few neon signs survived an "anti-blight" purge that began in the 1960s. Most of the classics that remain are on the Hastings strip in the Downtown Eastside, like the Only seafood restaurant's orange neon seahorse, the swirling circles of the Ovaltine restaurant, and the giant pink pig and dollar signs of Save on Meats.

Thankfully, several neon classics were saved after their businesses closed, and are in the collection of the **Vancouver Museum**. One of the most renowned is the sign from The Aristocratic, which beckoned from Granville and Broadway for decades. The Aristocratic was Vancouver's premier restaurant chain from the '30s to the '60s, and was known for its stylish neon signs featuring

Photo: VPL 81669

On either side of the stage are a pair of arches atop grated façades. These are organ screens, discreetly hiding dozens of pipes powered by the Orpheum's amazing Wurlitzer 240 organ. The organ cost $45,000 in 1927, and is a magnificent piece of equipment – organ fans come from all over North America to see it. It is the only original vaudeville organ still in operation at its original theatre. It was first situated in the orchestra pit in front of the stage, which disappeared when the stage was pushed forward in the 1970s renovation. The organ is now hidden beneath the stage, and is raised on a platform when needed.

"The wonderful thing about the organ is that it's on a hydraulic system," says Young. "It's got the original water pipes that control it. When the organ is up, at intermission when people flush the toilets, the organ drops about three feet. The whole platform just drops."

At the top of the arches nearest the balcony is an "O," for the Orpheum Theatre Circuit. The Orpheum name is a blend of two ancient Greek words. "The Oprh was from Orpheus, [a mythical character] who went to hell to save his wife," explains Young. "He played the lyre, he could make streams come alive, trees come alive…. He went to hell to save his wife, Eurydice. He was taking her back, but it was like Lot [in the Bible]. He's told not to look back, but he does, and she has to go back to hell. *Odia*, or *odeum*, is the Greek word for theatre. They put them together, the "orph" off Orpheus and the "eum" off odeum, and it became the Orpheum.

In the mid-1970s, the building was saved from demolition and redevelopment by the biggest heritage preservation movement in Vancouver history. One of the building's original painters, Tony Heinsbargen, was brought back to oversee the restoration of the building in 1976. Heinsbargen saw that the Orpheum was restored to its original glory, but he added a dramatic touch: the original dome in the theatre was white; Heinsbargen decided to paint a mural instead. The conductor in the mural is Ron Nelson, one of the architects who worked on the restoration. The three children are the offspring of another architect, Paul Merrick. The tiger is a loving nod to Heinsbargen's wife, whom he called his tiger. He painted most of the mural on canvas at home in Los Angeles, and installed it on the dome like wallpaper.

Risty, a dapper little man in a top hat, tuxedo, and monocle. The Vancouver Museum saved Risty from the scrap heap when the last Aristocratic closed in 1997. But an unforeseen problem arose when they tried to move it. The sign is so big – 10 feet high, 11 feet long, and one foot deep – that it wouldn't fit through any doors at the museum.

It wound up being stored at another site, and when the Museum mounted a neon exhibition, was displayed outside – which was only fitting, 'cause neon signs are supposed to be outside. (An Aristocratic neon sign is on display on the second floor of Chapters at Granville and Broadway, site of the last Aristocratic.)

Photo: Solo

When Sylvia Ablowitz was a little girl growing up in the West End, her father used to take her for nightly walks along Beach Avenue. Every night, he would stop at the corner of Beach and Gilford "and just stand there and look." One night Sylvia asked him what he was looking at. He replied: "I'm going to build a building there some day."

The building that arose became one of Vancouver's most beloved landmarks, the **Sylvia Hotel** (*1154 Gilford St., 604-681-9321*). Abraham Goldstein named the building after his daughter, who died in 2002 at the age of 102. Construction of the Sylvia started in 1912. Her father's original idea was to build a hotel, but the city would only give him a permit for an apartment block, so it opened as the Sylvia Court Apartments on May 3, 1913.

The eight-storey building would dominate the West End skyline for decades. After it was converted to a hotel in 1936, the eighth floor was turned into a restaurant that advertised "dining in the sky."

The Sylvia was built at the end of one of Vancouver's biggest booms (the population grew from 27,000 in 1901 to 100,000 in 1911). The outbreak of the First World War resulted in an economic depression, and Sylvia's father lost his dream building because he couldn't keep up the mortgage payments. He had planned to build two more hotels and name them after his other children, Cecil and Aileen, but they were never built.

The Goldstein family moved to Los Angeles in 1922 in search of better weather and economic fortune. Cecil became an entertainment lawyer, and Aileen wound up marrying Cal Eaton, of the department store Eatons. After Aileen's husband died, she became a renowned boxing promoter. She died in 1987, but her legacy was

BIG SIGN GUY

Vancouver's best-known billionaire, Jimmy Pattison (Save-On Foods, Ripley's Believe It or Not!), is known for thinking big. So it should come as no surprise that he was behind the **BowMac** sign on Broadway – the biggest commercial sign in Vancouver.

The year was 1957. Pattison was working as the general manager of Bowell Maclean (BowMac) auto dealers on West Broadway. Faced with stiff competition from Black Motors to the east and Dueck's to the west, Pattison and his advertising manager Wilf Ray decided to erect a monumental sign no one could ignore. "Black's sign was 25 feet and Dueck's had two 60-foot towers," relates Ray. "So we went with this 100-foot BowMac."

honoured when she became the first woman to be inducted into the Boxing Hall of Fame in 2003.

Sylvia worked for a labour union in California, but returned to Vancouver in 1928. On a boat cruise for Jewish singles, she caught the eye of real estate salesman Harry Ablowitz. They married and she remained in Vancouver until her death, although she rarely visited the hotel that bore her name.

"We opened it with [radio host] Jack Webster, who went to the top of it," says Pattison. "I'll never forget it, because Jack hit his head on one of those girders going up the sign and cracked his head open. He went up, did his broadcast, and there was blood all over him. A typical Jack Webster deal."

"There was enough cement in the base of that sign to pave 40 home driveways," says Ray. "It had 10 miles of wiring, and you could see it 10 miles away. It went into the *Guinness Book of World Records* in 1959 as the world's largest free-standing neon sign." BowMac is no longer in business, but the sign is still there, sharing the location with a giant Toys "R" Us sign. The city opted for the unique double sign as a way of saluting the past, while acknowledging the present.

Project Too Dumb

There have been some bizarre plans in Vancouver's history, but few were wackier, or more ill-conceived, than Project 200, a 1960s plan to revitalize the downtown waterfront. It drew its name from a 1965 proposal by the Canadian Pacific Railway and some partners to spend $200 million on what would have been the biggest urban renewal scheme in Canadian history.

The plan changed over the years, but the basic gist was to construct a bunch of bland cement highrise towers over the CPR tracks between Carrall and Burrard. In tandem with the office towers, a freeway would have been built along the waterfront, with a link to another freeway that would have ripped through Vancouver's east end to link up with the Trans-Canada Highway in Burnaby.

Proponents envisioned a virtual city within the city of "tall, majestic buildings and great plazas." Eighteen towers were proposed, with a total floor space of eight million square feet. About 84,000 people were expected to live or work in or visit Project 200 each day. There was even a plan for moving sidewalks that would take people from one part of the project to another. The estimated cost of the plan rose to $300 million by 1968.

The downside was that most of Gastown and Chinatown would have been leveled to accommodate the towers and the freeway system. Critics also assailed the project for turning its back on the rest of downtown; American urban planner Allan Temko described the development as "waterfront vandalism" that would cut off views and wouldn't "enhance anything but the CPR's bank balance."

An outraged public put the kibosh on the plan, and only a handful of Project 200 buildings were ever built: these include the CN/CP Telecommunications building at Cambie and Cordova and the Woodwards parking garage on Water Street.

Photo: Courtesy Roedde House Museum

The **Roedde House Museum** (*1415 Barclay St.,
604-684-7040*) in the West End was built in 1893 for
Gustav Roedde, Vancouver's first bookbinder, by his
friend, Sir Francis Mawson Rattenbury. If the name
sounds familiar, it's because Rattenbury, just 25 years old
at the time, was in the midst of a proposal for another
project: Victoria's Parliament Buildings. Architects were
asked to submit proposals under a pseudonym;
Rattenbury, who had recently arrived from his native
England, submitted his under the cheeky reference "a
Canadian architect." He won the commission.

Rattenbury went on to design Victoria's Empress Hotel
and the building that became the Vancouver Art Gallery
(formerly the Provincial courthouse) and he oversaw the
1901 facelift of the Hotel Vancouver, but Roedde House
is the only Vancouver residential building to his credit.
Built in the Queen Anne style, with garden and gazebo,

THE SUN RISES ON SKID ROW

The **Sunrise Hotel** used to be a
place where people got their teeth
punched out. Now it's where the
needy go to get their teeth fixed up.
A dental office opened in 2001 on
the main floor of the once-notorious
Downtown Eastside hotel at 101 East
Hastings, which has been cleaned up
since it was purchased in 1999 by
several government agencies and
turned over to the non-profit Portland
Hotel Society.

It's fitting that the dental clinic went
into the Sunrise, because in the
1910s it was the home to one of
Vancouver's most famous dentists,
Painless Parker. Parker was both a
person and a chain of dental offices
up and down the west coast. He had
several Vancouver locations on
Hastings and Granville Streets, but
the first one seems to have been on
the second floor of the Sunrise, which
was then called the Irving Hotel.

the house's unique domed cupola was used as a greenhouse by Roedde matriarch Matilda, and was Rattenbury's concession to her (she had wanted a basement) so she could have views of the beach and the sea. The Roeddes lived in the house for 32 years, leaving only when daughter Ann, a nurse, was killed by a psychiatric patient at Vancouver General Hospital at the age of 28. The house was sold in 1925 for $6,000 and went on to become, among other things, a boarding house. In 1976, it was designated a Class A heritage site, and in 1984, the Roedde House Preservation Society was formed to restore it to its former glory.

Now Vancouver's only house museum, it was fully completed in 2000, and is replete with artifacts typical of middle-class life in Vancouver at the turn of the century. These include such parlour curiosities as a stereoscope viewer (the predecessor to the television) and a working phonograph with First-World-War-era records. If the kitchen sink looks a little low, it's because it was custom-built for Matilda Roedde, who stood just 4'11". In the children's rooms there are bearskin gloves (possibly from the bears the Roedde sons used to shoot on Kits Beach at Yew Street when they were 9 or 10). As for Rattenbury, he returned to England in 1929, and was killed by his wife's young lover in Bournemouth, England, on March 27, 1935 by means of a croquet mallet. Part of Barclay Heritage Square, the Roedde House Museum is open for tours, concerts, and event rentals, or visit *roeddehouse.org* for a virtual tour.

Painless was quite a showman; he liked to wear the teeth he had extracted during the day on a necklace he strung around his neck. And one day a week, he would go out on the sidewalk with a little platform and invite passersby to get some free dental work, which would inevitably attract a big crowd. His second-storey offices also had a big window, which allowed the masses a front-row view of his painless methods. His motto was, "If it hurts, don't pay me."

The Irving Hotel was built in 1906 by Judge Arthur Wesley Vowell. It was a high-end hotel in the heart of the city's prime business and commercial district. Each room was equipped with a private bath, hot and cold running water, and a telephone — a pretty big deal in 1907.

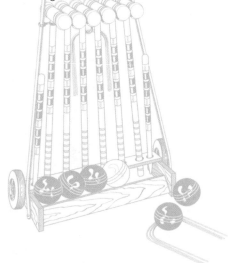

Transportation

You can use more than planes, trains, and automobiles to get in, out of, and around Vancouver. It's no surprise that citizens of Terminal City would promote a number of alternative transportation ideas: energy-efficient vehicles, cycle warriors, and electric scooters. But even here, old is new again.

Old is New Again

Photo: Mandelbrot

Vancouver (with the help of provincial and federal governments) is spending billions of dollars on new **SkyTrain** lines, and endlessly debating where they should go. But essentially, modern planners are trying to replicate the old Interurban and streetcar lines that ran throughout the Lower Mainland from the 1890s to the 1950s. In fact, the original SkyTrain line from downtown to New Westminster follows an old Interurban line.

The Interurban terminal in Vancouver was at Carrall and Hastings. In tandem with the North Shore ferry that used to dock at the foot of Columbia, the Interurban brought about 10,000 people per day to the old downtown core. When it shut down in 1954, Hastings started a long downhill slide economically, which hit bottom after the Woodwards department store closed in 1993. The Fraser Valley Interurban, meanwhile, used to bring shoppers in from the Valley to Columbia Street in New West. When it shut down, Columbia Street went downhill as well.

Vancouver is now trying to bring back the streetcar as a downtown tourist attraction. A pair of restored old Interurban cars run on weekends from Granville Island to the southern end of False Creek, and the city has plans to run the streetcar line down Quebec Street to Columbia, and up Cordova to the CPR station. If money can be found, there are all sorts of possible streetcar lines, such as one that goes along the waterfront from Gastown to Stanley Park, and down Beach Avenue to Pacific Boulevard.

By the way, many of the beautiful green boulevards in the middle of streets like King Edward and Pender are old Interurban or streetcar lines, and the jog in Trafalgar Street at 14th Avenue is due to a former streetcar line.

Dive! Dive! Dive!

One of the world's greatest deep-sea submarines is beached outside the Vancouver Maritime Museum on Kits Point. And it has a big connection to both *Star Trek* and the *Titanic*.

The **Ben Franklin** was a marvel of deep-sea exploration in the late 1960s, capable of plunging to depths of 3,000 feet. *Titanic* explorer Robert Ballard made his first deep-sea dive on the sub, which was built by Swiss inventor/scientist Dr. Jacques Piccard, a favourite of *Star Trek* creator Gene Roddenberry, who named the captain of the second Starship Enterprise Jean-Luc Picard in his honour.

Its landmark voyage was a month spent drifting in the Gulf Stream from the Bahamas to Nova Scotia, submerged at an average depth of between 300 and 400 metres. The voyage was made by seven crew members and was partly paid for and monitored by NASA, which wanted to study the effects of being cut off from the world for prolonged periods.

Unfortunately, the sub emerged on August 14, 1969, about the same time man landed on the moon. Its exploits were relegated to the back pages, and a hoped-for boom in underwater exploration fell by the wayside as the U.S. government concentrated on the headline-grabbing space race.

The *Ben Franklin* was damaged in a gale in 1970 after it ran aground on a reef. It was subsequently bought by a Vancouver businessman named John Horton, who hoped to convert it into an underwater diving platform. But his plans never materialized and it lay abandoned and forgotten in a couple of Vancouver shipyards for three decades.

In December 1999, Vancouver Shipyards was cleaning up, and wanted the 120-tonne sub moved. Horton offered it to the **Vancouver Maritime Museum** (*1905 Ogden Ave., 604-257-8300*), and director James Delgato gladly accepted it. For a couple of years, it languished on the beach, looking like an abandoned old propane tank, but in 2002, the exterior was scrubbed up and repainted, bringing it back to life.

LITTLE RASCAL

While Vancouver is famous for being the birthplace of the Ballard fuel cell that will one day power commercially viable hydrogen-run cars and buses, it was a 1972 invention called "the Rascal" that was the first energy-efficient car to be invented, by a Vancouver man named Blythe Rogers. The 3-wheeled, bright orange convertible car was to sell for just $2,700, but though there were 400,000 willing buyers lined up, the financing never came through.

The Best Old Car in Canada

Photo: VPL 12695

TAKE A BEACHCOMBER TO GIBSONS

Vancouver has a new fast way to get to the Sunshine Coast from downtown. Georgia Strait Transit runs the *MV Bruno Gerussi*, a 40-passenger catamaran that makes a 50-minute trek between a berth west of Canada Place and the government wharf in Gibsons. The ferry is named for the legendary BC star of the CBC television series *The Beachcombers*, which was, appropriately, set and filmed in Gibsons. The *Gerussi* makes four round trips daily; cost is $17 one-way, $30 same-day round-trip.

Vancouver's mild climate is perfect for old cars. And on any given day you'll find a bunch of them hanging around in various states of repair at **False Creek Automotive** (*370 W. First Ave., 604-879-1711*), just east of the Cambie Bridge. False Creek specializes in fixing up vintage cars, and in finding the parts to fix them up with. And if they can't find the part, they'll make one.

As it happens, False Creek owner Vern Bethel owns the best old car in Vancouver, and arguably Canada – the McLaughlin-Buick Royal Tour Car. In 1939, McLaughlin-Buick (a Canadian company that built stylish cars from 1908 to 1942) was called upon to build two cars for the cross-Canada tour by King George VI and his wife Elizabeth. The Royal Tour is the limousine of limousines. It's more than 20 feet long (six metres), weighs 5,800 pounds (2,630 kilograms), and has power to spare, roaring from zero to 60 miles (95 kilometres) per hour in 18.5 seconds.

Royal maroon in colour, it features exotic wood trim, wool broadloom seats, a divider window between the chauffeur and the back seat, and a dictograph, which allowed the royal couple to converse with the chauffeur. It also had extremely high windows, to accommodate the head dress of the royals. Its top speed is 85 mph (135 kph), and it gets seven miles (11 kilometres) per gallon in the city, 11 in the country. The original cost was $15,000 wholesale, $25,000 retail.

In 1940, the car was bought by Helen Palmer, a wealthy socialite in Victoria. It remained in her family until 1972, when Bethel tracked it down and bought it in "restorable, unrusted, but rough shape." (Bethel has a thing for '39 Buicks – he's had 22 of them.) He's loath to say what he paid for it, but admits he's sunk more than

TRANSPORTATION 49

$50,000 into restorations, which are extremely expensive because it's such a high-end car: "The top alone would run over $10,000 if it were done." Building a similar car today would probably cost about $250,000.

Carrying on the royal tradition, Bethel took the car to the Commonwealth Games in Victoria (where it carried the Queen) and Expo 86 (it was used to chauffeur Prince Charles and Diana). All told, eight members of the royal family have ridden in the car. It is currently on loan to the Royal British Columbia Museum in Victoria.

When Bikers Sob

Photo: Solo

There aren't many things that can make a big, fat hairy biker cry like the **Trev Deeley Motorcycle Collection**. It is located off the beaten track (*1-13500 Verdun Place, Richmond, 604-273-5421*), but if you're into motorcycles, it's nirvana.

There are 300 motorcycles in the collection, beginning with a 1913 Harley Davidson that looks more like a bicycle than a chopper – it has long, thin bike handle bars, a skinny frame, and an old bike-style rack that sits atop the rear tire.

Harleys form the basis of the collection – there are 70 of 'em, including 10 models from the '20s, 14 from the '30s, and nine from the '40s. You can see the evolution in motorcycles from decade to decade, and will be amazed at how powerful some of the early models were – there's a 1920 Harley with a 1000cc engine.

Many aren't mere modes of transport, they're works of art, painted in vivid colours. The 1935 Harley, for example, has a two-tone job in sky blue and cream. The 750cc beast could clip along at 85 miles an hour, and sold for $345.

There are plenty of motorcycles from well-known manufacturers like Norton, BSA, Kawaski, Yamaha, and Honda. But what's really special about the collection are the rare cycles like the 1929 Scott Squirrel, the 1949

HAZARDS OF THE ROAD

One of the scourges of drivers with older cars is the provincial government's **Aircare** program. If your car doesn't pass, you usually have to spend at least $200 fixing it up to get a "conditional" pass. (Hint: a tank of premium gas might also do the trick if you are borderline.)

The theory behind Aircare is sound: keeping beaters spewing blue smoke off the road. But in practice, the standards wind up killing off numerous old cars that seem to be in fine shape, either because they'll never measure up to the Aircare standards or get collector plate status from ICBC (where one's car has to be in almost mint condition).

Some people take their cars to mechanics, who adjust them to Aircare standards, then once they've passed Aircare, return to the mechanics to have them adjusted back to the way they were before. Why? Because many old cars run really rough if they're tuned according to Aircare's requirements.

Other old car owners register their vehicle outside the city (like Vancouver Island or the Okanagan), where Aircare is not required. Another alternative is to claim you're in transit, between addresses. ICBC then assesses you in Region Z – the region of no fixed address – and the land of no Aircare.

Photo: Solo

Whizzer moped (which had bicycle pedals for when you wanted to save on gas), and the 1926 Excelsior Super X, a stylin' jet black number made by Schwinn, the famed Chicago bike manufacturer.

For sheer weirdness, there is a 1987 Harley Davidson three-wheeled car and the Sidecar Taxi, a bizarre bike from the '50s that was custom-made in Bellingham and features a mini-car attached to the side of a motorcycle.

MOST TRAVELLED BUS ROUTES

1. 19 into Stanley Park

2. 250 to Horseshoe Bay

3. 41 to UBC via Shaughnessy and South West Marine Drive

4. 4 to UBC via Kitsilano

5. 236 to Grouse Mountain and Capilano Canyon Dam

6. 212 to Deep Cove

7. 351 to White Rock

8. 401 to Steveston

9. 254 to British Properties

10. 229 to Lynn Canyon

11. From Vancouver 160 to Port Moody Station. Change to C-26 to Belcarra Park

Beached Beaver

Photo: CVA BO.P.495.N.507

The most famous shipwreck in Vancouver history was the *Beaver*, which ran aground off Prospect Point in Stanley Park in 1888. The *Beaver* sat on the rocks for four years, and souvenir hunters picked at her bones until the wake of the steamer Yosemite pushed her off the rocks and she sank to the bottom of the First Narrows.

The *Beaver* was built for the Hudson's Bay Company in 1835 and was the first steamer on the North Pacific. She was there during the founding of Fort Victoria in 1843, and also did duty during the Fraser River gold rush of 1858.

The Vancouver Museum has much of the ship, including her anchor, both paddlewheels, a four-by-ten-foot section of railing,15 ribs, and lots of knick knacks that people fashioned from her wood, like walking sticks and canes. But the bulk of the ship is still sitting where it sank in 1892, just off Prospect Point.

Photo: Solo

If Glen Clark had built the **SeaBus** instead of the fast ferries, he might still be premier of British Columbia. The modest catamarans have proven remarkably efficient since they were launched on June 17, 1977, missing only one day of service in 25 years.

Each day, the SeaBus runs between 6:02 a.m. and 1 a.m. the following day, taking commuters and tourists from the foot of Lonsdale in North Vancouver to the Canadian Pacific Railway station in downtown Vancouver, and back again. Skimming along the water at 11.5 knots, the SeaBus carries four crew and up to 400 passengers across the 1.7 nautical mile crossing, which takes 12 minutes. The two SeaBuses make a total of 126 crossings each day, carrying an average of 17,000 passengers daily, which rises to 21,000 during the summer.

The vessels were designed by Case Existological Laboratories, and built at Yarrow Shipyards in Victoria. They were named *Beaver* and *Otter*, after historic Hudson's Bay Company ships. The cost of the entire SeaBus project was $35 million in 1977, including $3.7 million to build each vessel.

At the time, the SeaBuses, like the fast ferry project, generated controversy. The original idea was launched by Dave Barrett's NDP government, and when Bill Bennett's Socreds took power in 1975, it looked at putting a stop to the project. But it was too far along, so it was completed, much to the chagrin of *Vancouver Sun* columnist Doug Collins, who quoted unnamed sources as stating the SeaBus "was a great civil service boondoggle that no one wanted to straighten out."

Criticism like this prompted a reply from another former *Sun* columnist, Alan Morley. "Let the prophets of doom stand back lest I turn my burning gaze upon them and shrivel them where they stand," he wrote. "I've had my first ride on the SeaBus, and happy days are here again."

The public evidently agreed. In April 2002, the SeaBus carried its 100 millionth passenger.

THE NANAIMO CONNECTION

The history of the ferry route between Vancouver and Nanaimo on Vancouver Island has not been a happy one. The fast-ferry fiasco sponsored by Glen Clark's NDP provincial government soured the public on finding solutions to getting to the island (and back) real quick; the ferries created huge waves for nearby residents, the conditions on-board were cramped and crowded, and the cost overruns were indeed a scandal. Now there's a new attempt at getting it right: the 300-passenger high-speed ferry *HarbourLynx* launched in September 2003; it makes the trip in 70 minutes, 25 minutes faster than the BC Ferries, and connects Vancouver at the downtown SeaBus terminal rather than Horseshoe Bay. Run by the Nanaimo Harbour Link Corporation, cost for the trip is $25 one-way, $45 round-trip.

CRASH-O-RAMA

Driving in Vancouver ain't no picnic, but is easier if you know what collision hot spots to avoid. Here are the 10 Vancouver intersections that were the busiest in 2002:

1. Cambie Street & West 41st Avenue: 439

2. Grandview Highway & Rupert Street: 347

3. Knight Street, Knight Street Bridge, SE Marine Drive, SE Marine Drive Onramp: 280

4. Oak Street & West 41st Avenue: 255

5. East 41st Avenue & Victoria Drive: 255

6. Boundary Road & Kingsway: 246

7. Main Street & SE Marine Drive: 228

8. Main Street & Terminal Avenue: 223

9. Joyce Street & Kingsway: 214

10. East 49th Avenue & Knight Street: 206

information courtesy ICBC

Recycled Ferries

You find the oddest things floating in the Fraser River, like a 1920s ferry being used as a houseboat. The ferry in question is the *Comox*, which used to take passengers from Whytecliff Park in West Vancouver to Snug Cove on Bowen Island. The wooden ship was built in 1924, and looks it, but owner Keith Thorp says it floats just fine.

He bought the old ferry in 1971, and has lived on it ever since. The *Comox* is moored in a picturesque floating village off Queensborough in New Westminster. Some houseboats in the 'hood are like floating palaces, but just as many are weather-beaten relics of another age.

To get there, head to the foot of Jardine Street by Dyke Road, walk past a big blue garbage bin, and trundle down a wooden walkway. If you have the nerve to portage across a couple of funky-looking planks, you'll find the *Comox* and other boats. Be careful, though; Thorp slipped and fell in the water a couple of years ago, and might have drowned were it not for his dog Hunter, a pint-sized pomeranian-corgi cross who barked and howled until a neighbour came to pull Thorp out.

SeaBus Stats

The double-ended catamarans, Burrard Beaver and Burrard Otter, that are the SeaBus ships, cross Burrard Inlet sailing from Waterfront Station at the edge of Gastown to Lonsdale Quay in North Vancouver. The 1.75 nautical mile crossing takes 12 minutes. But here's the best part: SeaBus has never missed a sailing due to weather conditions.

End of the Roads

Have you ever wondered why Vancouver streets like Burrard and Hemlock stop dead cold at 16th Avenue? It's because 16th was the original southern boundary of the city of Vancouver. Beyond it was South Vancouver and Point Grey, which were separate municipalities until 1929.

Forget your $400,000 Ferraris, Porsches, and Lamborghinis. The fastest car on the road just might be a souped-up Volkswagen Beetle from Langley's **Marcel Horn**.

Honest. Horn specializes in "after market" conversions that can turn a small compact into a lean mean racing machine. For US$25,000 to US$100,000, you can get a modest car with immodest power, a 500-horsepower monster that rips down the highway at warp speed, going from zero to 100 km per hour in four seconds.

Horn's conversions have developed a fanatical following among an elite group of corporate executives who love to rev their engine at stop lights and then blow away some hapless greaseball in a regular hot car.

How fast do Horn's conversions go? Well, Horn took a Golf to Germany a couple of years ago to be tested by the German government, which strictly regulates after-market conversions. The bureaucrat who wrote out the report took the car up to 310 km an hour.

Horn got his start in the hot car market in high school. Unable to afford a bitchin' Camaro or Trans-Am, he souped up a 1976 Rabbit into a pocket rocket. After high school, he started doing it for other people. His big break came in 1996, when he decided the new Volkswagen Beetle was a perfect candidate to modify into a supercar.

He borrowed money from the bank, bought a Beetle, redid it, and sent it to the auto press for testing. Rave reviews in *Road & Track*, *Motortrend*, *European Car*, and *MAXpower* followed, and the phone started ringing.

"We take a new Beetle, put four wheel drive into it, put a V-6 motor into it, add a twin turbo package," he says. "It runs a quarter-mile in under 12 seconds, has a sticker price of about US$100,000. But it will out-run the Vipers, the G22 Porsches, the Ferraris, anything with $400,000 price-tags. It can out-brake, out-perform, out-accelerate, and out-corner them. And you've got the nostalgia of a little harmless Beetle rolling up on all the big bad boy toys."

CARS WANTED

Thinking about getting a new car? A used car? Keep this list in mind: the top stolen vehicles in B.C.

1. Honda Civic, 88-00
2. Dodge Caravan, 91-95
3. Toyota Camry, 84-91
4. Plymouth Voyager, 91-95
5. Honda Accord, 86-94
6. Jeep Cherokee, 88-94
7. Toyota Pickup, 84-88
8. Oldsmobile Cutlass, 85-88
9. Honda Prelude, 86-88
10. Acura Integra, 90-95
11. Dodge Spirit, 90-92
12. Plymouth Acclaim, 90-92
13. Toyota 4Runner, 88-89
14. Ford Mustang, 89-90
15. Chevrolet Camaro, 84-87
16. Chevrolet Cavalier, 90
17. Dodge Shadow, 91
18. Chrysler Dynasty, 91
19. GMC Pickup, 89
20. Nissan Pulsar, 87
21. Dodge Neon, 95
22. Toyota Le Van, 85
23. Toyota Tercel, 86
24. Plymouth Sundance, 91
25. Nissan Sentra, 87

information courtesy ICBC

Float Your Own Boat

Photo: Mandelbrot

Getting out on the water can turn your whole day around. There's something incredibly pacifying about floating about and taking in the sights. Sadly, not many of us can afford our own yachts, or even little boats, but thankfully, there are lots of options.

The cheapest, quickest way to get on the water, and to get from downtown to Granville Island, is to hop either a **False Creek Ferry** from the West End or an **Aquabus** from Yaletown. For $2 to $5, depending on how far you want to go (you can get from Vanier Park to Science World), the little boats will zip you across False Creek.

Option number two is to rent a power boat or kayak at one of the many marinas in town. In Deep Cove, for example, you have the option of renting from about 100 vessels from **Deep Cove Canoe and Kayak** (*2007 Rockcliff Road, 604-929-2662, deepcovekayak.com*), at $28-30 for a two-hour minimum.

If you want a power boat, **Deep Cove Marina** (*2890 Panorama Drive, 604-929-1251*) rents a 14-foot boat with a 40 horsepower motor for $85 for three hours, plus gas. Deep Cove is a good place to go boating, because it's at the entrance to Indian Arm, an 18-kilometre-long fjord with calm water and spectacular scenery. Five minutes out of the cove, you can be surrounded by complete wilderness. But there are also plenty of man-made attractions, such as the Wigwam Inn, the Buntzen Lake power station, and all sorts of cottages.

There are inflatable two-person kayaks available for rent at **Granville Island Boat Rentals**. Totally funny looking (army green), but a neat way to spend an afternoon with your honey.

AUTOMATED ELECTRIC

Vancouver's SkyTrain is made up of two lines, the Expo and the Millennium, that together create the longest automated electric train system in the world. The Expo line, which runs from Waterfront Station to King George Station, is 28.3 km long and takes 39 minutes to ride. The Millennium Line runs from Commercial Drive Station to Columbia Station, is 19.2 km long, and takes 25 minutes to ride. At Columbia Station the Millennium Line joins the Expo line to continue back to Waterfront Station.

Photo: Mandelbrot

Faster Than Ferries

Building a fast ferry to cut the time commuting from Vancouver to Nanaimo sounded great on paper, but proved disastrous in execution when costs soared and the media went ballistic on the NDP government.

They should have seen it coming. Ferries are always late, are often breaking down, and people complain about them to no end. And prototypes like the fast ferry project always cost more than anticipated.

Besides, if you want to get to Victoria or Nanaimo quickly, you can take a plane or helicopter. **Harbour Air** offers one-way float plane trips to Victoria for $99, to the Gulf Islands for $74, and to Nanaimo for only $54.

Helijet Airways offers one-way helicopter trips to Victoria for $99 to $159. You can also fly Helijet one way from Vancouver Harbour to Boeing Field in Seattle for $307 to $354, or from Vancouver to Whistler for $143 to $179.

Flying to Victoria on a sunny day is an incredible experience – you pass over the Gulf Islands and sometimes can see pods of whales swimming in the Strait of Juan de Fuca. Flying time is about half an hour, downtown to downtown.

Precious Cargo

Can't bare to put a drugged Fluffy in the aircraft's hold when the family goes on vacation? The new California-based **Companion Air**, which flies up and down the West Coast with stops at YVR, will give the family dog a seat beside you.

companionair.com

Air Pirate

If you see a dark, strange-looking float plane emblazoned with a skull and crossbones landing in the harbour, do not be alarmed. Air pirates are not invading the city. It's only the owner of the California-based Oakley sportswear empire (whose logo is a skull and crossbones). He sometimes stops in Vancouver on the way to his to his recreational property up the coast.

MOUNTING A CRITICAL MASS

The revolution will not be motorized. Or so says **Critical Mass**, a bike protest movement that was launched in San Francisco in 1992 and now has a sizeable Vancouver following, with 250 riders turning out for some events. Critical Mass rides happen on the last Friday of every month, with riders meeting at the Vancouver Art Gallery around 6:00 p.m. And they ride, rain or shine. Critical Mass cyclists typically shut down a bridge or street in a "celebratory reclamation of public space." They have protested events like the war on Iraq and the Molson Indy car race, and have showed their support for causes like the Woodwards squat by homeless people in 2002. You don't have to be on a bike to participate: skateboards and in-line skates work just as well.

Cab Grabs

Catching a cab in Vancouver can drive anyone to distraction. The worst time of all is between 3 and 3:30 p.m. (shift change for Yellow Cab, the largest company). If you are downtown and have been fruitlessly trying to flag a taxi for hours, head to one of these three hotels with cab loops. Chances are all the cabbies will be lined up here reading the newspaper or having a snooze.

Sutton Place Hotel
854 Burrard St.

Fairmont Hotel Vancouver
900 W. Georgia St.

The Four Seasons Hotel
791 W. Georgia St.

Photo: Solo

Scooter Sensation

Photo: Solo

When Dean Kamen unveiled the Segway scooter on *Good Morning America* in December 2001, the event came after a year of speculation about the supersecret project he had been working on for ten years. All that was known was that his new invention had something to do with transportation. Coming from the man who created a portable dialysis machine and reinvented the wheelchair with his Ibot, which enabled users to climb stairs and travel offroad, imaginations ran rampant. So it's no surprise that when people saw the machine, they were underwhelmed. Sure, the electric-powered two-wheeler was an engineering marvel, but it's a scooter, and while Kamen predicted that his invention was going to revolutionize human transportation, the Segway has done anything but. Attacked by critics as heavy (80 pounds), limited (about ten miles, no more than four hours, on one charge), and expensive (CDN$6,950 before tax), the Segway has become little more than an expensive toy. But they're fun to ride, and now you can try one for yourself (by the way, women learn faster than men, for some reason). **Future Human Transport Solutions** near Granville Island (*604-734-9280, segwaybc.com*) has a stable of more than 10 scooters that you can rent for your tour of the seawall.

Arrive in Style

The **C & N Backpackers Hostel** (*927 Main St., 604-682-2441, cnnbackpacker.com*) gives weary travellers a break from public transit. If you book for three nights, they'll arrange to pick you up for free at the airport or downtown in their own white stretch limo labeled with the "C & N Backpackers Hostel" logo. Once at the hostel, your bed is $16.

Sports & the Outdoors

Photo: Solo

One of the great Vancouver clichés is that you can go skiing in the morning and sailing in the afternoon, or go golfing in the morning and snowboarding at night, or go drinking in the morning and pass out at night. It's true, of course, but no one ever does. Nonetheless, Vancouver is a sports paradise, even if our pro teams usually stink.

Forget About 2010, What Happened to 1976?

Vancouverites are either excited or scared (or both) about the potential impact the 2010 Olympics will have on the city. The boosters think it will usher in an era of economic prosperity, the doubters think it will make the city more crowded and expensive and lower the city's much-vaunted quality of life.

There were similar feelings about Expo 86, which was a big financial success but led some locals to ruefully joke "we invited the world, but they didn't go home." There was a civic vote about whether to have the Olympics, which the "yes" side won decisively, 64 percent to 36. Oddly enough, Vancouver was the first place where an Olympic plebiscite was successful: one was defeated in Colorado in the 1970s, and Bern dropped out of the running for 2010 after citizens gave the thumbs-down to the games.

The Colorado vote could have had major implications for Vancouver. Whistler had mounted an unsuccessful bid for the 1976 Winter Games, which went to Denver. When Colorado dopped the games, organizers quietly asked the province if B.C. was still interested, but Dave Barrett's NDP government refused. The 1976 Winter Games were eventually held in Innsbruck, Austria – which had not even originally bid for the '76 Winter Olympic Games.

Whistler would have looked a lot different if the Games had come in 1976. Bid organizers proposed building a 50,000-seat outdoor stadium in Whistler for opening and closing ceremonies, along with a 10,000-seat hockey arena, a 5,000-seat figure skating arena, another 2,500-seat hockey arena, a speed skating oval, a figure skating practice rink, and an eight-rink curling facility – all in Whistler. Vancouver would have been the site of some cultural events and little else.

Free Parking

The first act of the first Vancouver city council in 1886 was to ask the federal government to set aside a 1,000-acre military reserve for a park. At the time, it probably seemed like an odd request. After all, the fledgling city had only 2,500 inhabitants, and virtually the entire Lower Mainland was still wilderness. But the feds complied, and on September 27, 1888, Mayor David Oppenheimer officially opened **Stanley Park**.

The official version of the creation of Stanley Park is that it was dreamed up by some far-sighted politicians. The more cynical take, however, is that the Canadian Pacific Railway talked the federal government into forming the park as a way of luring the masses to its big real estate holdings in the West End.

In any event, Stanley Park quickly became the focal point for the booming city, and an internationally-known symbol of Vancouver – a natural wonderland of towering trees, beautiful beaches, and jaw-dropping vistas.

But the canopy of giant trees covering the park is not old growth. Stanley Park was logged several times from the 1850s to 1880s when it was a military reserve, and the logging skid roads (where trees were dragged away) form the basis of its trail system.

It also may be a bit of an accident that there's so much forest in the park. The eastern side of the park was developed in its early days with several British-style sports facilities – a cricket pitch, a rugby field, tennis courts, a golf course, and a lawn bowling green.

But the park was so big, its western side was largely left untouched, and the second-growth forest grew. Subsequently, public attitudes towards trees changed, and instead of developing the western side of the park, it was allowed to remain in its (largely) natural state.

Photo: Dan Scott/Vancouver Sun

UNCOUTH 'TENDER

The NHL's Vancouver Canucks have made some mysterious trades over the years, but one of the strangest was when the team's head honchos got rid of goalie Gary "Suitcase" Smith while he was at the top of his game in 1975.

It seems Smith was invited to a Christmas party at the West Vancouver waterfront home of Canucks owners Frank and Emily Griffiths. Emily was introduced to Smith as the daughter of Dr. W.R. Ballard, whose famous pet food line featured a dog on the label.

"I see the resemblance on the can," deadpanned Smith, who was nicknamed Suitcase because he had played with so many teams.

A month or so later, he proved his nickname when he was traded again.

Taking the Plunge

Photo: Stuart Thomson, CVA 99-1783

Vancouverites are known to do crazy things, but in terms of mass lunacy, nothing compares to the annual **Polar Bear Swim** on New Year's Day. Every year, 1,500 to 2,000 people shake off New Year's hangovers, doff their clothes, and make a mad dash into English Bay. On a sunny day, the beach can be packed with 10,000 onlookers. Not bad, considering that only six people were at the first swim in 1920.

The Polar Bear Swim was the brainchild of Peter Pantages, longtime co-owner of the Peter Pan Cafe on Granville Street. Born in Andros, Greece, Pantages moved to Vancouver in 1919 to work at the Pantages Theatre on Hastings Street, which was owned by his cousin Alexander.

An avid swimmer, he became a charter member of the Vancouver branch of the Royal Lifesaving Society, and vowed to swim every day of the year, no matter where he was. Looking to get his friends together for a celebration, Pantages came up with the idea of a Polar Bear Swim in English Bay, which can be as cold as three degrees above freezing.

In the early years, Polar Bears would change into their swimsuits in the basement of the Sylvia Hotel before sprinting across to English Bay. Some years it was held on New Year's, other times on Christmas. After the swim, the revellers would be invited back to the Peter Pan Cafe for a hot toddy, which became almost as big an event as the swim itself.

The Vancouver Park Board took over the swim in the 1950s, and it continues to have a strange attraction for Vancouverites eight decades after it was founded. Several members of the Pantages family still live in Vancouver and take part in the swim.

Basil Pantages first took the New Year's plunge in 1938, when he was only five years old. His advice to would-be Polar Bears is not to drink any alcohol beforehand. "All drinking does is warm up your blood, so when you hit the water you feel the cold even worse," he explains.

WHO NEEDS PROFESSIONALS?

When it comes to the performance of Vancouver's professional sports teams, there isn't much to brag about. But in the world of **Ultimate**, Vancouver teams are tops. Ultimate, the game where teams throw and catch discs (known to many by the brand name Frisbee), is much like football without the steroids, and in the 2003 Canadian National Championships, held in Quebec, Vancouver teams won the two major categories. Furious George took the open division (they won the world open championship in 2002), and Prime (their Tanis Frame is pictured below) came away with the women's division trophy (they won the world women's crown in 2000). Ultimate is now Vancouver's largest team sport. Even better: you can watch games for free. Check the Vancouver Ultimate League website (*vul.bc.ca*) for game times and locations.

Photo: Scobel Wiggins

The Best Hockey Team in Vancouver

The Canucks have had some good teams over the years. But it's doubtful if they will ever come up with a squad that matches the accomplishments of Vancouver's first Stanley Cup winners, the 1914-1915 **Vancouver Millionaires**.

The Millionaires are one of hockey's great unheralded teams. At a time when teams only carried about 10 players, seven Millionaires made it into the Hockey Hall of Fame: Fred (Cyclone) Taylor, Frank Patrick, Frank Nighbor, Hugh Lehman, Mickey Mackay, Barney Stanley, and Si Griffs.

Hockey was a far different game back then. There were two main professional leagues, the six-team National Hockey Association in the east and the three-team Pacific Coast Hockey Association in the west. The winners of the leagues played in a "World's Series" for the Stanley Cup.

The Millionaires were the champs of the PCHA, which also included the Victoria Aristocrats and the Portland Rosebuds. The league had been founded by the Patrick family, which financed teams and arenas in Vancouver and Victoria by selling off the family lumber business in Nelson.

In the west, hockey was played with a seventh player on the ice, called a rover. Defencemen were called point and cover point. Players often played a whole game, without a break, as soccer is played.

NAME THAT TEAM

The New Westminster Salmonbellies may have the best local sports name, but the **Vancouver Canucks** have the best story behind theirs. The year was 1945, and the infamous Coley Hall had snookered a back-door deal with his drinking buddy, auto dealer and Pacific National Exhibition president Mackenzie Bowell (of BowMac fame), for the rights to play hockey at the PNE Forum. The catch was that the Vancouver franchise for the newly formed Pacific Coast Hockey League had already been awarded to Arrow Transfer owner Chuck Charles.

With no rink to play in, Charles was forced to hand over the franchise rights to Hall, a local sports legend known for his quick temper and quick fists (Coley once broke the nose of a local sports editor, then gave him a Cadillac so he wouldn't sue). In August 1945, Hall was duly awarded the PCHL franchise. He then went to his favourite bootlegger's to have a beer to celebrate. Hall told the bootlegger, Art Nevison, of his new team, and asked what he should call them.

"Call them the Canucks," said Nevison, after comic book hero Johnny Canuck, who fought the Nazis and symbolized Canada's war effort.

So he did.

The east played with six players, and had a curious system where penalized players were replaced by substitutes while they served penance for their sins. This made for some rough play; the really bad boys would receive a three-minute penalty instead of the standard two minutes, which wasn't much of a deterrent.

The "World Series" was a three-game affair, with odd games to be played under western rules, even under eastern. The Ottawa team was a powerhouse, with future Hall of Famers Art Ross (of Art Ross Trophy fame), Clint Benedict, Eddie Gerard, Jack Darragh, and Harry (Punch) Broadbent. They oozed confidence when they arrived on the coast, but were in for a shock. From the moment the puck was dropped, the younger Millionaires outskated, outhustled, and outplayed Ottawa. They won the first game 6-2, took the second 8-3, and annihilated Ottawa 12-3 in the finale.

Cyclone Taylor lived up to his nickname, making several sensational dashes up ice from his rover position and leading Vancouver with seven goals and three assists. Nighbor matched him in points by racking up four goals and six assists, while Stanley had the best single game, knocking in five goals in the game three blowout.

The Millionaires looked to have the makings of a dynasty, but were edged out by Portland and the Seattle Metropolitans in succeeding years. The Millionaires won the PCHA title in 1918, 1921, 1922, and 1923 (after the team's named was changed to the Maroons), but lost the Stanley Cup each time. (The last B.C. team to win the Stanley Cup was the Victoria Cougars in 1925, who beat the Montreal Canadiens three games to one.)

The NHA became the National Hockey League in 1917, and when it decided to expand to the U.S. in 1926, the Patricks sold virtually the entire league to the NHL for about $300,000. The Millionaires ceased to exist, but the Victoria Cougars – which had started out in 1911 as the New Westminster Royals – became the Detroit Cougars, and later, the Red Wings.

The Prettiest Little Ballpark in the World

It isn't as majestic as the Lions Gate Bridge, as magnificent as the Marine Building, or even as distinctive as the B.C. Hydro Building. **Nat Bailey Stadium** is a more modest landmark – a small baseball park tucked between Main Street and Queen Elizabeth Park.

From the outside, it's fairly nondescript, a semicircular concrete wall. Inside, the concourse is kind of cramped, and the stands aren't exactly luxurious. But to many Vancouver baseball fans, it's a treasure, the prettiest little ballpark in the world.

The stadium was built in 1951, but its roots go back much farther. The infield sod was transplanted from Athletic Park, Vancouver's main baseball field from 1913 to 1951, located beneath where the Granville Street Bridge now stands. On October 19, 1934, a barnstorming crew of major-leaguers including Babe Ruth, Lou Gehrig, and Connie Mack stopped off at Athletic Park on their way to Japan, playing an exhibition game in a torrential rainstorm.

Built of wood, Athletic Park burned to the ground twice, in 1926 and 1945. After the second fire, local promoters and politicians started talking about building the concrete baseball park that became Nat Bailey.

Nat Bailey's ancient, hand-operated scoreboard and light standards were imported from Sick's Stadium in Seattle, which was built in 1913 and torn down in 1979. It was only fitting that Nat Bailey should get part of Sick's Stadium, because Sick's Stadium's blueprints were used to build Nat Bailey. Both stadiums were built by beer barons Emil and Fritz Sick of Seattle.

Nat Bailey was originally named Capilano Stadium, after the Sicks' local brewery. It was renamed in honour of Bailey, founder of the first drive-in restaurant in Canada (White Spot), a co-owner of baseball's Vancouver Mounties, and a big-time supporter of the sport.

BANNED BIKE ROUTE

Vancouver is a great place for bicycling, if you can avoid the bloody big hills and getting soaked to the skin when it rains. The city has a network of designated bike routes where cyclists can (hopefully) avoid too much interaction with cars, as well as a network of seawalls around the downtown core which offer beautiful scenery and the freshest fresh air in the city. A map of the cycling routes can be accessed on the City of Vancouver's website (*city.vancouver.bc.ca/engsvcs/transport/cycling/routes.htm*).

Photo: Solo

You Can Park Here
(But There's No Park Here)

Photo: Solo

Alas, the waterfront downtown bike route ends at Dunlevy Street in Japantown, where you run into the Canadian Pacific Railway tracks and the Port of Vancouver. But some bikers aren't deterred by the Port facilities. They sneak in through a gate, cycle around the stacks of containers, and emerge at Commissioner Street on the other side of the tracks where there is an industrial road that leads all the way to New Brighton Park by the Second Narrows Bridge. Problem is, the Port police have shut off public access to Commissioner, so you'll have to be careful, and feign innocence if you're caught.

The city of Vancouver has spent a fortune on new park space downtown: a one-square block park at Davie and Seymour that cost $18 million. Meanwhile, one of Vancouver's oldest parks is being used for a parking lot.

Larwill Park sits next to the Queen Elizabeth Theatre, on the block bounded by Georgia, Dunsmuir, Beatty, and Hamilton. Many Vancouverites know it as the site of the Greyhound Bus Depot, which leased it from 1943 to 1993.

On Easter Monday, 1887, the four-and-a-half-acre site was host to the first athletic competition in the city of Vancouver, a rugby game between Vancouver and New Westminster. (There had been a track and field meet scheduled for the summer of 1886, but it was cancelled when the fledgling city burned to the ground that June.)

In the early days, sports groups rented it from the Canadian Pacific Railway for $5 per year. They spent $310 clearing it of trees and stumps, and kept cows and goats on the site to maintain the field. (Okay, they ate the grass.)

In 1931, city archivist Major J.S. Matthews wrote that the park "has seen untold numbers of celebrations, ceremonies, carnivals, circuses, cricket, lacrosse, baseball, and football matches, trooping of the colors, memorial parades, civil commotion, even riots and battered heads. Quack doctors have thumped their drums and bawled out the marvelous cure-all qualities of their 'pink pills for pale people.'"

For Vancouver's first half-century, it was called the Cambie Street Grounds, but in 1943, it was renamed Larwill Park in honour of pioneer Al Larwill, who lived in a cabin in the northeast corner of the park and looked after the sports equipment.

Later that year, though, the city turned it into a bus depot. The parks board officially had ownership of the site until the mid-1990s, then sold it to another city body, the Property Endowment Fund, for $8.6 million. The parks board used that money to purchase future park land by the Fraser River.

The city almost sold the land to a developer in 1998, who was going to put a shopping mall on the site. But the deal fell through, so Vancouver's oldest park remains a parking lot.

Vancouver is a city of masochists. How else to explain the popularity of the **Grouse Grind**? The Grind involves hiking 900 metres (2,800 feet) straight up to the top of Grouse Mountain. The elevation gain from the base is 275 metres (900 feet), which means that most of the Grind is ridiculously steep. Moreover, it's unrelenting: there are no flat bits where you can catch your breath. Dubbed nature's stairmaster, it runs straight up, at what seems to be a 45-degree angle.

For some reason, this appeals to Vancouverites, who have turned the Grind into a local phenomenon. More than 100,000 people do the trek every year. On a sunny weekend, the trail is the hiking equivalent of Robson Street, attracting over 1,000 people per day.

Horror stories about the Grouse Grind abound. One woman took her svelte mother from Winnipeg up the Grind; halfway up, Mom broke down in tears. Another woman asked a guy to join her for the hike, and he thought it was going to be easy. He was sweating and cursing by the top, and never phoned her again.

The hike begins at Grouse's lower gravel parking lot. (You can tell where it starts, because there's an Evian water vending machine.) The first bit joins up with the less-severe Baden-Powell trail, but soon it forks to the left, where the real grinding starts.

People have been hiking up the mountain since 1894, when a hunting party shot a grouse and named the mountain in its honour. The first big wave of hikers came in the 1920s and 1930s, when thousands climbed the mountain to reach cabins in Grouse Mountain Village.

The Grind was cut out of the wilderness from 1981 to 1983 by mountaineers Don MacPherson and Phil Severy. The trail they chose ran underneath the Grouse gondola, which provided a quick and easy descent to the bottom without any strain on the knees. (It used to be free, but a couple of years ago, Grouse noticed the huge numbers of hikers, and started charging for it.)

Numerous Vancouver Canucks have done the Grind, including Trevor Linden, Jyrki Lumme, and Tim Hunter. Houston Rockets basketball star Hakeem Olajuwon was a regular Grinder. Canucks conditioning coach Peter Twist says the Grind is an excellent aerobic and anaerobic workout.

MOUNTAIN BIKE MECCA

If Vancouver is mountain bike heaven, then Mecca is the **Cove Bike Shop** in Deep Cove. The store dates to 1980, when a trio of high school buddies Chaz Romalis, Doug Lafavor, and Ashley Walker scrounged $7,000 to open Canada's first all-mountain-bike store. Romalis is the only original owner left, but he isn't so much a canny businessman as someone who lived the lifestyle, understood where the trend was going, and profited from it. But success didn't come easy — in the early days he lived at the store, which he shared with several rats. Romalis's big break, literally, came when he broke his ankle and couldn't ride his road bike. So he nicked his mom's three-speed cruiser and started venturing off-road. He loved it, but kept wrecking bikes. So he started looking for tougher frames and rims. He imported parts from the U.S. and built his own bikes with his friends.

At the same time, some similar ne'er-do-wells were building the first mountain bikes in California. Romalis spotted one in Osoyoos and saw the future. Lafavor went to San Francisco and returned with a $750 bike. When they couldn't interest any local bike stores in carrying them, they started their own store. It was a labour of love for several years, but took off in the mountain bike explosion of the late '80s. In 1995, Romalis decided the company had to begin producing its brand of bikes.

The first design was called the Hummer: "Don't let summers be a bummer, get a Hummer." Now Cove rakes in about $5.5 million in sales internationally. And 40-something Romalis gets to spend his mornings mountain biking on the North Shore, and winters in Mexico.

At the top, after checking out the view and savoring your triumph, standard operating procedure is to go have a drink or a snack at Grouse's Bar 98 bistro/bar. Tuesday and Wednesday nights are unofficial "singles" nights on the Grind, and Bar 98 is where the fit singles meet to check out each other's pecs, thighs, and abs.

If staring at your feet for an hour and a half isn't your idea of a hot date, take the gentler Baden Powell trail beside the Grind. It takes slightly longer, but is prettier and ends up at the same place. Plus it's free.

It Ain't St. Andrews

Golfing is a ton of fun, but ridiculously expensive. And when you want to get on a course at a normal time, it's usually booked, anyway. But that's *ball* golf. *Disc golf* is a whole other story.

Disc golf is played with a Frisbee, or flying disc. Unlike ball golf, disc golf courses are free, and there's usually no waiting. Ball golf courses are also packed with networking business executives; disc golfers tend to be alternative lifestyle enthusiasts: they play the game for the vibe as much as the sport.

The rules are the same as golf, and so is the attraction — you can commune with nature walking around a lush green course, testing your skills while getting some exercise.

Players aim for a 1.5-metre-high metal basket with galvanized chains hanging down its sides. The idea is to send the disc into the steel chains and have it land in the basket. The holes are from 60 to 100 metres in length. Avid disc golfers usually carry around several special discs, like a Stingray or Cyclone (for long-distance driving), a Rock (for chipping), and a Rattler or Aviar (for putting).

If you're interested, Vancouver has several disc golf courses — Queen Elizabeth Park and Jericho in Vancouver, Win Skill Park in Tsawwassen, Semiahmoo High School in Surrey, and Moody Park in Coquitlam.

Vancouver's First Sports Palace

Photo: VPL 17042

Much was made of Arthur Griffiths' decision to build **General Motors Place**, home to the Vancouver Canucks, downtown in 1995, where the masses could walk to the game from work. But it isn't the city's first downtown hockey arena.

Vancouver's first big sports palace was the Denman Arena, which stood at the foot of Georgia and Denman from 1911 to 1936. It was built by hockey legends Frank and Lester Patrick, who needed an arena for the Vancouver entry in their new Pacific Coast Hockey Association. (The three-team league, which also featured teams in Victoria and New Westminister, folded in 1926.) The arena was made of wood, but had a brick façade. It had 10,000 seats, featured the first artificial ice in Canada, and cost $300,000 to build. It opened December 21, 1911, but burned to the ground August 20, 1936.

It was at the Denman Arena that the Vancouver Millionaires won Vancouver's first Stanley Cup in 1915. Rudolph Valentino once judged a beauty contest there and Jack Dempsey boxed at the arena in 1931.

Hockey games moved out to the PNE Forum after the Denman Arena burnt down (its remains are pictured above), but there were endless proposals for downtown arenas. In 1953, Coley Hall, owner of the Vancouver Canucks (the team that preceded the present-day one), wanted to build an 11,000 seat arena on the present site of the CBC; in 1964, Toronto Maple Leafs owners Harold Ballard and Stafford Smithe tried to get the city to give them downtown land in return for an NHL franchise, but the city declined. In 1967, Erwin Swangard built the $3 million Pacific Coliseum on the PNE grounds, three years before Vancouver was granted an NHL franchise.

Incidentally, the scoreboard at GM Place cost $6 million in 1995 – double the price of the entire Coliseum 25 years earlier.

WHISTLER MOUNTAIN BIKING

Think you need skis or a snowboard to justify a trip to Whistler? Think again. The **Whistler Mountain Bike Park** means the mountain is occupied year 'round. In 1998, 15,000 mountain bikers took advantage of the lifts to make downhill more fun (imagine having to *ride* up before crashing down). Dave Kelly is the man responsible for creating a *terrain park*, which means mountain biking here is more than pedalling along a trail. Kelly and his crew use dirt, wood, and rock to sculpt the hill to enhance the riding experience. Take A-Line, for example, perhaps the most popular downhill mountain bike trail in the world, which features jumps from top to bottom. But it's not all about bikers trying to hurt themselves; Kelly has diversified the types of runs at the Park, to the point where the double black diamond (expert), blue square (intermediate), green circle (novice) classification of runs familiar to skiers and snowboarders is now used for mountain bike trails. Mountain bikers seem to like it. In 2003, more than 60,000 mountain bikers hit the trails. Says one mountain bike aficionado, "When a mountain biker dies and goes to heaven, it will look just like Whistler."

Delta Delight

To most Vancouverites, **Deas Island** is an afterthought, a spot of land you pass by when you drive through the tunnel connecting Highway 99. But if you take the time to leave the freeway and explore the 70-hectare island, you'll find a unique park.

Deas Island Regional Park is an excellent spot for a picnic or a family gathering. It offers a front-row seat to the natural and industrial life of the Fraser River. And it has a trio of heritage buildings that provide a glimpse into turn-of-the-century life in Delta.

Walking along the Island Tip trail on a sunny day feels like being in the Mississippi delta, particularly after leaving the developed eastern portion of the island for the relatively natural western side. Take away the boats ripping along the river and it's pretty much the way it must have been when the island's first settler, John Sullivan Deas, arrived in 1873.

Deas was a freed black from the United States who started a cannery on the island. Sockeye salmon were plentiful around the island and for a couple of years his cannery flourished, producing the most tins of salmon on the Fraser River. But competition and inefficient equipment forced the cannery to close in 1880. Deas moved to Portland, where he died the same year.

Other canneries operated on the island until the First World War. Farmers tilled the rich delta soil until the late 1940s, and some fishermen built shacks on the banks of the Fraser, living there into the 1950s. By the late '50s, though, Deas Island was abandoned, its remaining buildings falling into disrepair. But big changes lay around the corner. The Deas Tunnel was built in 1959, and the northeast corner of the island was stabilized by dumping tons of rock on to the shoreline. For several years, the land was used for grazing by local livestock. In 1981, it became a park.

The most impressive heritage building on the site is Burrvilla, built in 1906 for Henry Burr, an early settler in the area who is an ancestor of the actor Raymond Burr. The Queen Anne farmhouse is big and grand, with an incredible sunburst design atop the front entrance. Originally situated east of Deas Island, it was moved to its present site in 1982.

An eagle's nest is one of the island's most popular natural attractions, along with great blue herons, great horned owls, and cooper hawks. The island's "flood plain forest" is filled with cottonwood and alder trees, ninepark, red osier dogwood, honeysuckle, and spirea. Rabbits and deer live in the forest and can often be spotted from the trails. Because the island is flat and not big, the trails are fairly easy. The Island Tip trail is the most scenic walk, and also seems to be the least populated. The Dyke Loop trail offers a look at Deas Slough, which is filled with rowers from the Delta Deas Rowing Club and/or water skiers. And Tinmakers Walk is a nice stroll through a cottonwood forest.

Free Snowshoe Trail

If you call Cypress Mountain for information about snowshoeing, they'll be happy to tell you about the snowshoeing trails, which cost a bundle to access and meander around the cross-country ski area. All well and good if you like crowds and dangerous patches of thin ice. When the snow levels drop, they'll often tell you that the snowshoeing trails are closed. But they won't tell you about the free snowshoeing trail that is always open, which starts at the base of the cross-country ski area and heads straight to the top of Hollyburn Mountain. Not only is it less crowded and free of charge, but there's a better payoff in the 360-degree panoramic mountain views once you get to the top (in about an hour). As you pass the ticket booth, head to your left up the steep logging road where the skiers are coming down. You'll follow a path through the woods for a bit, before coming upon wide open banks. Follow in the footsteps of those who have gone before, and you emerge on a sunny mountaintop with a dozen or so other snowshoers. Hint #2: rent your snowshoes at **Three Vets** (*2200 Yukon St., 604-872-5475*) where they are a fraction of the price and better quality than those on the mountain.

Basketball Diaries

A lesser-known haunt for celebrity-spotting is the **Pacific Palisades Hotel** (*1277 Robson St.*). The hotel twigged to the fact that a lot of stars travel with basketballs, so they installed a hidden hoop behind one of the towers, accessible only from inside the hotel. Celebrities who've done lay-ups here include Scott Speedman (*Felicity*) and Eminem's nemesis, Moby.

SKI FREE

On opening day at **Whistler Blackcomb** (*whistlerblackcomb .com*), the pole position at the Wizard Express chairlift at the base of Blackcomb Mountain is coveted, with people lining up a day in advance. To make the wait more exciting, the famous mountain resort initiated a competition for something even more coveted: a free season's pass. In 2002, the Freeze Factor event required competitors to engage in 24 hours of activities including a foot race in ski boots and the eating of crickets. Only one season's pass was awarded; the second and third place finishers received express cards, which allow for discounted lift tickets. For those who are less competitive, the hill also has an online competition every year.

A Beery Good Snooker Player

There are many sports stars, but few become folk heroes like **Big Bill Werbeniuk**. The 300-pound Werbeniuk was once the seventh-ranked snooker player in the world. But he is chiefly remembered for the prodigious amount of beer he drank to counteract a hereditary condition known as benign essential tremor, which caused his arms to shake. This made him a folk hero in snooker- and beer-mad Britain, where he moved in the mid-'70s. His fame only grew when he split his pants on a national TV broadcast.

His beer drinking was on doctor's orders. He also combatted his condition with Inderal, a beta-blocker. But his career ended in 1992 after the World Professional Billiards and Snooker Association declared Inderal a banned substance.

How much beer he drank has become the subject of debate: some say 30 pints a day, others 40, others 50. He claimed he once drank 76 cans of beer during a marathon session at an Australian tournament, when he and English player John Spencer teamed up to win all the prize money from the other competitors after the official competition ended.

Werbeniuk was born and raised in Winnipeg. Playing pool was in his blood: his grandfather owned a pool hall on Logan Avenue in the city's tough core, and young Bill was a pool shark by his early teens. Legend has it he took an older pool shark for $600 when he was only 12. He moved to B.C. when he was 20, and quickly became B.C. champion – he was the first person to run a perfect game in tournament play. By 1973, he was Canadian and North American Champion.

In 1982, he teamed up with Victoria native Cliff Thorburn and Kirk Stevens to win the World Cup of snooker. He was ranked in the top 16 in the world for eight years before his run-in with the authorities over Inderal. After his retirement he lived with his family in Pitt Meadows until his death in 2003.

UNKNOWN TENNIS COURTS

You will soon see why they're nicknamed the ghetto courts. On the roof of a False Creek parkade there are four public tennis courts where you can almost always find a vacant one – unlike everywhere else in the city. The walls that surround the courts are almost entirely covered in graffiti. At last check there was a weird-science-type mural of a wacky inventor with reproductions of Da Vinci's *Vetruvian Man*. The Vancouver Parks Board periodically paints over the graffiti, and they've recently taken to locking the doors at night, but for graffiti artists, where there's a will, there's a way. To find the tennis courts, follow the little path where Ash Street intersects 6th Avenue. Cross the Vancouver Historic Railway tracks and the parkade will be on your left. Take the stairs up to the roof.

Photo: Solo

The White Elephant

When it was built in 1983, **BC Place Stadium** was hailed as a state-of-the-art sports palace where the teams and fans could enjoy games without being soaked by the ever-present rain. It worked for a couple of years before sports fans realized it sucked watching football indoors, and BC Place turned into a white elephant, good for trade shows and not much else.

In retrospect, you have to wonder what the hell they were thinking, spending $100 million on a football stadium that could only be used a dozen or so times per year. Well, the truth is, it wasn't built as a football stadium. One of the big reasons BC Place was built was that somebody convinced Bill Bennett's Socred government that Vancouver could land a major league baseball franchise if only it had a proper stadium.

A few games were played at BC Place – Seattle Mariners star Edgar Martinez ripped up his knee on its awful turf – but baseball's powers-that-be quickly realized that indoor stadiums in general didn't work. The indoor stadium trend died, and Vancouver never got its major league team.

You Are Here: Geocaching Mania

Geocaching is a world-wide game made possible by the invention of inexpensive hand-held Global Positioning System devices used primarily by sailors and hikers. Players hide tiny objects in Tupperware containers, post the co-ordinates on the website (*geocaching.com*), and other players try to locate them. Once they've identified the object in the cache (say, a little pig eraser or a Chinese coin), they replace it with something new, and so on. Naysayers complain the game is so popular that soon the world will be covered in Tupperware containers. Hence, new rules dictate that you can only place caches where you can easily maintain them (there are 923 in B.C.). One of Vancouver's pioneer geocachers (she's credited with placing the first cache on Prince Edward Island) is filmmaker Mary Ungerleider. If you're playing, here's a hint: Ungerleider oversees six caches and lives in False Creek. If your GPS signal points to the water, don't start swimming. As investigative reporter Justin Beddall revealed in a story about crab poaching in *Vancouver* magazine, poachers are using GPSs to locate traps they have hidden with an underwater float.

Annual Races and Sporting Events

Adidas Vancouver International Marathon

A 42-km loop through Stanley Park and parts of downtown Vancouver. There's a half-marathon option and a 5-k route for kids. May. *604-872-2928, adidasvanmarathon.ca*

The Alcan Dragon Boat Festival

On the third weekend in June, the largest dragon boat races outside Hong Kong take place at False Creek's Plaza of Nations. June. *604-688-2382, adbf.com*

The AT&T Wireless Open

Stanley Park hosts the largest public tennis tournament in Canada with competitors as young as 10. July. *Tennis B.C.: 604-737-3086, tennisbc.org*

My First Triathlon/My (Almost) First Triathlon

For novices and second-timers only. June, July, and August. *triathlons.net*

North Shore Triathlon

On Victoria Day weekend 500 to 600 participants compete, swimming, biking, and running their way to the finish. May.
604-980-0251, nstc.ca

Quicksilver/Roxy Surf Jam

Tofino, Canada's top surfing destination and home to its only female surf school (surfsister.com) attracts both male and female competitors. July.
B.C. Surfing Association: bcsa.ca

Slam City Jam

Vancouver's Pacific Coliseum holds the North American Skateboarding Championships. May.
604-280-4444, slamcityjam.com

UBC Triathlon and Duathlon

Remember, UBC is located on the top of a really big hill. March.
604-822-1688, legacygames-ubc.ca

Wreck Beach Bum Run

Canada's first and only nude run. Body paint optional. August.
wreckbeach.org

Vancouver SunRun

The second-largest 10-km race of its kind in North America with 50,000 runners. April.
604-689-9441, sunrun.com

Lost and Found

Photo: Solo

Have an annoying habit of getting lost? Well in Vancouver, you don't have to look for moss growing on the north side of tree trunks to get your bearings. Thanks to BC Hydro, you can determine your position on the earth in latitude and longitude as long as you can find a wooden power pole. At eye level on every pole is a metal plate with two lines of numbers stamped into it. On the first line, the first four numbers provide your longitude (all parts of B.C. are west of 110 degrees, so the "1" has been dropped): 2307 means you are at a longitude of 123 degrees, 7 minutes. The second set of numbers provide your latitude: 4916 places you at 49 degrees, 16 minutes. The third set of numbers is a BC Hydro location map, and is of little use. The second line of numbers are correction values, so you can better pinpoint your location on earth. Each number has had its last "0" dropped: 010 and 429 would tell you you're standing 100 feet west and 4,290 feet north of the latitude and longitude described in the first line. So there's no reason you should ever got lost in Vancouver (provided you can remember these instructions!).

by
Murray
Bancroft

Finding a good meal in an unknown city can prove challenging even to the most intuitive belly. It's a search with no shortage of pitfalls and false starts. Take, for example, the brunch restaurant with a crowd of people lined up outside in the rain – more likely a result of an inadequate floor plan and a mob with a sheep mentality than of anything tasty inside. You could flip through the ads in the entertainment papers, but restaurants that advertise often need to for good reason. This chapter will introduce you to the Japanese chef who invented the California roll, take you to the Italian restaurant where Hollywood celebs tussled with the mob, and help you sample the local larder. So read on, and jump the line, because your table is ready.

Dining Undercover

With the gritty appeal of a booze can and the electrical ingenuity of a Vancouver grow-op, this secret dining club even has its own T-shirt. Having worked as a cook for touring rock bands, a man set up shop in his Vancouver home, and for over a decade has been practicing his own brand of underground dining. He calls his customers once a year to give them the date they'll be dining and lets them know what they'll be eating. Each evening comes with its own theme. From Thai to "Back Woods Americana," it's a little like Forrest Gump's proverbial box of chocolates – you never quite know what you're going to get. What's the catch? The following five strict rules that, if broken, will result in being cast forever from the list:

1. Don't call him … he'll call you
2. You may invite up to eight guests, but you are responsible at all times for their behaviour
3. Don't show up at the same time, and don't ring the door bell
4. Don't ask for recipes
5. Don't ever write about it (I am so off the list)

Violating any of these infractions is punishable by immediate expulsion from the group. The good news is if, like myself, you happen to break one of these rules, there are countless other options in the quest for a decent meal in this city. I suggest that you pay a visit to any of the following restaurants, where you and your guests are more than welcome to show up together.

Photo: Solo

Bishop's

John Bishop is well on his way to offering a menu comprised of 100 percent organic ingredients, and is the harbinger of seasonal cooking in Vancouver. Executive chef Dennis Green creates weekly menus to accommodate fluctuations in supply, while profiting from seasonal ingredients in their prime. And you'll profit too, from a well-honed wine list (which includes several organic selections) and simply handled, exquisite local fare. Bishop is also author of a number of bestselling cookbooks.
2183 W. 4th Ave., 604-738-2025

Bis Moreno

All too often a restaurant will open in Vancouver that shares striking similarities to a popular spot in New York or San Francisco. Some even share the same name. Enter Bis Moreno, a new kid on the block that is truly unique to our city – and it came to us via Prince George. With two successful restaurants under their belt in the mecca of northern B.C., restaurateurs Moreno and Cinzia Miotto felt that they had something to offer Vancouverites. As it turns out, it's an offer we can't refuse. An effective marriage of local ingredients and Italian technique results in multi-course tasting menus that attract attention. The Miottos have given a welcome wake-up call to Italian cooking in Vancouver.
1355 Hornby St., 604-669-2812

Photo: Solo

Photo: Solo

FIRST NATIONS FEAST
Famous Vancouver architect Arthur Erickson designed the room at **Liliget Feast House** (*1724 Davie St., 604-681-7044*), where First Nations dishes like oolichan, fiddleheads, and alder-smoked salmon are served in a longhouse setting.

Photo: Hamid Attie

C

Regulars like David Suzuki give a nod of approval to chef Rob Clark's commitment to enviro-friendly fishing practices, while Tina Turner rented the entire room for a private birthday party (no word on her private dancer), but supplied her own macrobiotic chef. A controversial year included a scathing review from Jacob Richler (*National Post*) and competing chef Rob Feenie's disparaging comments in a *Globe and Mail* article. But what is undisputed is Clark's willingness to take risks and his aggressive sourcing of fresh seafood.
1600 Howe St., 604-681-1164

WILL THE REAL TANDOORI KING PLEASE STAND UP?

Feuding brothers-in-law opened Tandoori King restaurants just steps from each other. The first, and best, is the **Original Tandoori K. King** (*689 E. 65th St., 604-327-8900*), close to the **Tandoori King** (*8017 Fraser St., 604-327-3355*). An ongoing lawsuit between the two is getting hotter than a tandoori oven.

Le Crocodile

Chef/proprietor Michel Jacob recently celebrated his restaurant's 20th anniversary, along with a loyal clientele. Known as the godfather of French cooking in this city, Jacob kickstarted the careers of Rob Feenie (Lumière; Feenie has a tattoo of a crocodile on his leg as a memento), David Hawksworth (West), and Don Letendre (Elixir), to name a few. Professional servers may direct your attention to Alsacian classics like onion tart; take their advice.
100-909 Burrard St. (entrance on Smithe), 604-669-4298

Photo: Solo

Lumière

Lumière is the first free-standing restaurant in Canada to earn the Relais Gourmand distinction (others are in hotels), and the only one in Vancouver. Chef/proprietor Rob Feenie established the modern-style tasting menu in this city, with his French, Asian, and West Coast ingredients. A post-meal discussion with guests Robert Redford and Brad Pitt lasted into the wee hours, causing Feenie to be a no-show for the taping of his Food Network cooking show *New Classics* the next morning.
2551 W. Broadway, 604-739-8185

Tojo's

Self-proclaimed inventor of the California Roll (something Martha Stewart claims to have confirmed when she visited in September 2003), chef/proprietor Hidekazu Tojo has earned his reputation as Nobu of the North. Perhaps that's the reason that celebrities, food editors, and politicians alike invariably stop by to show some respect to Tojo-san and sample inventive dishes like the hot-and-cold Northern Lights Roll. Those who prefer to see Tojo eye-to-eye take a seat at the bar ... but keep an eye on the bill, as perfection comes with a hefty price tag.
777 W. Broadway, 604-872-8050

THE SAFEST SEAT IN TOWN
Perched high atop Queen Elizabeth Park, the aptly named **Seasons In The Park** (*33rd Ave. & Cambie St., Queen Elizabeth Park, 604-874-8008*) has been host to a U.S./Russian presidential summit, and a dinner for I.O.C. delegates that may have helped us win the 2010 Olympic Winter Games. There's only one way in and one way out, making security a simple task. A floor directly below the restaurant houses secret service and acts as a temporary press gallery.

Vij's

The best Indian food in Canada, period. A famished John Cleese, knowing that it would be the only visit of his trip, ordered "one of everything" from the entire menu. Proprietor Vikram Vij is every bit as hospitable as the toothsome room. A strictly-enforced no-reservation policy also makes for a hopping bar. If you enjoy good food, allow Vij to make the big decisions … then sit back and enjoy the ride.
1480 W. 11th Ave., 604-736-6664

West

New York's "The Fat Guy" recently completed a cross-Canada grazing (evidently not on foot) and rated this as one of the top three restaurants in the country. Chef David Hawksworth returned to open West having spent a decade earning his chops in London at such esteemed spots as Marco Pierre White's Canteen. Hawksworth's ever-evolving menu reflects the best of our local ingredients. Perhaps that's why he and his crew were able to wrestle the Restaurant of the Year award at the 2003 *Vancouver Magazine* Restaurant Awards from five-consecutive-year-title-holder, Lumière. However, a spirited hockey match between the two restaurants just weeks before the awards ended in a convincing win for Lumière by a score of 13 to 4. You can't win 'em all.
2281 Granville St., 604-738-8938

Photo: Solo

THE MOST DANGEROUS SEAT IN TOWN

Unlike some new designer diners, **Helen's Grill** (*4102 Main St., 604-874-4413*) has as much street cred as rapper 50 Cent. A word to the wise: if the high calorie intake doesn't get you, the corner booth wedged way out into the busy intersection of King Edward and Main Street just might.

For years the izakaya (roughly translated: eating and drinking place) has provided refuge for stressed-out wage slaves in Japan looking for small dishes that pair well with drinks; it's their version of tapas. In Vancouver the izakayas offer a more convivial, and rowdier, alternative to the ubiquitous sushi counter. With small dishes of everything from grilled fish and stews, to potato gratin and deep fried chicken, it's everyday kind of food. After working as a stockbroker for over a decade in Tokyo, Justin Alt grew tired of trading in Sony and Mitsubishi and decided to return to Vancouver to open **Happa Izakaya** (*1479 Robson St., 604-689-4272*), where he now trades in flame-torched mackerel and Japanese beer. Alt, with wife Lea, decided to help Vancouverites decompress in the *izakaya* tradition. And guests remain decompressed even after the bill arrives.... With no

dish costing more than $8, and draft sake in bamboo for the same amount, you may not want to leave.

Japanese language students look for a taste of home at **Guu** (pictured right) and **Guu with Garlic** (*838 Thurlow St., 604-685-8817; 1698 Robson St.,*

604-685-8678), but on Friday or Saturday nights, you'll be looking for a seat.

Heavily frequented by club kids and off-duty chefs, the **Gyoza King** (*1508 Robson St., 604-669-8278*) has become a landmark for late-night, noisy dining. Slip into a pair of the house slippers while you eat, just don't forget to grab your shoes on your way out.

MAJOR LEAGUE LOBSTERS
Chef James Walt of **Blue Water Café & Bar** (*1095 Hamilton St., 604-688-8078*) had a request, from a rather peckish guest, for a 12-pound lobster. Not wanting to disappoint a customer, Walt was able to locate such a creature, but added that "each claw was as big as a catcher's mitt."

Why Vancouver's Dim Sum is Better Than Hong Kong's

Photo: Solo

Renowned foodie (and *Vogue* food editor) Jeffrey Stiengarten's latest book *It Must Have Been Something I Ate* makes reference to Vancouver as having some of the best Chinese restaurants in the world. Leading up to the repatriation of Hong Kong, large quantities of people, money, and chefs fled to Vancouver.

Waiters at the **Imperial** (pictured above, *325 Burrard St., 604-688-8191*) balance trays of sticky rice and fresh watermelon juice in this lofty room in the Marine Building.

What **Kirin Seafood Restaurant** (*201-555 W. 12th, 604-879-8038; 200-7900 Westminster Hwy., Richmond, 604-303-8833*) lacks in drama (no push carts or waiters with trays of food), it more than makes up for with fresh ingredients and tasty dishes.

Good quality dim sum at bargain prices (and atmosphere) are aplenty at **Royal King Chinese Seafood** (*3560 Fraser St., 604-876-0028*). When someone has finished eating, the bus boy will take each corner of the plastic table cloth that covers each table and carry it off (dirty plates and all) to his station. That's the reason your meal was so cheap. Just don't forget your cell phone on the table or you may be fishing it out of a bus pan.

Highly acclaimed local architect Bing Thom designed the building that houses the Main Street **Sun Sui Wah** (*3888 Main St., 604-872-8822; 4940-#3 Rd., Richmond, 604-273-8208*), but the Richmond location has slightly better food and is well worth the drive.

Photo: Solo

The year-round rooftop patio at **Joe Fortes Seafood & Chop House** (pictured left, *777 Thurlow St., 604-669-1940*) offers white linen service and seafood towers. Take a seat under the tent, gaze out onto the herb garden, and ask yourself why more restaurateurs don't take advantage of their rooftop square footage.

Budget or time-conscious lunch breakers hit the patio and cafeteria-style **Gallery Café** (pictured below, *750 Hornby St., 604-688-2233*) atop the Vancouver Art Gallery. Enjoy the classical music, canvas umbrellas, and art gallery architecture. Beer and wine prices will make you want to take the rest of the afternoon off.

Finally the top floor of **The Beach House At Dundarave Pier** (*150-25th St., West Vancouver, 604-922-1414*) is open for alfresco dining. A large patio (with a tent if it's needed) is so close to the water, you could almost catch your dinner.

Photo: Solo

The Breakfast Club

Alibi Room

First-rate brunches like eggs benny on potato latkes are gobbled up by film biz crowds.

157 Alexander St., 604-623-3383

Photo: Solo

Clove

If you prefer turntables over a jukebox when you take your breakfast, look no further than this laid back, Indian-influenced eatery.

2054 Commercial Dr., 604-255-5550

Photo: Solo

Havana

The original owner started this Cuban hot spot in order to finance an independent film project, and it worked. The new owners didn't change a thing. A large sidewalk patio facilitates great people-watching on the Drive.
1212 Commercial Dr.,
604-253-9119

Tangerine

A free-ranging Kitsilano crowd flocks into this healthy-yet-hip neighbourhood stop for organic pancakes and healthy eggs.
1685 Yew St., 604-739-4677

Tomahawk

Firmly in the diner category, this North Shore landmark employed a young Bryan Adams as a dishwasher (back in the summer of '69?). Feeling macho? Order the Skookum Chief hamburger: egg, bacon, wiener, beef, and cheese. But don't blame me for the heartburn.
1550 Philip Ave., North Vancouver,
604-988-2612

Photo: Solo

Opened as a project by young Colombian architects, the light and breezy **Baru Latino** (*2353 Alma St., 604 222-9171*) offers tasty, South American dishes like ceviche as well as Latin-inspired cocktails.

It's fitting that **Monsoon** (*2526 Main St., 604-879-4001*) was the brain child of a former nightclub owner. A casual, warm room creates a tropical vibe through Vancouver's rainiest of nights. Share small plates of yam fries with soy chili sambal or chai brulé and, of course, anything from the drinks menu.

Photo: Solo

A layover in Memphis in 1999 is what inspired George Siu and Park Heffeifinger to open **Memphis Blues Barbeque House** (*1465 W. Broadway,* *604-738-6806; 1342 Commercial Dr., 604-215-2599*). And a layover is what you may require to regroup after sampling their famous barbecue classics like Cornish game hen or slabs of ribs. Heffeifinger is one of the city's finest wine consultants and educators, so take his advice on what to pair with the barbecue brisket. But Diet Coke and beer seem to be the crowd favourites.

Communal Tables

Photo: Solo

Step up to the communal table at **Soupspoons** (*2275 W. 4th Ave., 604-328-7687; 990 Denman St., 604-328-7687; 680 W. Broadway, 604-328-7687*), where single lunch-breakers often wind up with soup, sandwich, and a phone number: how's that for a lunch combo?

Seattleites may lay claim to the first **Alibi Room** (*157 Alexander St., 604-623-3383*), but ours (in Gastown) boasts a sleeker design and Canadian prices. Long communal tables are a throwback to the space's former days as a clubhouse for the local taxi driver's union.

Photo: Mandelbrot

A Raw Deal

You can have anything you want at the **Raw Organic Health Café** (*1849 W. 1st Ave., 604-737-0420*), just don't complain that your fries are cold. As the name would suggest, all of the dishes on offer are uncooked, and made almost entirely from organic ingredients. The menu reads like the personals section of a new age magazine with options like "eccentric veggie delight" and "organic sexy smoothies." Look for raw food celeb groupies like Demi Moore and Donna Karan, who coughs up $1,000 a day for her personal raw food chef.

Cheap and Cheerful

Photo: Solo

Café Crêpe

Three locations strong and growing, the crêpes and French-style grilled sandwiches keep them lining up at the sidewalk take-out windows, especially while waiting to get into the nightclubs on Granville. Inside, the scaled-down bistro rooms provide just enough joie de vivre.
2861 Granville St., 604-488-1326; 1032 Robson St., 604-488-0045

East is East

Go West, to the far reaches of Kitsilano, to try some Eastern Afghan-Indian fusion, like the lamb kebab roti rolls, in an exotic room.
3243 W. Broadway, 604-734-5881

Photo: Solo

Fiddlehead Joe's

After a game of tennis, take a seat on the refreshingly casual sea wall patio as the world roller blades by. One of the best deals in town for a quality Caesar salad, a glass of beer or white wine – and an ocean view.

2-1012 Beach Ave., 604-688-1969

Hon's Wun-Tun House

Most popular for their potstickers, order half a dozen and then move on to a number of tasty noodle dishes. Everything is made fresh at their own factory. The Robson Street location boasts a separate vegetarian-only kitchen.

280 Keefer St., 604-688-0871; 1339 Robson St., 604-685-0871

Photo: Solo

Bistro Bargains

By no means a traditional bistro, but chef/proprietor Rob Feenie has never been reined in by tradition. **Feenie's** (*2563 W. Broadway, 604-739-7115*) is a modern bistro (next door to his more formal Lumière) that offers cozy dishes like calamari salad and duck confit shepherd's pie. Feenie's Weenie (cheese smokie) comes as is, or fully dressed. Snappy service and a well-appointed, contemporary room round off the experience. This could be the best value for your dollar in the city.

In the heart of the wealthiest postal code in Canada, **La Regalade** (*103-2232 Marine Dr., West Vancouver, 604-921-2228*) offers incredible value by any standards. Chef/proprietor Alain Raye had a Michelin star in France – now he's the star of West Vancouver with his rustic brand of French comfort food.

The steak-frites and salad ($8.99) at **Salade des Fruits** (*1551 W. 7th Ave., 604-714-5987*) remains one of the best deals in the city. Unlike the food, the room is low rent thanks to its location in the lobby of the French Cultural Centre. A bare bones wine list makes for quick decision-making: red or white.

Naked Lunch

No shirt, no shoes, no pants … no problem. This Greek food stand known as **Nudius Foodius** (*Wreck Beach*) has been a landmark at the clothing-optional beach – as have the numerous vendors peddling beer, watermelon, and various hallucinogens. Most vendors and food stand staffers opt out of wearing uniforms with the exception of leather hip purses. Where else would they keep the change?

Posh Picnics

Catch the sunset at English Bay, but not before stopping by the take-out window of **Raincity Grill** (*1193 Denman St., 604-685-7337*) for a packaged picnic like a Prince George lamb sandwich, matchstick potatoes, and a chocholate brownie with seasonal fruit ($10).

Yaletown rollerbladers take a quick detour from the seawall to **Provence Marinaside** (*1177 Marinaside Cr., 604-681-4144*) and fill their backpacks with inexpensive antipasto dishes like roast chicken and grilled asparagus, bottles of San Pelligrino, and desserts like tarte aux pommes.

Famous Flops

The restaurant business is always a gamble with notoriously bad odds. The **Moustache Café** on Granville Street had beaten those odds and was finding its place as one of Vancouver's finest restaurants. That is, until the proprietor lost it lock, stock, and wine cellar due to bad gambling debts. Most of the staff congregated in the living room of a prominent Vancouver food critic, who was a sure bet to help place them in other, less risky ventures.

The **Century Grill** in Yaletown may have started big, but soon everyone involved was being served summons rather than their trademark chicken picanté. After numerous lawsuits, the restaurant collapsed like a bad soufflé. A trail of disgruntled investors made limited partnership a dirty word.

On South Granville, **Gianni's** was keeping the Shaughnessy set in truffles and Chianti when GST back taxes (reportedly in the six figures) put an abrupt end to the party. Several cooks retrieved their knives (and possibly a few truffles) from the kitchen minutes before the padlocks went on the doors.

Tea Time

Don't Show the Elephant Gallery Café

This modern Asian tearoom has a minimalist decor with a large selection of teas, all filtered through a glass pipe on the wall. A display of Scandinavian CDs adds to the café's global character. The name comes from a Chinese proverb about the importance of modesty.
1201 Hamilton St., 604-331-1018

Secret Garden Tea Company

Known for their British-style teas and excellent tea sandwiches.
5559 West Blvd., 604-261-3070

Tearoom T

Quickly building an international reputation in the connoisseur market, they provide tea blends to five star hotels in Paris, London, Berlin, Hong Kong, Shanghia, Tokyo, and others.
1568 W. Broadway, 604-730-8390, tealeaves.com

Photo: Solo

WE ARE FAMILY

The first restaurant of the **Earls** chain (*1185 Robson St., 604-669-0020 and other locations*) opened in 1982; there are now 52 restaurants. Pizza ovens offer something for the kids but their trump card is their Product Development chef Kathleen O'Connor.

For the tweens, try the **Cactus Club** (*1530 W. Broadway, 604-733-0434 and other locations*) which is 50 percent owned by Earls but has a slightly hipper look. The new Yaletown location will have a built-in DJ booth. The restaurant at Broadway and Granville was noted by a local modeling agency as a top location to scout new talent.

In Vancouver, you'll find that coffee shops and cafés are often more crowded than bars. Whether it's a first date, or full-blown speed dating, the next time you visit your local java joint you may leave with more than just a caffeine buzz.

Sit amongst the Italian garden sculptures at **Calabria Coffee Bar** (pictured above, *1745 Commercial Dr., 604-253-7017*) and name the Italian celebrities whose headshots grace the walls. One of the proprietors, Vince Murdocco (who works with his brother and father), is the kickboxer-cum-actor who stared in the oft-overlooked *Flesh Gordon and the Cosmic Cheerleaders.*

For the best coffee in town, stop by either location of **Café Artigiano** (*763 Hornby St., 604-696-9222; 1101 W. Pender St., 604-685-5333*), where they take equal pride in the presentation. For two years running they've taken home the gold at the Las Vegas Latte Art Competition by pouring lattés with a perfect rosetta behind their back or while wearing boxing gloves. This year they will compete in the world championships, but if all of this doesn't impress, just try the coffee.

At **Café Abruzzo Cappuccino Bar** (*1321 Commercial Dr., 604-254-2641*) it's all soccer, all the time … and you'd better be rooting for the Italians. Italian sausage in a bun and strong coffee act as brief interruptions to talk of AC Milan's latest trade.

At **Café O** (*302 Davie St., 604-694-2240*) at the new Opus Hotel in Yaletown, there are lots of papers to read over a French-style café au lait. Unlike the Seattle-based shop across the street, this one also serves wine by the glass. Put that in your non-fat-decaf-double-caramel-venti-mocha and shake it.

seal the deal business lunches

Cioppino's Mediterranean Grill

A smart room with outstanding Italian food and tables big enough to write on. Tip: on a hot summer day, get a table far away from the dumpster near the patio.
1133 Hamilton St., 604-688-7466

The Imperial

It may be an old classic, but this downtown Chinese eatery's dim sum lunch fits in with the times: inexpensive and quick.
355 Burrard St., 604-688-8191

The Smoking Dog

Veteran restaurateur Jean-Claude Ramond stocks developer Peter Wall's preferred Montrachet, and can always come up with a Cuban cigar for

Photo: Mandelbrot

your American business partner.
1889 W. 1st Ave., 604-732-8811

West

Call ahead and reserve table #10 and look onto Granville Street through the floor-to-ceiling window. If you can't close the deal here, it probably won't happen.
2881 Granville St., 604-738-8938

HERO WORSHIP

It's better known for its cheeses and imported olive oils, but order a grilled sandwich as you do your shopping at **La Grotta del Fromaggio** (*1791 Commercial Dr., 604-255-3911*) and you won't regret it.

When on the North Shore, join the queue at **La Galleria Fine Food** (*3055 Highland Blvd., North Vancouver, 604-990-9162*) for one of their specialty baguette sandwiches.

French-style sandwiches like chicken salad or ham, Swiss cheese, and hard-boiled egg sell out early in the day at **Patisserie Lebeau** (*1728 W. 2nd Ave., 604-731-3528*).

keep your eyes on these fries

Belgian Fries

An ex-flight attendant opened shop after many layovers in Brussels. It's a good thing he backed out of his first plan to sell small packs of stale pretzels and over-priced drinks. Served the European way, with mayo, not (gasp!) ketchup.
1885 Commercial Dr., 604-253-4220

Café de Paris

The unofficial French consulate in Vancouver – not because of the food but due to the dozens of Frenchmen who have owned it at some point. Despite the many changes of ownership, the pommes frites, which are served with all main courses, have never suffered.
751 Denman St., 604-687-1418

Earls

A recent update to thin-cut French fries is cause for celebration. High-quality shoestring fries, especially for a restaurant chain.
1185 Robson St., 604-669-0020 and other locations

Pastis

Served on their own in a basket, or log cabin-style with their famous steak tartare and cornichons.
2153 W. 4th Ave., 604-731-5020

SOUP'S ON

In a bull or bear market, the best place to eat on Granville Island is **The Stock Market** (*1689 Johnston St., Granville Island Public Market, 604-687-2433*). Try the red snapper soup and you will not be surprised to learn the proprietor is a classically-trained chef and makes everything from scratch. Chefs and food critics alike have been known to use his ready-to-go stocks and crème fraîche in a pinch.

Circolo

This private room, called Circolino, comes with its own open kitchen and chef.
1116 Mainland St., 604-687-1116

Photo: Solo

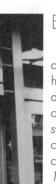

Photo: Solo

Enoteca

This room can accommodate an entire hockey team, and often does. Canucks and out-of-town teams alike swing by for pre-game carbs and post-game cool downs.
1129 Hamilton St., 604-685-8462

The Fish House in Stanley Park

One evening, acting on a dare, a woman removed her top and continued her meal in a silk bra. To the wonderment of the male guests (not to mention several waiters), the other female guests followed suit. For the remainder of the evening, the group received the most attentive service imaginable.
8901 Stanley Park Dr., 604-681-7275

Il Giardino

A stellar room with a private courtyard is favoured by celebs and politicians alike.
1382 Hornby St., 604-669-2422

Feenie's

Chef/proprietor does it your way with the Feenie burger ($12) ... but his way is to add seared foie gras and short ribs (and an extra $25 to your bill).
2563 W. Broadway, 604-739-7115

Hamburger Mary's

Known for their organic burgers and drag queens, not always in that order.
1202 Davie St., 604-687-1293; 2184 Cornwall Ave., 604-677-6767

Moderne Burger

A cool green retro diner with all the trimmings ... minus the grease. The owner was once a props guy in the film industry.
2507 W. Broadway, 604-739-0005

Photo: Solo

exotic gourmet to go

Choa Phraya

Spice up your next TV dinner by leaving the wok work to the pros and have them drop off tasteful Thai dishes like barbecue chicken with fresh herbs (gai yang) or sautéed garlic prawns (koung pad khing).
2325 Cambie St., 604-732-3939

Photo: Solo

Habibi's

For your next Middle Eastern soirée, spend your time setting up the Moroccan tea glasses and bartering with the belly dancer and order food here. For tasty, and healthy, take-out, try the shoumadar (beet salad), foule (baby fava beans in lemon and garlic), and Lebanese-style hummus.
1128 W. Broadway, 604-732-7487

Rubina Grill

Pick up your reusable metal tiffin (two- or four-tiered stacking lunch boxes from Bombay) and they'll fill 'em up with tasty Indian fare and send you on your way. With prices like this (from $4 to $7.50), you may want to get rid of those brown bags.
1689 Johnston St., Granville Island Public Market, 604-662-7778; Capilano Mall Food Court, 935 Marine Dr., North Vancouver, no telephone

Vij's Masala

It took proprietor Vikram Vij eight years to open another eatery but, like his style of cooking, he believes in a long, slow braise over a quick flash in the pan. Vij's newest venture serves succulently simple lunches and ready-to-eat Indian dishes. Take-out for the taste-conscious.
1488 W. 11th Ave., 604-736-5711

Vera's Burger Shack

The co-owner plays for the Canadian Football League, and was recently traded from B.C. to Toronto. The company motto is "You can't beat Vera's meat" and you'd better not argue with that.
1935 Cornwall Ave., 604-228-8372; 2506 Bellevue Ave. (at Dundarave Pier), North Vancouver, 604-603-8372

West

If you're looking to go high end, try the Wagu beef burger (from hand-massaged cattle that listen to classical music). The problem with most cows today? Too much rap.
2881 Granville St., 604-738-8938

White Spot

Their Legendary Burger is, well, just that. In fact, in a recent polling of Vancouver food critics it was one of their most popular guilty pleasures.
1616 W. Georgia St., 604-681-8034 and other locations

Photo: VPL 59417

design of the times:
Vancouver's sharpest rooms

Lumière Bar

When chef/proprietor Rob Feenie earned the prestigious Relais Gourmand classification at Lumière, one of the recommendations was that he build a proper separate entrance. Feenie took the space next door, and to offset the cost of a new entrance, built the tasting bar. There are 12 items on the menu at $12 each, in a very smart room with great service and even better drinks. Like everything Feenie lays his hands on, Lumière Bar was an instant success.
2551 W. Broadway, 604-739-8185

Tangerine

Opened as a side project by two brothers-in-law (an architect and a graphic designer). Things worked out so well that they formed a design company that now creates rooms for other restaurateurs.
1685 Yew St., 604-739-4677

Vij's

The first contemporary Indian room in this city. Much like the restaurant, it's in a class of its own.
1480 W. 11th Ave., 604-736-6664

Photo: Rob Melnychuk

Elixir

The steak-frites is the big seller at this busy brasserie-fashioned restaurant at the Opus Hotel.

322 Davie St., 604-642-0557

Photo: Solo

Hy's Encore

This classic steak house is known both for its well-aged servers and well-aged beef.

637 Hornby St., 604-683-7671

Morton's of Chicago

American decor, American portions ... but you may need to earn American dollars to afford it.

757 W. Hastings St., 604-915-5105

The Smoking Dog

The peppercorn steak is almost as notorious as gregarious proprietor Jean-Claude Ramond.

1889 W. 1st Ave., 604-732-8811

shuck & slurp:
Vancouver is your oyster

Photo: Solo

Bacchus

Across from to the Vancouver Courthouse, Bacchus at the Wedgewood Hotel attracts judges, lawyers, and "not guilty" verdict revelers.
845 Hornby St., 604-608-5319

Elixir

Accordion-style folding windows open up to the sidewalk in the I-can't-believe-it's-not-Paris Garden Room. Chef Don Letendre serves up French classics at this Opus Hotel eatery, like onion soup and salade Niçoise.
322 Davie St., 604-642-0557

The Lobster Man

This seafood market on Granville Island is the only place to get your oysters when you want to do the shucking yourself. Knowledgeable staff will walk you through the dozen or so varieties and provide you with recipes and shucking instructions. Live tanks are fitted with ultraviolet lights to kill any possible bacteria, so shuck with a clear conscience.
1807 Mast Tower Rd., Granville Island, 604-687-4228

Showcase

Paul Simon knew of 50 ways to leave his lover but executive chef Bruce Knapic can produce at least six ways to win her back. His "6 Oysters prepared 6 Ways" combines hot and cold variations like lobster Rockefeller or fresh on the half shell with champagne foam. In the Marriott Pinnacle Hotel.
1128 W. Hastings St., 604-684-1128

Rodney's Oyster House; The Mermaid Room;
The Screaming Oyster

Photo: Solo

When you're looking to make the oyster your world, any of these locations will do. The boys behind the bar at Rodney's have been known to shuck in the buff (except for their aprons) for an enthusiastic group of single forty-somethings. The Mermaid Room is a private room above the restaurant with clamshell chairs and a floor that resembles the beach. The Screaming Oyster is new in Whistler.
Rodney's/Mermaid: 1228 Hamilton St.,
604-609-0080
Screaming: 2102 Lake Placid Rd., Whistler,
604-938-6687

splendid sushi

Aki

The room is the nicest of any sushi restaurant in the city with an extensive menu that more than holds its own.
745 Thurlow St., 604-682-4032

Blue Water Café & Bar

Step up to the separate sushi bar at this seafood haven and order the Blue Water Roll (crispy prawn) or the humorous Caterpillar Roll (salmon topped with avocado and capers for eyes that appears to crawl across your plate).
1095 Hamilton St., 604-688-8078

Honjin Sushi

A newcomer to Yaletown, but already known for innovative dishes and the chef's enthusiasm to provide regulars with a new experience each visit.
138 Davie St., 604-688-8808

Shijo's

Consistent, great quality sushi in Kitsilano.
1926 W. 4th Ave., 604-732-4676

Tojo's

Bring your appetite, but don't forget your wallet. Try his inspired Rainbow Roll.
#202-777 W. Broadway, 604-872-8050

VEGETARIAN DELIGHTS
Although the **Naam** (*2724 W. 4th Ave., 604-738-7151*) may be a Vancouver vegetarian landmark in the heart of Kitsilano, some of the laid-back servers have short-term memories. So leave yourself lots of time and order a few extra tofu dishes as they may not all arrive.

If you're looking for something a little less groovy, try **Habibi's** (*1128 W. Broadway, 604-732-7487*) for fresh, modern, and award-winning Lebanese vegetarian fare.

Buddhist inspired I-can't-believe-it's-not-meat dishes are available at **Bo Kong** (*3068 Main St., 604-876-3088; 80-8100 Ackroyd Rd., Richmond, 604-278-1992*).

For vegetarians on-the-go, Vancouver's **Yves** vegetarian hot dogs are sold by most street vendors and their veggie burgers just got picked up by McDonald's.

Midnight Snacks

Photo: Hamid Attie

Bin 941 & Bin 942

Brush elbows in either of these busy rooms with post-shift restaurant workers and late-night bar hoppers. Flavourful, inventive tapas-style dishes are the trademark of chef/proprietor Gord Martin.
941: 941 Davie St., 604-683-1246
942: 1521 W. Broadway,
604-734-9421

Wild Rice

At this modern Asian restaurant, stick to the simple dishes with fewer and less esoteric ingredients. A beautiful turquoise resin bar was custom-made by acclaimed Vancouver designer Martha Sturdy.
117 W. Pender St., 604-642-2882

sweet teeth: chocolatiers

Thomas Haas

Well-known for his chocolates, Haas supplies **Senses Bakery** (*801 W. Georgia St., 604-633-0138*) and oversees the dessert cart at **Diva at the Met** (*645 Howe St., 604-602-7788*). On the North Shore, keep an eye out for Haas's chocolate factory (set to open spring 2004; *128-998 Harbourside Dr., North Vancouver, 604-904-7479*) that will include a *"salon du chocolat"* where you can sample the latest batch.

Thierry Busset

Having worked throughout Europe with some heavyweights like Albert Roux and Marco Pierre White, Busset touched down in Vancouver (in part due to a love for kayaking and the outdoors) and makes the finest pastries in town. The fruits of Busset's labour can be sampled at **CinCin** (*1154 Robson St., 604-688-7338*).

Literature & the Arts

Galleries, bookstores, museums, theatre, dance: Vancouver's got it all, and more. For the straight story on readings and openings, not to mention the scoop on where you can learn to act and dance up a storm yourself, read on. Special bonus: the story of the rock stars who evolved.

Unknown Cybersource

When local cyberscribe **William Gibson** was writing *Virtual Light*, set amongst San Francisco's bike courier scene, he went straight to the source, working his way through a stack of back issues of the SF messenger zine *Mercury Rising*. So his depiction of the life of couriers is pretty accurate, except for one thing. His characters use the word "proj" to mean "hurry up" or "let's go," whereas even rookie couriers know the phrase is slang for weed. (Guess Gibson misinterpreted the fact that everybody leaves the room whenever the word is spoken.) By the way, the character J-Bone in Gibson's short story "Johnny Mnemonic" – played by Ice-T in the film – is almost certainly borrowed from real-life San Francisco messenger Jason "J-Bone" Abernathy, more recently of the Denver Professional Bike Messengers Association.

The Case of the Bibliophile

Ever wonder what happened to Celia Duthie, Vancouver's most famous book purveyor? After selling her eponymous store to her sister, she began studying woodland management, natch. Perhaps all those years shifting paper drove home the fact that there's a need to develop value-added wood products in B.C., rather than shipping out the raw materials and buying them back as something else. Her love of silviculture and reading have recently merged in a range of book furniture. Called **Duthie Bookcases**, the line is made on Vancouver Island from native woods like alder, fir, and yew. Her first customer was Canadian author Nancy Richler (*Your Mouth is Lovely*) who bought a dictionary stand. Products include a new revolving bookcase and an Arts and Crafts model, and may expand to include library desks and barrister bookcases. Order them at **Duthie Books** (*2239 W. 4th Ave., 604-732-5344, duthiebookcases.com*).

totally booked

THE VANCOUVER CANON

Writing fiction, unlike investment banking, is a vocation that can be done from anywhere on Earth, so you may as well pick somewhere beautiful. Perhaps that's why Vancouver and its surrounding islands are home to an astonishing number of novelists and poets. And virtually no investment bankers. Famed Canadian novelist Margaret Atwood was even inspired to write poetry here: "We ran west/wanting/a place of absolute/informed beginning." But as a city barely more than 100 years old, there are very few romantic, wistful, or even disdainful references to Vancouver in fiction. Vancouver is a nice place to live, but the action happens elsewhere. But that's all changing. Here's how some Vancouver-based writers have seen our city in fiction:

Author: William Gibson
Story: "The Winter Market," 1984
Landmarks mentioned: In this short story set in the future, the world famous science fiction writer (and coiner of the term cyberspace) creates a dystopic **Granville Island** (The Winter Market). Looking North towards downtown, the character Rubin sees "the city beyond the Market a clean sculpture of light, a lie, where the broken and the lost burrow into the gomi [garbage in Japanese] that grows like humus at the bases of the towers of glass…" Sounds a little like Concord Pacific, the condo development right across the water that had not yet been built when the story was written.

Author: Douglas Coupland

Book: Girlfriend in a Coma, 1998
Landmarks mentioned: North Vancouver's **Sentinal Spartans** football team, **Handsworth High School**, and **Lions Gate Hospital** all appear on page one. As a North Shore native, Generation X author Coupland was

THE ANTI-VANCOUVER CANON

Lee Henderson *(leehenderson .com)* is a talented young author noted for his award-winning first book of short stories, *The Broken Record Technique*. He grew up on the Prairies, but now resides in Vancouver with his wife. But don't expect him to be loving up this city in his prose. A quote: "For me, if I'm writing about Vancouver or Saskatoon, it's because of a deep-seated hatred of these places. I have no romantic feelings about it. I've hated almost every place that I've lived and I hate Vancouver — I hate everything about it. So that comes out in the writing" (*The Globe and Mail*, June 28, 2003). Fine, then.

THE NON-VANCOUVERITE VANCOUVER CANON

On the flipside, there's civic booster and American science fiction legend, **Philip K. Dick**. It's well-known that the author of the 1968 book *Do Androids Dream of Electric Sheep?* (on which the movie *Blade Runner* is based) hung around Vancouver for a time after delivering his landmark lecture "The Android and the Human" at a 1972 science fiction convention. Things went from bad to worse for the depressive drug addict, who attempted to commit suicide and checked himself into a rehab for heroin addicts called X-Kalay. While in Vancouver, he also attempted to seduce a Vancouver woman named Andrea who is immortalized as the character "Jamis" in his book *The Girl With the Black Hair*. But not all the memories were bad, apparently. In his 1981 book *The Divine Invasion*, he writes:

"Let us go," she said, "hand in hand. Like Beethoven and Goethe: two friends. Take us to Stanley Park in British Columbia and we will observe the animals there, the wolves, the great white wolves. It is a beautiful park, and Lionsgate Bridge [sic] is beautiful; Vancouver, British Columbia is the most beautiful city on Earth."

a pioneer of incorporating real Vancouver places into his internationally acclaimed work.

Photo: Rosalee Hiebert

Author: Michael Turner
Book: The Pornographer's Poem, 1999
Landmarks mentioned: Along with real streets and high schools, the **Venus Theatre**, an old 16-mm porn theatre at 720 Main Street, was immortalized in this novel. It's autobiographical, so now even his mom knows about his misspent youth. Luckily he grew up to redeem himself with the books *Hard Core Logo*, about a punk band (Turner was in the band Hard Rock Miners), and *American Whiskey Bar*. The former was made into a film directed by Bruce McDonald and the latter into a live TV drama broadcast on Toronto's CityTV.

Author: Timothy Taylor
Book: Stanley Park, 2001
Landmarks mentioned: The main character opens a restaurant on **Cambie Street** and visits his father, a squatter in **Stanley Park**, where real places like **Siwash Rock** are part of the story. The book has been optioned as a film, so Vancouver will play Vancouver on screen—an equally rare occurrence.

Author: Kevin Chong
Book: Baroque-a-Nova, 2001
Landmarks mentioned: The town in the book is loosely based on **Ladner**, a Vancouver suburb where Chong spent part of his childhood. The book is named for a song on a jukebox at **Helen's Diner** on the corner of Main Street and 25th Avenue in Vancouver. Wong and other young Vancouver fiction writers are known to hang out at this retro diner.

Wealthy and Well Read

West Vancouver is the wealthiest postal code in Canada. The **West Vancouver Memorial Library** (*1950 Marine Dr., 604-925-7400, westvanlib.org*) has the highest lending rate in the country. We set out to unravel the mystery. Was the lending rate indicative of the population's tight-fistedness, and hence unwillingness to actually buy books? Were they signing out get-rich-quick paperbacks that we should know about immediately? In our scientific, double-blind study that consisted of one call to the West Van reference librarian Ted Benson, he attributed the high lending rate to the fact that the community is literate and wealthy, and to the quality and diversity of the collection. The most popular books? Michael Moore's *Stupid White Men*, and anything by Bernard Lewis. *The Life of Pi* and *Angela's Ashes* were also heavily in demand. Upon further investigation with the Adult Desk, we also discovered that the library has the best Persian book collection in North America, a great mystery collection, and since it has such a nice ambiance with natural light and a courtyard, many well-known people are regulars who do their work and the library – such as author/illustrator Nick Bantock (*Griffin & Sabine*) as well as the artist Susanna Blunt (she did the new portrait of Queen Elizabeth for Canadian coins).

Public Words

Photo: Ken Paquette

Want to know what 40,000 literature fanatics look like en masse? Head to the area around Library Square in downtown Vancouver between 11 a.m. and 6 p.m on the last Sunday of September. The **Word on The Street** festival is almost 10 years old, and includes readings by well-known writers, discussion panels, music, children's tents, magazines and lots of free stuff for those who buy the famous book bags. Local book and magazine publishers and retailers also set up booths. *thewordonthestreet.ca*

Booked Up

Vancouver has a bookstore for every kind of taste, from graphic novels to high-end cookbooks.

Banyen Books
Everything you ever wanted to know about your aura, your chakras, or downward-facing-dog.
2671 W. Broadway, 604-732-7912, banyen.com

Photo: Solo

Barbara jo's Books to Cooks
All the best cookbooks in the world, plus great magazines and cooking demonstrations from celebrity chefs.
1128 Mainland St., 604-688-6755

Black Bond Books
Canada's largest independent bookstore chain, with 12 outlets.
1-5562-24th Ave., Surrey, 604-536-4444 and other locations

An "A" for Press Coverage

Graduates of the **UBC creative writing program** famously dominated *Toronto Life* magazine's 2002 summer fiction issue (dubbed *Vancouver Life*) and continue to be a prolific and vaunted group. In 2003, the Danuta Gleed Literary Award for Canadian Short Fiction was awarded to Lee Henderson (*The Broken Record Technique*) and the runners-up were Timothy Taylor (*Silent Cruise*) and Nancy Lee (*Dead Girls*); all three graduated from the program. Other notable grads include Eden Robinson (Governor General's Award and Giller Prize shortlists for *Monkey Beach*), Stephanie Bolster (Governor General's Award for *White Stone: The Alice Poems*), Anne Fleming (Governor General's Award and Danuta Gleed shortlists for *Pool Hopping and Other Stories*), Tammy Armstrong (Governor General's Award shortlist for *Bogman's Music*), Lynn Coady (Governor General's Award shortlist for *Strange Heaven*), and Madeleine Thien (Ethel Wilson Fiction Prize and City of Vancouver Book Award winner and Commonwealth Writers Prize regional finalist for *Simple Recipes*).

Blackberry Books

Granville Island's resident bookstore carries a lot of hard-to-find small press titles.
1663 Duranleau St., 604-685-6188

Book Mark

Most of the books are next door at the Vancouver Public Library, but there's all kinds of other stuff geared to the bookworms hanging around the area.
350 W. Georgia St., 604-331-4040

Chapters/Indigo

The Canadian megachain offers coffee, selection, and some offbeat book tables (e.g., "Small Ideas That Shook the World," "Frankly, My Queer," "Whatever Turns Your Crank").
788 Robson St., 604-682-4066; 2505 Granville St., 604-731-7822; 8171 Ackroyd Rd. Richmond, 604-303-7392; other locations; chapters.ca

The Evils of Bad Grammar

As if you needed another reason to keep your kids away from Surrey, the Vancouver suburb with the highest rate of violent crime in the country. The staunchly conservative and small-minded Surrey School Board has been in the eye of the national media for some time, since banning story books called *Asha's Mums*, *Belinda's Bouquet*, and *One Dad, Two Dads, Brown Dad, Blue Dads* from its classrooms. All, you may have guessed, deal with same-sex families. The issue went all the way to the Supreme Court of Canada, where a judge warned the school board against using religious arguments to ban books. So the trustees changed their tack. Their new set of arguments for banning said books centres around the shoddy spelling, grammar, and storylines. *Asha's Mums* switches tense on one page, uses the American spelling of "favourite," and when Asha puts on her red sweatsuit, the accompanying black-and-white illustration shows her in white, they argued. What's more, the Belinda in *Belinda's Bouquet* is overweight, which suggests that is okay, a board member said. The books are still banned.

1991 was a good year for **Nick Bantock**. He was toiling away as an obscure-but-talented illustrator of book covers on Bowen Island just off Vancouver, but always made time to meet up with the local boys for their regular poker games. Since old Bantock was the starving artist of the group (and a legendary miser), his pals covered for him when it was his turn to provide the libations. Then came 1991. It was the year he published the first book in his *Griffin & Sabine* trilogy, the gorgeous adult picture books that document, in postcards and pictures, a surreal love story between the characters Griffin Moss and Sabine Strohem. The books went on to sell more than 3 million copies and spend 100 weeks on the *New York Times* bestseller list. So when it next came round to Bantock's turn to bring the hooch to the poker game that year, his buddies let it be known that now, he'd have to bring his share. But it seems that the windfall did nothing to change his miserly ways. The story goes that he pulled a bottle of the cheapest whiskey he could find out of his back, poured everyone a sip, then screwed on the cap, and put it back in his bag for good. He's since gone on to write and illustrate more than two dozen books and moved to the rolling hills and gold-paved lanes of West Vancouver.

Photo: Solo

Book Warehouse

New titles start at twenty percent below the list price and go down from there, so dig deep in those bargain bins. A good selection of local and Canadian authors.
*2388 W. 4th Ave., 604-734-5711
and five other locations,
bookwarehouse.ca*

Dead Write

Whodunnit?
*7374 W. 10th Ave., 604-228-8223,
deadwrite.com*

Duthie Books

A comprehensive bookstore with a literate staff. How, er, novel.
*2239 W. 4th Ave., 604-732-5344,
duthiebooks.com*

Photo: Solo

Photo: Jess Atwood Gibson

Photo: Solo

Granville Book Company

A little bit of everything right in the heart of the Granville strip. Tried and true, this store's been around forever.

850 Granville St., 604-687-2213

Hager Books

A literary bookstore that will do special orders from as far away as Europe.

2176 W. 41st Ave., 604-263-9412

Lawrence's Used Books

A great antiquarian bookstore with a very loyal following.

3591 W. 41st Ave., 604-261-3812

If you think you see Margaret Atwood pinching tomatoes at the Granville Island Public Market in October – it probably is. More than 70 international writers and 11,000 readers converge annually on Granville Island over five days in late October for the **Vancouver International Writers (and Readers) Festival**, one of North America's top literary events. Artistic director Alma Lee has an uncanny ability to book appearances from authors right before their Giller and Booker Prize nominations are announced. Then-unknowns Richard Ford, Ian Rankin, Jack Whyte, Witi Ihimaera (writer of the movie *Whale Rider*), Elizabeth George, Evelyn Lau, Nino Ricci, Rohinton Mistry, Vikram Seth, Sheri-D Wilson, Wayson Choy, Gail Anderson-Dargatz, Elizabeth George, Diana Gabaldon, and many more have made their public debuts (sometimes emboldened by backstage swigs) over the festival's 16-year history. The literary talent on display can be dazzling – perhaps too dazzling, such as the time when *Sex and the City* author Candace Bushnell caused a male volunteer to faint.

604-681-6330, writersfest.bc.ca

**Little Sister's Book
and Art Emporium**

Legendary importers of "obscenities"
— according to Canada Customs —
and possibly one of the finest gay
and lesbian bookstores anywhere,
with a wide selection that appeals to
the straight crowd too.
*1238 Davie St., 604-669-1753,
lsisters.com*

The rarest B.C. collectible is a complete set of
1862 British Columbia gold and silver coins – $10
and $20 pieces in gold and silver – minted at the
height of the Fraser River gold rush, but never issued.
Only a handful have survived, and many of them
are in museums, making the privately owned coins
ultra-rare and ultra-expensive.

The coins date to a pre-Confederation era when the
province was divided into two colonies, Vancouver
Island and British Columbia. Vancouver Island's capital
was located in Victoria, while British Columbia's was in
New Westminster. The colonies boomed in 1858 after
word reached the California goldfields that gold had
been discovered in sand bars along the Fraser River.

Before the gold rush, Fort Victoria had a population of
about 300 and the mainland was even more sparsely
populated. By the time of the 1861 census, the non-
Native population of Vancouver Island had reached
3,024, while the non-Native population of the mainland
was 10,600.

But the gold rush produced a problem in that miners
needed a way to convert their gold dust to currency. In
1861, Governor James Douglas wrote to Britain about
the need for a B.C. coin, and sent colonial assayer
Francis Claudet to San Francisco to buy coin-making
equipment. The dyes for the coins were made in San

Macleod's Books

An antiquarian bookstore that
specializes in rare editions and once
banned books – like Henry Miller's
Tropic of Cancer.
455 W. Pender St., 604-681-7654

Photo: Solo

Francisco by Albert Kuner, who had done many coins in the American West.

The B.C. mint was set up in the assay office in New Westminster in June 1862, and some sample coins were made and sent to Douglas. One side featured the British crown and the legend, "Government of British Columbia." On the reverse was "20 dollars, 1862," surrounded by a wreath. But Douglas had changed his mind about the need for a B.C. coin, and decided not to issue them. A small batch was made for an exhibition in London, but that was it.

B.C.'s premier monetary expert, Ron Greene, says about four to six copies of each coin are known to exist. The rarest coin is the $10 gold piece; Greene says there are only two known examples outside museums, and one of them hasn't been seen since it was sold in Amsterdam in 1937.

How the coins ever got out of government hands is a mystery. One theory is that the provincial government sold them to government ministers as mementos. Former premier John Robson used to carry a $10 gold coin on a watch chain; it is now in the B.C. Archives, which has the only other full set of the coins. B.C. coins can also be found in the collections of the Bank of Canada, the Canadian Imperial Bank of Commerce, and the British Museum.

The British Museum's two gold coins were donated in 1864 by Douglas' successor, Frederick Seymour. (Seymour is the only governor in B.C. history who is believed to have died from an overdose of laudanum, a 19th-century "medicine" that mixed opium with alcohol.) King Farouk of Egypt once had a B.C. coin, while American Virgil Brand had seven in his collection of 350,000.

Toronto businessman Sid Belzberg is the only private collector with a complete set. He tried to sell them at auction in 2003, but the estimates of US$250,000 each for the gold coins and US$35,000 and US$50,000 for the silver coins weren't met, so he elected not to sell them.

The **Chan Centre for the Performing Arts** at UBC (*6265 Crescent Rd., 604-822-9197, chancentre.com*) was controversial from the start. Political science profs who overlooked the site from their ivory tower complained that Bing Thom's architectural masterpiece looked like a nuclear reactor. Whatever your impressions of the outside of the spherical building, you can't deny the brilliance of its architect. The building's developer requested that Thom cut down all the trees surrounding the building so that theatre patrons could have a view of the water from the lobby. Thom refused, explaining that since theatre events are held in the evening, the water would be in complete darkness anyway. He left the trees and installed special non-reflective glass used in airplane windshields in the lobby. Now you can look out into a magical stand of trees (rather than complete darkness) while sipping your intermission cocktails.

Read

This small shop within Granville Island's Charles H. Scott Gallery at the Emily Carr Institute of Art and Design stocks great art books and esoteric small-press titles.
1399 Johnston St., Granville Island, 604-844-3811

Sophia Books

Vancouver's premier foreign language bookstore, with titles in French, Japanese, and other languages, not to mention an unusual number of hard-to-find foreign fashion magazines (like street 'zines from Tokyo) and fashion books on pattern drafting, draping, and the like.
492 W. Hastings St., 604-684-0484, sophiabooks.com

Photo: Solo

Vancouver Art Gallery Store

Known for its superior selection of fine art books, even if the book section has been inexplicably downsized.
750 Hornby St., 604-662-4706

Vancouver Kidsbooks

There is a world beyond Harry Potter. A fabulous place to buy a gift book for a child; staff know exactly what they'll love and gift-wrapping is free.
3083 W. Broadway, 604-738-5335; 3040 Edgemont Blvd., North Vancouver, 604-986-6190; kidsbooks.bc.ca

Women in Print

Features books, magazines, and other media by, for, and about women.
3566 W. 4th Ave., 604-732-4128, womeninprint.ca

32 Books

Some of literature's biggest names come to read at this little independent on the North Shore.
3018 Edgemont Blvd., North Vancouver, 604-980-9032

Everything You Always Wanted to Know About Art (But Were Afraid to Ask)

Are you one of those people who go to art galleries and museums and wished you knew more about the artists and their work, but are too embarrassed to admit your humble ignorance? There's help available. The **Contemporary Art Society of Vancouver** (*casvancouver@hotmail.com*) is a non-profit organization founded in 1977 to promote an appreciation and understanding of twentieth and twenty-first-century art. Each year the CASV organizes lectures by prominent artists, critics, collectors, dealers, and museum people from all parts of North America and around the world. Recent lecturers have included Seattle video artist Gary Hill, the Berlin-based architecture collective Graft, Los Angeles-based artist Sandeep Mukherjee, and curator Wayne Baerwaldt of the Power Plant in Toronto. Events are often held at the Emily Carr Insitute of Art and Design on Granville Island.

DIY Gallery Tour

The full-colour **Art Guide to BC** (*art-bc.com*) provides a road map to more than 300 artists, artisans, and galleries in British Columbia. Published by Trudy Van Dop – who also runs the **Van Dop Gallery** (*421 Richmond St., New Westminster, 604-521-7887, vandopgallery.com*) – the guide is organized by provincial region, so if you've got some time to kill at Granville Island, you can visit the venues there. The listings include photographs, descriptions, and coordinates, and the guide is available at BCAA offices, BC Ferries terminals, tourist centres, and hotel kiosks.

cool collector galleries

Catriona Jeffries Gallery

She's known as a cultural ambassador for Vancouver and as a mentor of new talent.
3149 Granville St., 604-736-1554, catrionajeffries.com

Diane Farris Gallery

An institution in the Vancouver art scene, when West 7th (at Granville) is blocked with limos, you know where their owners are shopping.
1590 W. 7th Ave., 604-737-2629, dianefarrisgallery.com

Monte Clark Gallery

The latest crop of art stars in combination with international names like Graham Gilmore. Check out the little room off the back lane where the most edgy installations are to be found. Artists' openings are always celebrity-studded. Recently opened a new gallery in Toronto that was the talk of the town.
2339 Granville St., 604-730-5000, monteclarkgallery.com

Simon Patrich Galleries

Courteney Cox paid $18,000 for a Michael Abraham painting here in 2001 for husband David Arquette's 29th birthday. She went back in 2003 to buy another of his pieces for $11,500.
2329 Granville St., 604-733-2662

Edgy Little Galleries

Art Beatus
The Vancouver branch of an esteemed Hong Kong gallery, featuring contemporary Chinese art.
M1-888 Nelson St., 604-688-2633, artbeatus.com

Photo: Solo

Artspeak
A small but always interesting artist-run centre.
233 Carrall St., 604-688-0051, artspeak.bc.ca

Belkin Satellite
If you love the UBC location, love its little sister, too, located in the Contemporary Art Gallery's former space.
555 Hamilton St. 604-687-3174

Bfly Atelier

Gold ceilings and hardwood floors
make the warehousey Gastown spot
a stunning venue for fashion shows
as well as art.
341 Water St., 2nd floor,
604-647-1019

Centre A

That's "A" as in Asian — a centre for
contemporary Asian art.
849 Homer St., 604-683-8326,
centrea.org

Photo: Solo

Gallery 83

Editorial photographers showcase
their personal creative work at this
quiet little jewel in hectic Chinatown.
83 E. Pender St., 604-605-3166

The most successful band from Vancouver's new wave period didn't sell any records, but it probably had more world-famous artists in its ranks than any rock group in history. **UJ3RK5** (known as the Ujerks) was an eight-piece troupe that worked the quirky, arty side of the new wave explosion, *à la* Talking Heads, Devo, or Pere Ubu. Songs like *UJ3RK5 Work For Police* and *Eisenhower and the Hippies* were catchy and jerky and hilarious — music that made your brain dance along with your feet.

The lead singer and main songwriter was Frank Ramirez, an unusual fellow with a unique lyrical sensibility and a bizarre sense of rhythm. The band put out a six-song EP on Quintessence Records, and contributed a song to the *Vancouver Complication* compilation, but folded soon after Polygram Records picked up the EP and people started to take them seriously.

So keyboardist **Jeff Wall**, guitarist **Rodney Graham**, and bassist **Ian Wallace** went back to their cameras and became the mainstays of the "Vancouver school" of photo-conceptual art. While their profiles in Canada are still growing, in Europe they're art superstars whose work sells for tens of thousands of dollars apiece.

Forgotten Sculptor

Sculptor **Charles Marega** may not be a household name, but his works remain beloved Vancouver landmarks, six decades after his death. Marega's lions guard the entrance to the Lions Gate Bridge. His statue of Captain George Vancouver stands in front of Vancouver City Hall. And he's all over the West End, with a statue of American President Warren Harding and a bust of early Vancouver mayor David Oppenheimer in Stanley Park and the Joe Fortes fountain at English Bay.

But one of Marega's most notable works is hidden away in the Vancouver archives, and likely will never see the light of day – a bust of the Italian dictator Benito Mussolini.

Marega was born in Gorizia in what is now Italy on Sept. 24, 1871, and arrived in Vancouver in 1909. But he never forgot his Italian roots, and created the Mussolini statue in the 1930s, when Il Duce was still respected by Italians around the world.

When Canada and Italy went to war in 1939, the sculpture of the fascist leader was quietly taken out of public sight. Marega wasn't around to argue – he had died on March 27, 1939, five months before the start of the Second World War.

Art Appreciation

Attention commitment-phobic art buffs: the **Vancouver Art Gallery** operates a little-known rentals department whereby gallery members can rent artwork from its archives to hang in their own homes for a month at a time. The rentals collection consists of more than 800 works, including paintings, photographs, and sculpture. Fees can be as low as $8 per month (they are based on a percentage of the art work's value) and for businesses, rental fees are tax-deductible. If you decide you can't part with your new Sheila Norgate acrylic-on-canvas, your rental fee will be deducted from the purchase price. Call 604-662-4746.

Grunt

An artist-run space at the bottom of a building of live/work studios.
116-350 E. 2nd Ave.,
604-875-9516

Onepointsix Design Studio and Gallery

A Monte Clark protégé opened this tiny shrine to sleek furniture design and contemporary art.
878 Homer St., 604-684-0478,
onepointsix.com

State

Widely thought to be the best photography gallery in town. A recent show travelled to L.A.'s hip downtown Standard Hotel.
1564 W. 6th Ave., Upper Floor,
604-632-0198

some artsy types

The Vancouver School

Pictures of empty Vancouver streets and suburban condo developments collector's items? Bet your bottom dollar they are. The Vancouver School of photographers, populated by Stan Douglas, Roy Arden, Ian Wallace, Ken Lum, Arni Haraldsson, Jeff Wall, and others is especially popular in Germany and other parts of Europe where photography is a more highly valued art form. Look for Jeff Wall's stunning back-lit cibachrome prints at the Vancouver Art Gallery.

Vikky Alexander

Contemporary artist specializing in lush postmodern landscapes, from French gardens to Vegas to the West Edmonton Mall.

Chris Gergley

Part of the "New Vancouver School," his fine art photography of South Granville apartment lobbies is an ongoing project. He is also heavily collected in Germany. Look for exhibits at Monte Clark.

Graham Gilmore

Though he now resides in New York, he occasionally exhibits his work here. His paintings of words arranged in patterns resembling intestines sound gross but are actually gorgeous.

Brian Jungen

First Nations artist, whose startling works bridge Native and consumer culture – such as "Cetelogy," a giant whale skeleton made from plastic chairs. Subject of a Vancouver Art Gallery show in 2005.

Atilla Richard Lukacs

The *enfant terrible* of the Vancouver art scene used to convert his allowance from his conservative father into gold dust and throw it on his homoerotic paintings in art school. Gay skinheads in combat boots is his signature subject, such as the vaunted "Adam and Steve," but his work is wide-ranging (and often controversial). His career has spanned from Europe to New York, but he has now relocated to Vancouver.

Scott Macfarlane

He's in his mid-twenties and his art career is only three years old, but the National Gallery of Canada acquired three of his photo-based works in 2003, and Jeff Wall named him "the" artist to watch.

Jack Shadbolt

Photo: VPL

The late, celebrated painter had a studio on Hornby Island where he turned out his highly valuable primitivist paintings of monsters, beasts, and bugs. He is known at the founder of West Coast modernism.

Chris Woods

A resident of Chilliwack, his world-famous work now focuses on mass-consumerism, with subjects like McDonald's and doughnut chains. You can see 14 of his mystical works permanently displayed in St. David's Anglican Church on Vancouver's Eastside.

Play Time

Catch stagings of classics and avant garde pieces at these venerable live-theatre venues.

Photo: Mandelbrot

Photo: Stan Douglas

Arts Club Theatre
1585 Johnston St., Granville Island, 604-687-1644, artsclub.com

Firehall Arts Centre
280 E. Cordova St., 604-689-0691, firehallartscentre.ca

Havana Restaurant and Gallery
1212 Commercial Dr., 604-253-9119, havana-art.com

Performance Works
1218 Cartwright St., Granville Island, 604-687-3020, granvilleisland.com

Frederick Wood Theatre
6354 Crescent Rd., UBC, 604-822-3880, theatre.ubc.ca

Vancouver East Cultural Centre
1895 Venables St., 604-251-1363, vecc.bc.ca

Vancouver artist **Stan Douglas** drew international acclaim for his 1999 work *Le Detroit*, a series of photographs of once magnificent buildings and neighbourhoods in Detroit that had fallen into ruin. He decided to turn his attention closer to home with *Every Building on 100 West Hastings*, a 16-foot-long panorama of the south side of the 100 block West Hastings, taken at night.

The block was once one of Vancouver's most vibrant shopping streets. Located across from Woodwards department store, it was home to a wide variety of stores, restaurants, and hotels, and contained some of the city's finest turn-of-the-20th-century commercial buildings. But since Woodwards closed in 1993, the street slid progressively downhill. Aside from pawn shops, the block is largely vacant, its handsome buildings slowly rotting away.

Douglas's inspiration for photographing the block was Edward Ruscha's famed piece, *Every Building on the Sunset Strip*. Working from 10 p.m. to 4 a.m. on August 27, 2001, Douglas virtually shut down the 100 block for the shoot. He lit the buildings with movie lights, set up in front of each building in the block, snapped 21 images, then blended them on computer. The result is a departure from a true panorama, where a camera rotates around from a single point, resulting in some distortion. In Douglas's photo, the streetscape is flattened out, because all the photos were taken from in front of the façade. The faded grandeur of the block really comes out in the photo, which was purchased by the Vancouver Art Gallery for its collection.

all the world's a stage

Vancouver is known as a hotbed for independent theatre. Here are some of the poor players who strut and fret their hours on the stage.

Electric Company Theatre
Their recent, award-winning play *The One That Got Away* was mounted and performed in a swimming pool. Splashy! The founders met at renowned local acting school, Studio 58 and formed the resident company of the Vancouver East Cultural Centre.
1885 Venables St., 604-253-4222, electriccompanytheatre.com

Gateway Theatre Society
The third largest theatre company in the Lower Mainland mounts four annual productions as well as the Pacific Piano Competition. The Gateway Academy for the Performing Arts is its theatre school.
6500 Gilbert Rd., Richmond, 604-270-6500, gatewaytheatre.com

Metropolitan Cooperative Theatre Society
This non-profit, amateur troupe has been performing styles from farce to English pantomime for more than 40 years.
604-266-7191, metrotheatre.com

Pink Ink Theatre Productions Association
The company's mandate is to produce French Canadian scripts in translation, so watch for anything by Robert Lepage.
604-872-1861

Théâtre la Seizième
B.C.'s only professional francophone theatre company operates out of the French Cultural Centre.
1545 W. 7th Ave., 604-736-2616

Act Facts: Theatre Schools

Arts Umbrella
Giving kids license to act up on Granville Island since 1979. Recently started an outreach program for east-side kids with the help of Sarah McLachlan.
1286 Cartwright St., Granville Island, 604-681-5268, artsumbrella.ca

Studio 58
A top rated school located in the basement of the Main Building at Langara College.
100 W. 49th Ave., 604-257-0366

UBC Department of Theatre, Film, and Creative Writing
6354 Crescent Rd., 2nd floor, 604-822-5985, theatre.ubc.ca/contactus.htm

Vancouver Youth Theatre
Innovative theatre training for young people ages 5 to 18.
100-6129-Windsor St., 604-877-0678, vyt.ca

Everybody Dance Now

GOH Ballet Academy

A beautiful ballet academy for novices to professionals. Specializes in adult classes. Drop-in: $15. 2345 Main St., 604-872-4014, gohballet.com

Harbour Dance Centre

Well-known for its great hip-hop, break dancing, and ballet classes. Membership: $28/year. Drop-in: $10/hour, non-member $11/hour. 927 Granville St., 3rd Floor, 604-684-9542, harbourdance.com.

Western Front

Jane Ellison leads dance classes affectionately called "boing boing" that include stretching, strengthening, and yoga to a wide variety of fabulous music. Drop-in: $7. 303 E. 8th Ave., 604-876-4146, front.bc.ca

Touchstone Theatre

Whether the play stars a forgotten war hero in a tiny Saskatchewan town or Franz Kafka, you'll be clapping. *604-709-9973, touchstonetheatre.com*

Rumble Productions

Risky and innovative are adjectives that come to mind when thinking of Rumble's plays; they focus on the works of emerging Canadian playwrights. *604-662-3395, rumble.org*

United Players of Vancouver Theatre Company

Classics from Dickens, Shaw, Coward, Molière, and their ilk. Founded in 1959, it's the resident company of the Jericho Arts Centre. *1675 Discovery St., 604-224-8007, unitedplayers.com*

Vancouver Theatre Sports League

Question: "Name a flavour of ice cream you would not want to eat." Answer: "Fish." So began one memorable sketch from this improvisational troupe that gets its inspiration from the audience. Operating from the Revue Theatre Cabaret on Granville Island. *1601 Johnston St., Granville Island, 604-687-1644, vtsl.com*

Cheap Date Nights

New York's MoMA does it, and so too the **Vancouver Art Gallery** (*750 Hornby St., 604-662-4719*). Dubbed "cheap date night," the gallery stays open till 9 p.m. on Thursdays, offering by-donation admission after 5. Watch for couples canoodling in the dark corners of the gallery's top floors. Regular admission is $12.50, so you might even have enough left to spring for a coffee afterward, big spender.

Shopping

成功

電話咭全部
九折!

Pop
e here

家庭用品★文具
HOUSE WARE ★ STATIONERY

神柜·拜神用品

Photo: Solo

From $3 bunches of dahlias to $5 million private islands, there are purchases here for every budget. From the wacky (underwear with a Prime Minister's face on it) to the tacky (*Garfield* memorabilia), we'll take you on a tour of an underground fashion empire, to the bowels of the rag trade, and to the core of the Japanese vintage market. Along the way, pick up a T-shirt with all of Bif Naked's tattoos on it, a supermodel snowboard, or a bag of primo pot seeds: it's all here for the taking.

Better Than
Canadian Tire Dollars

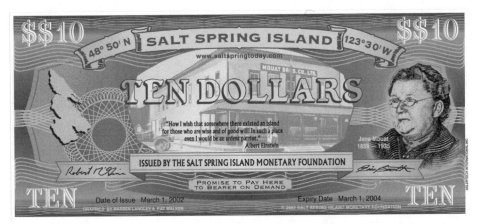

Shopping locally got a whole lot easier when Salt Spring Island, off Vancouver's coast, introduced its own currency in 2001 – thus creating the very first local currency in the world that is backed by a national currency. **Salt Spring dollars** are accepted at local banks and merchants at par with Canadian dollars. The bills, which feature orcas and historical buildings, are bought by tourists, who spend them on the island and often take whatever is left home as a souvenir – meaning free money for Salt Spring. But, in the typical bohemian island spirit, you may not need to buy their dollars at all, since Salt Spring (like several other Gulf Islands) also happens to be home to a store where everything is free.

Photo: Solo

Legendary New York window dresser Simon Doonan got reams of press for his controversial displays at Barneys New York, sometimes including homages to Madonna and sacrilegious imagery. The dream team of merchandisers at **Holt Renfrew** (*Pacific Centre, 633 Granville St., 604-681-3121, holtrenfrew.com*) also do great windows, but Vancouver audiences are far more sensitive than those in New York. A recent prom-themed display of a mannequin swinging from a chandelier had to be dismantled after passersby complained it looked like she was committing suicide. (?!) If you've ever walked past **Front** (*3772 Main St., 604-879-8431, front_company@hotmail.com*) and mistook the vintage clothing store for an art gallery, it's because one of the owners, Diana Li, is a professional artist. This past year saw displays such as a row of intricate dresses made entirely of paper (later shown at the Diane Farris Gallery), and a vast array of miniature tuxedos and ball gowns made of feathers. Installations have ranged from a display of custom-made corsets by Lace Embrace Atelier (*laceembrace.com*) around Valentine's Day to a huge model helicopter around the time of the war on Iraq. If you miss one of the displays, you can sometimes catch them when they move to **Loulou** (*3067 W. Broadway, 604-733-0466*), her family's quaint card and gift shop in Kits. The wacky windows at **Urban Empire**, (pictured above, *1108 Commercial Drive, 604-254-4700*) have included a bruised and bloodied Farrah Fawcett doll head, Mother Theresa breath freshener, and a flock of rubber ducks with signs protesting Premier Gordon Campbell. But owner Patricia Salmond's shining moment comes at Film Festival time in late September. The night before the festival opens she unveils what has been, since she started competing in 1997, the winning window display in the Festival's contest. Her victorious 2002 display was based on the premise of sleeping her way

WALK THIS WAY

It's way off the fashion radar, but a little-known store called **Scalie Shoes** in the otherwise unspectacular Kingsgate Mall (*102-370 E. Broadway, 604-877-0752*) has been shodding enterprising young fashion mavens on a budget for the past few years. You see, pointy toes and stiletto heels never went out of style at Scalie. Dubbed "skanky shoes," this stuck-in-the-80s shop may find you wrestling a drag queen or professional streetwalker for that last pair of leopard heels. But persist: they're just like the Dolce & Gabbana ones, really.

Local Wear Wares

Memorize this list of Vancouver designers and you'll thank us that you bought their clothing and jewellery when you could still afford it: **Mandula Moda, Dust** by **Heather Young, Allison Wonderland, Dace, Cake, Elsa Smith, Sunja Link, Anna De Courcy**, and **Isabelle Dunlop**. Now head to these great stores that always carry a selection from local designers:

The Block, *350 W. Cordova St., 604-685-8885, theblock.ca*

Bruce, *1038 Alberni St., 604-688-8802*

Dream Designs, *311 Cordova St., 604-683-7326*

Eugene Choo, *3683 Main St., 604-873-8874, eugenechoo.com*

to the top of the festival. The bordello-like installation included a bed (with the mandatory Film Fest poster screened onto the pillow) with sets of slippers tucked under it. There were gnarly, knobbly little hobbit slippers for *Lord of the Rings*, sack-o-potato slippers for *Sling Blade*, a rose-covered pair for *American Beauty*, and slippers made entirely of safety pins for *Sid and Nancy*. In 2003, the concept was rejected screenplays. When she put a sign in the window asking people to donate their old typewriters for the *mise-en-scène*, she got a serendipitous call from nearby Havana restaurant. They just happened to be mounting a play that involved destroying a different typewriter every night. The stacks of busted up typewriters made their way into what was slated to be the darkest, most perverse Film Fest window yet.

DIY Fashion

Photo: Solo

Ever looked at a tank top with a sparkly embellishment on it for $150 and thought, "I could make that!"? The problem is, most of us wouldn't ever get around to it. But now there's no excuse. If you have access to a hot glue gun and the address to **DressSew** (*337 W. Hastings St., 604-682-6196*), you're well on your way to becoming a fashion designer. Drop by nearby **Army & Navy** (pictured above, *27 W. Hastings St., 604-682-6644, armyandnavy.com*) for a pile of ribbed men's tank tops ($4-$10) then stop at DressSew for sequined decals in the shapes of birds and flowers, Swarovski crystals, and all manner of gauzy ribbon to glue on. For less than $15, you'll be the height of fashion.

Photo: Solo

People regularly complain that Vancouver's shoe stores don't do us justice. But boots? No complaints there. Not only was the first Canadian distributor of Dr. Martens based in Vancouver, but both **Dayton Boots** and **John Fluevog Boots & Shoes**, now known around the globe, started here. Daytons were originally made as boots for loggers but caught on in the film industry. The stars saw the crew wearing them, and before you knew it, everyone from Angelina Jolie to Johnny Depp (who loves them so much he even requested a factory tour) was sporting Daytons. For a taste of the company's heritage, visit the original Dayton location in the Downtown Eastside (*2250 E. Hastings St., 604-253-6671, daytonboots.com*) with the fluorescent boot sign and dozens of signed celebrity photos. For a taste of the modern image of Dayton, visit the newly opened flagship store (*872 Granville St., 604-682-2668*) near John Fluevog; the modular store showcases the solid leather boots like works of art. As for John Fluevog, his 14-eyelet boots came in crazy colours during the '80s punk movement, and his Angels (Fluevog is a devout Christian) have inspired many people to perform otherworldly feats while wearing them. They are known as 'vogs by their devout wearers, who will remember when the store was called Fox and Fluevog. There are Fluevog stores in London, New York, and Toronto, but the Granville location (*873 Granville St., 604-688-2828, fluevog.com*) is the original.

Photo: Solo

WHO IS THE REAL EDWARD CHAPMAN?

In a bizarre case of borrowed identity, there's trouble brewing among the blue-rinse set who shop at the storied **Edward Chapman's Ltd.**, established in 1890. Warring factions are opening retail locations right near each other with the late clothier's name on them, selling approximately the same labels. While the two families (one Chapman's decendants, one not) battle their way through the court system, you can take advantage of price wars at their competing stores at 2596 Granville Street (*604-732-3394*) and a block away at 2699 Granville Street (*604-738-0848*) as well as downtown at 833 West Pender Street (*604-685-6207*) and down the way at 750 West Pender Street (*604-688-6711*).

Photo: Solo

CHEAP THREADS

The relatively new **Fashion Exchange** building *(1951 Glen Dr.)* is a to-the-trade-only building full of fashion showrooms. But not only are there regular sample sales here, the main level has several showrooms, open to the public, that offer inexpensive Asian imports (designer knock-off purses, shoes, etc.) and accessories on a cash-and-carry basis. When this tip was first published in *Vancouver FASHION Magazine*, readers started calling to find out how they could access the building. Here's the answer: walk right through the front door.

This fable begins and ends with legendary Vancouver fashion retailer Chip Wilson. He founded boarder shop **Westbeach**, then sold it to a Japanese company that sold it to an American snowboard firm, who then hired Wilson back to work for them as a consultant so that he effectively got paid twice. Meanwhile, Wilson was busy with his sportswear line, **Homeless**. The Japanese were eager to buy that too, and during the negotiations, he twigged on to part of its appeal: the letter L in the name; the consonant does not figure into the Japanese language, so it is difficult for them to pronounce. Novelty plus North American equals cool. So when Wilson set off to launch a women's sportswear line in 2000, he naturally looked for a name with a large number of Ls – hence, **Lululemon Athletica** *(2113 W. 4th Ave., 604-732-6111; 1148 Robson St., 604-681-3118; lululemon.com)*. In just two years, the Lululemon brand grew from one to six stores across Canada and in California – without the help of the Japanese. But now Wilson is on to other stunts, such as getting into a tiff with the *Yoga Journal* over their reluctance to print his ad featuring a naked man in a yoga pose, as well as inviting people to arrive at his Robson Street store naked on opening day to win free Lululemon clothes. This resulted in hordes of naked 15-year-olds huddled on the street in the early morning while their horrified, yet powerless, mothers opined to news crews.

designer sample sales

Vancouver is home to a half-dozen of the country's top designers. Trouble is, most of them sell almost exclusively in the U.S. where they can access a bigger market and the high fashion buyer is less price-conscious. The flipside is that most of them offload extra stock and samples in Vancouver so as not to taint the U.S. market. Welcome to the big designer sample sale in the sky. As a side note, designers such as Catherine Regehr and Patricia Fieldwalker price their garments the same in the U.S. and Canada, so if you buy them here, they are automatically about 30 percent off. Here is a list of Vancouver designers who hold sample sales seasonally:

Jacqueline Conoir Designs

An appointment-only studio, you can book alone or with a group of friends. A beautiful, airy environment lets you wander warehouse aisles for edgy workwear, yoga wear, and the new eveningwear line at 30 percent less than you'd pay at department stores. Or sit back on the couch sipping wine and let the sales associates do the running around. Note: the changing room is communal. *46 W. 6th Ave., 604-688-5222, jcstudio.ca*

Yumi Eto

Canada's most celebrated young couturier, who sells at stores like Browns in London and Tokyo's Isetan. Most discounted pieces run around $500 but scoring an asymmetrical white coat for $150 is possible. Contact *yumieto@yumieto.com* to be added to the email list. *305-1008 Homer St., 604-689-8320, yumieto.com*

Patricia Fieldwalker

Gorgeous silk lingerie trimmed with French Calais lace, as seen in countless films and *Sex and the City*. Arrive early for larger sizes and her U.S.-only ready-to-wear line. Call to be added to the mailing list. *402-343 Railway St., 604-689-1210 or 888-689-SILK, pfieldwalker.com*

EVERYONE'S A WINNER

The Canadian discount chain **Winners** only recently arrived in the West but already we've discovered the ground rules. Suburban stores (like Surrey) carry larger sizes only, and if you're looking for designers more notable than Liz Claibourne, don't even bother. Instead, head to the tonier locations on the North Shore where the best buys are shoes, luggage, and lingerie. If you can approximate your size, skip the dressing room. Scan the housewares section for high-end cooking pots such as Le Creuset and Henkel knives. C by Chloe trousers (not even available in Vancouver) and a Ferré suit were recent finds at the Richmond location. These four locations are the best of the existing ten: Downtown (*798 Granville St.*), Richmond (*5300 No. 3 Rd., 604-279-9466*), North Vancouver (*1199 Lynn Valley Rd., 604-990-8230*), and West Vancouver (*2002 Park Royal South, 604-926-0944*).

Ron Leal

Production garments in a full range of sizes (remember, these were destined for the U.S. market, so a size 4 fits more like a Canadian 8). Prices are not bargain-basement cheap, but the quality is very good. Phone to join the fax or email lists.
305 W. 8th Ave., 604-669-2511, ronleal.com

Zonda Nellis

Drapy, flowy eveningwear for the artistic set since the 1980s. Call to be added to the customer database.
2203 Granville St., 604-736-5668, zondanellis.com

Catherine Regehr

Go early and go often to the quarterly sales and score a strapless silk dress for $75 (the beadwork on it alone would have cost more) or a black evening coat for $200. The best buys are her wedding dresses (retail $1,500) that have been known to go for $100. Sizes run 8 to 12. Watch local papers for sales four times a year.
111-1529 W. 6th Ave., 604-734-9339, catherineregehr.com

Martha Sturdy

The chunky resin jewellery that Sturdy invented in the 1980s could not be more the height of fashion again, judging from the number of fashion magazines that have been pulling from her archives for editorial spreads lately. Find gold and silver jewellery and her highly coveted housewares in discontinued colours and shapes. Watch local papers for sales four times a year.
12 W. 5th Ave, 604-872-5205, marthasturdy.com

Yaletown Sample Sales

Bi-annual sample sales open to the public are advertised on showroom doors along the 1000-blocks of Mainland and Hamilton Streets in Yaletown, usually in April and October. These aren't like the fake sample sales in New York's SoHo that run all year long. Keep your eyes peeled for signs indicating deals on coveted labels such as Miss Sixty, Diesel, Kenneth Cole, and Sinequanone. Clothing sizes are usually 4 to 6, but accessories fit everyone.

Photo: Solo

ONE PRICE FITS ALL

Walk into either of the **Exos** fashion stores, peruse the racks of bright, trendy clothing, and something will feel strange. Then it dawns on you: there are no price tags. Don't get excited, it's not free. But it's understood by regular shoppers that everything for sale here is $20. Pants? $20. Tank top? $20. Dress? $20. This may also explain the preponderance of polyester.
1947 W. 4th Ave., 604-730-9603; 1682 Robson St., 604-682-3011

Mac Cadillac's Underground Fashion Empire

"Mac Cadillac has retired," said Craig Doyle recently, when pressed. "When I turned 30 I decided to get serious." But it was his doppelgänger Mac Cadillac's free-spirited ways that paved the road to the bourgeoning **Bang-On** empire (*961 Robson St., 604-602-0371, bang-on.ca*) he now commands. Cadillac played in bands and traded in vintage clothing, opening tiny stores in bad neighbourhoods with names like **Cherry Bomb** (*843 Granville St., 604-408-2424, bang-on.ca*) and Vive Le Rock – named after the Adam Ant song. Suddenly, the decalled T-shirts and '80s pop-culture paraphernalia he was selling became all the rage. Now, Mac Cadillac is Craig Doyle, owner of the flashy new Bang-On flagship right beside MTV Canada that sells T-shirts with vintage decals to the likes of Avril Lavigne (skulls and skaters) and Eminem's band (George Bush, *American Psycho* shirts for the Grammys). There are stores in Toronto, New York, and Monterrey, Mexico – but to see where it all started, climb up to the original **America Upstairs** (*8-712 Robson St., 604-633-5393, bang-on.ca*). "I don't know why I keep it. I guess it's a shrine," says Doyle. And, if you're hankering for a Ricky Schroeder, Mr T, or Michael Jackson T-shirt, this is where you'll find it.

Deals & Steals

Photo: Sole

If you hit the **Designer Warehouse** after a recent shipment, lucky you. You'll get first dibs on in-season dresses from BCBG and Oscar knock-offs from A.B.S. by Allen Schwartz. The young proprietor, Tamaragh Fox, was once a fashion designer and has lived in New York, so she knows a deal to see one. One American woman walked away from here with 14 Versace dresses.
1011 Mainland St., 604-609-0955

Main Street Vintage

Front & Co.

This vintage store keeps expanding down the block, currently occupying three storefronts: one for men's and women's sportswear; one for dresses and designer items; and one for new and vintage housewares. Note: this is where many fashion industry insiders (editors, photographers, designers) consign their clothes.
3772 Main St., 604-879-8431, front_company@hotmail.com

Madison on Main

A relatively new consignment shop, you can sometimes find great accessories here, like 1980s ruched purses. An amazing vintage raincoat in perfect condition was selling for just $37.
3728 Main St., 604-873-4100

offbeat bidding

There's an auction to suit your every need. Here's a few:

S E R F (Surplus Equipment Recycling Facility)

This is where UBC's old desks, microscopes, computers, bulldozers, etc. go to rest. The once weekly sales on campus will now be held 24/7, via the Internet at *serf.ubc.ca*.

Vancouver Police Auction

Held at Riley Park Arena on a Saturday in April, this is where to buy back all the stuff that got stolen from your car downtown. There are no reserve bids, and items on the block in 2003 included golf clubs, digital cameras, DVD players, and – now we're talking – loose gemstones, banknotes, and silver bars. Call *604-594-2253*, or visit *ableauctions.ca*.

Warehousing and Asset Investment Recovery

Government waste found here. Mostly office furniture (can anyone say cutbacks?) is available at Thursday sales. *8307-130th Street, Surrey, bcsolutions.gov.bc.ca*

My Orange Bag

A young husband-and-wife team started this store after completing a cross-continent road trip collecting nostalgic items – many in their original packaging – and dead stock clothing from the 1960s and 1970s. Vintage magazines and catalogues are great inspiration for budding fashion designers. Just try to keep your boyfriend away from the Ataris. *4332 Main St., 604-879-4472, myorangebag.com*

flea markets

21st Century Flea Market

Not much in the way of furniture, but among the 175 tables you'll find whole sections devoted to *Garfield* memorabilia, camp '60s romance novels, vintage beauty products, jewellery, even unopened packages of Lucky Strike cigarettes for four dollars. A great spot for funny little gifts. Held in January at the **Croatian Cultural Centre**, *3250 Commercial Dr., 604-879-0154, croationculturalcentrevancouver.com*

Vancouver Flea Market

Photo: Solo

It's a bit dingy, but it's the best way to unload your stuff when you move. As you start setting up your reserved $15 table, regular dealers will come and buy all your junk from you for a flat rate (if you are lucky they'll buy it in the parking lot straight from your car). It's cheaper than advertising a garage sale, less hassle, and you're at the beach by 10 a.m. If you go there to shop, look for cheap razor blades of questionable origin (and you wondered why they locked them up at the drugstores?) vintage jewellery, and more junk like the stuff you just unloaded. Weekends only.
703 Terminal Ave., 604-685-0666

Burcu's Angels
2535 Main St., 604-874-9773

Cherry Bomb
843 Granville St., 604-408-2424, bang-on.ca

Photo: Solo

Deluxe Junk
310 W. Cordova St., 604-685-4871, DELUXJUNK.com

Fashion Junkees
438 W. Pender St., 604-899-2525

Legends Retro-Fashion
4366 Main St., 604-875-0621

Minx
430 Homer St., 604-806-3606

Prodigal Son
303 W. Cordova St., 604-688-8034

vintage vantage

Secondhand Safari

This guided bus tour takes you to four consignment stores where you'll stop and shop for designer labels. The $25 ticket includes lunch, prizes, gift certificates, and, you never know, a great deal in a vintage Yves St Laurent, perhaps?
604-222-1945, secondhandsavvy.com

Kawabata-Ya

Photo: Solo

The store's name is a Japanese phrase that means "Kawabata's place" and it's a best-kept secret of Vancouver fashion stylists. Impeccably clean, the store has always had the season's hottest vintage accessories, whether it was *Playboy* sunglasses from the '70s, or poorboy caps. Recently relocated to a subterranean spot in Gastown *(437 W. Hastings St., 604-806-0020)*, it is nestled among the city's crop of language schools. The store's owners have first "picking rights" to a clothing recycling plant in Burnaby that shreds wool sweaters and bundles denim for resale to developing countries. The "pickers," as they are called in the vintage clothing trade, have been known to rescue Hudson's Bay blankets, cashmere sweaters, and even a Dior evening gown. (Jonathon, whose reworked sweatshirts, scarves, and sweaters sell at the store, researched the Dior dress's origin and traced it back to a 1970s runway show in Paris. Given that the dress never made it into

THANKS FOR THE MEMORIES

Model Kate Moss wrote her autobiography before she turned 21, so why shouldn't your 5-year-old have one too? Now you, your pet, fiancé, or grandmother can have your own hardcover coffee table book, filled with personal photographs and stories. The team that creates these popular "Memory Books" conduct interviews with far-flung friends and family, then piece it all together with supplied photographs. Taking just six weeks to assemble, they are proving to be popular gifts for milestones, from bridal showers to 30th anniversaries. But, starting at $850, memories don't come cheap.
604-261-1858, echomemoirs.com

production, he surmises that it was probably the model who brought it to Vancouver.) Find designer and reworked vintage items at Kawabata-Ya's beautiful, airy new sister store MoBo-MoGa (Japanese-English slang for Modern Boy Modern Girl) in Gastown *(205-332 Water St., 604-806-0105).*

True Value Vintage

The largest vintage store in Vancouver got in a legal tiff with second-hand chain Value Village and had to put the word "True" in front of its name. The Gap's design team was caught riffling through the vintage denim in this well-organized store and the owner recently came upon a huge cache of vintage sunglasses. The store is divided into sections including leather, vintage sports clothes, and their reworked vintage line "Beyond Retro." Look up for some of the best stuff — it is displayed on the walls. It has a brand new outlet in New York and another in Japan named Zachary's Smile, after the owner's son.
710 Robson St., 604-685-5403

Old Stuff in New West

Downtown New Westminster is one of the Lower Mainland's best-known unknowns: Columbia Street is positively brimming with cool old buildings waiting to be turned into condos. But gentrication has been slow. New West's planners seem to have put their efforts into constructing new buildings on reclaimed industrial waterfront (Westminster Quay) or reclaimed prison lands (the old B.C. Penitentiary site). At present, the most happening part of New West is at the very bottom of the downtown hill, on Front Street, which has become an antiques mecca, largely because it offers dealers cheap rents. The shops tend to be a place for bargains as well, and feature more collectibles and Canadiana than the pricier, high-end European antiques found on Main and Granville Streets.

In New West's early days, though, Front Street didn't exist. The buildings on Columbia went right to the edge of the Fraser River, and had floating loading docks for ships. Today's Front Street storefronts are basically the rear basements of Columbia Street buildings. Over the years, the riverbank was filled in. After a fire devastated New Westminster's downtown in 1898, much of the rubble was pushed into the Fraser, and became Front Street.

GET A LIFE (STYLE)

Now that the lifestyle store is a mainstay of modern retailing, one does not need to cultivate a sense of style when one can simply charge it. We once witnessed an interior designer buy an entire living room display from **Caban** *(2912 Granville St., 604-742-1522, caban.com)* and a pro golfer once announced upon walking into **Bruce** *(1038 Alberni St., 604-688-8802)* that he was in need of 30 gifts for his girlfriend's 30th birthday (he found eight). Time and time again, though, these two stores deliver the epitome of products that fulfill the dictum that one's life should be filled only with things that are both useful and agreeable.

Photo: Solo

good thrift stores

SPCA Thrift Store

3606 W. Broadway. 604-742-1510, spca.bc.ca

Union Gospel Thrift Store

659 E. Hastings St., 604-254-8721

PET PORTRAITS

Artist and musician Kevin House has been making quite a name among celebs and locals for his vintage circus-style banners of pets and children (US$1,500). Local actors Sarah Strange *(Da Vinci's Inquest)* and Callum Keith Rennie *(Memento, Suspicious River)* have commissioned portraits of their pets, and you can too, via **Kevin House Banner Co.** *(kevinhouse.ca)*.

home and garden deals

The Dahlia Man

Known simply as The Dahlia Man, Pete sells immense bunches (enough for several bouquets) of dahlias from his Langley home for just $3. Locals say he hasn't changed his prices in years. He'll even do weddings with three weeks' notice.
604-946-2165

koolhaus Distribution Centre

One of the city's most impressive furniture stores located on West 4th Avenue has now opened a warehouse store where you'll find deals of 50-70 percent off modern designer furniture, such as coffee tables by Hom Design and sofas by Bombast. You'll have to go to the regular location *(2199 W. 4th Ave., 604-875-9004, koolhaus.com)* for beautiful hydraulic beds with dust-bunny-free storage space inside.
1425 Odlum Drive, 604-254-9008, koolhausdesign.com

Wonderbucks

This family-owned store was opened to protest the so-called dollar stores that rip you off by selling fifty-cent junk for a dollar. Now with several outlets, it sells stainless steel kitchen gadgets, simple teak patio furniture, good cloth napkins, cheap candles, and the like.
1803 Commercial Dr., 604-253-0515; 909 W. Broadway, 604-742-0510, wonderbucks.com

Photo: Solo

Why lug souvenirs from your travels home with you when these fine Vancouver stores sell them right here? There are many great shops selling wares from France, Indonesia, Thailand, and Italy. Australian goods rarely make it off the island, due to prohibitive duties and transportation costs, but **Roost Homeware** (pictured above, *1192 Hamilton St., 604-708-0084, roosthome.com*) sells Aussie house wares like bright resin bowls from Dinosaur Design. **Sate** (*1520 W. 13th Ave., 604-734-7283*), a new store owned by the restaurateurs behind the popular neighbourhood bistro, **Trafalgar's** (*2603 W.16th Ave, 604-739-0555, trafalgars.com*), deals in beautiful Vietnamese deco furniture and French lacquer work. Also consider the strands of oversized pearls, ground coffee that smells like chocolate, and dramatic silk clothing and bedding – all from Vietnam. **Blue Terra Home** (*1146 Commercial Dr., 604-253-1711, blueterrahome.com*) sells oversized archways and benches for your garden from Indonesia and Bali. Also find silk cushions, bird cages, and other exotic accessories.

BE CLOTHED AND B. NAKED

Vancouver rocker **Bif Naked** wants you to put on her clothes. It all began when fans started making their own T-shirts with the image of "Stick Girl" that appears on her album covers. When they wore the shirts to travelling music festival Edgefest, the entrepreneurial Bif (she's got a line of greeting cards too) thought she'd get in on the action by manufacturing her own b. naked line. Bif's own fashion look has changed dramatically recently; the raven-haired Godess of Goth has given up black in favour of pretty, girly pinks. But she's still got all those tatties – and so can you, with the men's and women's "Showin' Ink" shirts that have facsimiles of all her tattoos on them in the appropriate places. Buy them at her label's web site, *herroyalmajestysrecords.com*.

wacky gifts

PONY UP

J.Lo and P. Diddy have their own fashion lines, so why not Vancouver's **Nettwerk Records**? They were already making merch for their own artists to hawk at concerts, so it was natural to start making a line of screen-printed T-shirts and casual clothes to place on their roster of celebrities. Don't be looking for pleather pants and white mink coats; the faded images and simple patterns in the **Chulo Pony** clothing line are better suited to the more laid-back rock star, much like Sarah McLachlan (a Nettwerk Records artist) and Coldplay (who are managed by Nettwerk). Avril Lavigne, another Nettwerk Management client, has not yet taken up the Chulo Pony look — perhaps they ought to start thinking about neckties. Check it out at *nettwerk.com*.

Neighbourly Soap

What started as a neighbourhood joke recently became a serious business for Vancouver's **City Soap Company** *(1-866-770-7627, citysoapcompany.com)*. Vancouver was starting to get a reputation as "no fun city," so in an effort to prove we don't take ourselves too seriously, they made a soap called "Grime Stoppers" for residents of the gritty Downtown Eastside. The joke kept going, with a "Fruity Beauty" bar for the gay village, "Big Hair" shampoo bar for the suburb of Surrey, and an oatmeal and patchouli "Granola Bar" for Commercial Drive. The best-selling, hemp-based "BC Bud Bar" could represent just about any neighbourhood in these parts (and has been spotted for sale as far away as Paris). The company now has a city series for Toronto, and is expanding into the U.S.

Cocktail Cars

Putting a whole new spin on drinking and driving, the Vancouver-made Cocktail Cars, with a martini glass top and a wheeled vehicle base, are selling like hot wheels. Choose from Vespas, Harleys, and classic cars – or place a custom order. Fill 'er up and race them down the bar.
cocktailcars.com

Pierre Trudeau Underwear

The wacky duo behind the **Smoking Lily** fashion design company *(3634 Main St., 604-873-5459, smokinglily.com)* is obsessed with anything you would not normally want printed on your clothes. Like squid, for example. Their picnic skirt had ants crawling up the side of it, and their cute little hand-knit mittens had skulls on them. But what got the national media's attention was

the women's underwear they make that's emblazoned with the image of former Canadian Prime Minister Pierre Trudeau – a notorious womanizer who was famous for saying the government had no place in the bedrooms of the nation. But in their pants? No problem! Just be glad they didn't choose PM Jean Chrétien.

Photo: Solo

Celebrity Sprees

I know, we hate celebrity gossip as much as you do, and watching Michael Jackson's vulgar million-dollar shopping spree for baroque home accessories in the recent documentary was enough to turn our stomachs, but hey, some people want to know what one buys when money is no object. Here, then, are some celebrity purchases made in Vancouver:

Brad Pitt loves the resin vases at **Martha Sturdy Originals** *(3039 Granville St., 604-737-0037, marthasturdy.com)* and **Goldie Hawn** was seen scooping up handfuls of Sturdy's red, heart-shaped key chains right before Valentine's Day.

Speaking of Goldie, now that she's a resident, she's been shopping up the town, including buying an entire bedroom suite from the now-defunct store **Shout With Joy!** in Yaletown (she got a steal with a dark wood bed that was only $800). **Benjamin Bratt**'s Sonoma bed from local furniture company, **hom**, was quite a bit more. Find them at **koolhaus** *(2119 W. 4th Ave., 604-875-9004, koolhausdesign.com)*.

No word on whether the massive, dread-locked *Andromeda* star **Keith Hamilton Cobb** found a bed big enough at **Mihrab** *(2229 Granville St., 604-879-6105, mihrabantiques.com)* but he certainly found lots of other furniture, which he had shipped back home to L.A. when the shooting season was over. **Sarah McLachlan** is also a big fan of the Indonesian/Moroccan/Indian furnishings here.

When **Courtney Love** is in town she requests that her trailer be filled with lilies and other fragrant flowers. Local upstart **Oasis Flowers** *(2793 Arbutus St., 604-688-8802, oasisflowers.com)* obliges.

Singer **Chantal Kreviazuk** scooped up armloads of local designer Mandula Moda's clothes when she visited **Bruce** *(1038 Alberni St., 604-488-8802)*, but her dog left a mess for the staff to clean up. **Robin Williams** is also a fan of the store, where he most recently bought a pair of locally made Tweaked Sneaks customized running shoes.

Never one to mince words, **Arnold Schwarzenegger** once declared, "I love this store!" upon entering **Le Château** *(813 Burrard St., 604-682-3909, le-chateau.com)* puffing a cigar. He was probably also loving the low prices as he picked up gifts for his

Dope Threadz

Is funk your brother? Check it out now:

Photo: Solo

AntiSocial

World-ranked skateboarder Craig McCrank owns this new store that was designed not to look like a skateboarder's bedroom. Actually, it looks more like an art gallery. *2425 Main St., 604-708-5678, antisocialskateboarding.com*

Dipt Urban Hook Ups

If you're down with the posse, you know that Dipt means well-dressed. If not, you probably shouldn't be shopping here. *819 Hornby St., 604-669-9990, getdipt.com*

teenaged daughter. Not sure if his parting words were, "I'll be back."

Speaking of frugal celebrities, **Britney Spears** and her younger sister went shopping with their bodyguards at Burnaby's mid-market Metrotown Mall. The mall opened inexpensive Spanish fashion retailer **Zara** *(2285-4700 Kingsway, 604-484-6095, zara.com)* after-hours so that the girls could buy up a storm in private. Local stylists and make-up artists working with the Spears sisters on the project she shot here say the girls were very nice and polite, though their handlers instructed them not to utter either Spears name at any time, lest the media find out they were in town.

Photo: Solo

Global Atomic Design

With some local labels, and some international, this pioneer urbanwear store is still a leader.
1006 Mainland St., 604-806-6223, globalatomic.com

Thriller

This store is owned by a guy named Michael Jackson. Get it? He is also famous as the inventor of the original "Canada Kicks Ass" shirts that he says paid for his mortgage. His latest venture is shirts that say "Yoga Schmoga." He gave one to Goldie Hawn.
1710 W. 4th Ave., 604-736-5651, thrillershop.com

Soul2Soul

An entire wall of durags and a whole lot of Triple 5 Soul. The upstairs hair salon specializes in dreads and braids — they can do 200 patterns.
840 Granville St., 604-685-6545

Want to Buy an Island?

For several years, Vancouver has had the highest cost of living anywhere in Canada — mostly due to the price of real estate. But, for those in the running, one of the best remaining real estate deals is to purchase the islands that surround Vancouver. While a house in Kerrisdale can set you back $5 million, you can own an entire island for as little as $1 million. Of course, you'll have to buy the boat and seaplane to go with it, not to mention the desalination plant for water, but when you're in this market, that's chump change. Canada has the largest number of islands of any country in the world, and B.C. currently has more for sale than any other province. There are approximately 100 islands owned privately here (the B.C. government owns the rest), and at last check on *privateislandsonline.com*, twenty-four were listed for sale — starting at as little as $30,000 and going up to $17 million. Robin Williams is rumoured to own an island off the Sunshine Coast and musician Kenny G looked at property in the area. Shop for your island at *bcoceanfront.com* and *bcprivateislands.com*

Cash and Carry

British purse designer Anya Hindmarch will let you be your own bag. For a mere $500, you can have your photo emblazoned on one of her high-end canvas totes, so that passersby can comment on how well you carry yourself. Order them at **Holt Renfrew** *(Pacific Centre, 633 Granville St., 604-681-3121, holtrenfrew.com)*.

stoner Vancouver

It is not unusual in Vancouver to have a street person ask, "Spare a joint?" or sit with a sign saying, "Need money for pot." Pot culture is everywhere. Hydroponics companies advertise on the side of buses, and at the very least you'll probably smell the sweet smoke of ganja wafting out of the bushes in Robson Square (a notorious toking spot) or even from the dude who just walked by smoking what you thought was a cigarette. BC Bud's international reputation was launched unofficially by puffing Olympic snowboarder Ross Rebagliati, and ever since, pot tourism has flourished. Here's a tour:

Nice Big Bags

Photo: Solo

The best spot for inexpensive, non-gimicky camping and fishing supplies is **3 Vets** *(2200 Yukon St., 604-872-5475)*. That's no secret. The stainless steel coolers would look right at home in a Calvin Klein Home collection, and the military clothing and fur-lined hunting caps are the height of fashion. The fact that the owners also sell First Nations art from the store's back room – because of a long-standing trading arrangement with a local Native band that gets fishing supplies – was revealed years ago as well. What is unknown, however, is that the oversized canvas and camouflage duffel bags that fly out the door are popular for moving more than outdoor gear. The bags are inexpensive yet durable enough to transport pounds of weed between grower and seller. What's more, this is the store where cops buy their boots: it's located a block from a Vancouver police station.

BC Bud: A Consumer's Guide

Photo: Solo

Don't get caught buying inferior pot from the neighbourhood dealer. Herewith, a connoiseur's guide to the best strains of BC Bud on the open market:

Blue Truck (named for a truck it fell out of into the bush)
Jack Herer (a famous pot aficionado)
Willie's Wonder (ditto)
Great White Shark (it's actually red, and very smelly)
Purple Pineberry (grows well outdoors)
Sweet Tooth (gives you the munchies)
Hemp Star (a Kootenay classic)
The Jamaicans (too much of this around)
Juicy Fruit (same as above)
Grapefruit (an old classic)
Grape Punch (has a grape-y fragrance)

Sweet Skunk (rare, delicate, and expensive)

Crystal Globe (a hippie fave)

Champagne (bikers' weed)

Afghan Hash Plant (like Champagne, but from Surrey)

Abby Thunderfuck (from Abbotsford, sometimes referred to as Triple X)

Kush (the ultimate – but hard to find – local pot)

All the bongs, water pipes, hookas, scales, and smoking supplies you will ever need. Some pipes change colour as you use them. Trippy.

Puff Pipes Smoke Shop

3255 Main St. 604-708-9804

Puff Pipes Outta Sight Smoke Shop

upstairs, 712 Robson St., 604-6840-PUFF, puffpipes.ca

The New Amsterdam Café

301 Hastings St., 604-682-8955, newamsterdamcafe.com

Photo: Solo

Marijuana Party Book Store

307 W. Hastings St., 604-682-1172, bcmarijuanaparty.com/newstore

Pot TV

pot-tv.net, info@pot-tv.net

Seedy Neighbourhood

Photo: Solo

Next time you're walking through Vancouver's pot-tourism epicentre on West Hastings Street between the **Dominion Building** at 207 and **Blunt Bros.** pot café at 317, look up. You might see a little sign in a second-storey window advertising pot seeds. While these little seed stores are not strictly legal, police have bigger fish to fry in the neighbourhood and don't bother shutting them down. They're always moving, so your favourite seed shop may have moved down the street.

Board Games

The coolest cruise around is a long board made by the local company, **Landyachtz** *(Landyachtz.com)*. The longest of these wooden skateboards is almost 1.5 metres – so don't even think about pulling tricks at the park. The Chief series is emblazoned with Haida graphics, and the Mountain Board has eight-inch off-road wheels.

Gorgeous women on snowboards are not a new thing – remember the legendary Emma Peel board from the late '80s? But gorgeous women from Vancouver on snowboards – now that's worth an extra coat of wax. The designer for local **Endeavour Design** snowboard company has an eye for fashion (and pretty girls) so he asked Vancouver-born supermodel Noot Seear (a current face of Chanel) if she'd have her image printed on a snowboard. Being a rider herself, she agreed. The next board in the series is to have Vancouver actress Sarah Carter on it. For most local boys, this will be their only chance to ride these girls. Buy them at **The Boardroom** *(1745 W.4th Ave., 604-734-7669)*.

top shopping neighbourhoods

One-of-a-Kind Stores

If you hit anywhere in Vancouver for shopping, let it be one of these hot shopping districts known for small, independent stores and designers, and inexpensive ethnic goodies.

MAIN EVENT

Vancouver's hottest new shopping district, alternatively called "UpTown" or "SoMa" for South Main, has as its epicentre the intersection of 21st Avenue and Main Street. The fashion and homewares – both new and vintage – are available within a block's radius and are some of the city's most original. Among the cool little independent shops are:

The Barefoot Contessa

Owner Eva is an actress, and for her, all the store's a stage. A great place to find gifts for your daughters or girlfriends, like pretty and glittery necklaces, purses, and notebooks. The new upstairs atelier is open the last Sunday of the month and features crochet lessons and personal shopping.

3715 Main St., 604-879-1137,
thebarefootcontessa.com

Photo: Solo

Beauty Mark

Now with a new second location on Broadway and Granville, this is where to get cult beauty supplies like the ones Madonna uses (Ole Henriksen) or skin care products made from Maple Syrup. Asian flight attendants arrive and buy in bulk for their friends back home (the Philosophy line is a favourite).
1030-1120 Hamilton St.,
604-642-2294, beautymark.ca

Bed

If you hear a young man walking down 4th Avenue ask the girl beside him if she wants to go to bed with him, don't assume he's being fresh. He's just talking about buying some sheets. The local Bed company makes affordable mix and match, hand-dyed cotton muslin sheets, duvet covers, pillowcases, and

curtains. There's a rainbow of colour options, from pewter to blueberry to mocha. And, of course, a bed in the middle of the store should you get other ideas.
2151 W. 4th Ave., 604-736-3482, bed-online.com

Buddha Supply Store

Joss is what Buddhists burn at funerals to represent good things the deceased will want to take with them to the afterlife. Fake banknotes, paper tuxedos, and cardboard Mercedes are some of the items you will find here. The inexpensive stacks of gold leaf paper make great place mats for dinner parties. As long as you're not superstitious.
4158 Main St., 604-873-8169

Eugene Choo

A brother-and-sister team run this store named after a childhood friend. An excellent representation of established Vancouver and Canadian designers for women (Elsa Corsi jewellery, Comrags, Preloved, Damzels in this Dress, Mandula Moda, and Dust by Heather Young). Cool stuff for guys includes vintage shirts and lines like Spiewak. Minimalist and well-culled, it's a must-visit.
3683 Main St., 604-873-8874, eugenechoo.com

Mod to Modern

Owner Michelle has a talent for reconditioning furniture from the '50s to "the release date of Madonna's first album," her cut-off (i.e., circa 1984). Look for her Lucite clocks, 1960s TVs, modular lamps, and humourous displays of legwarmers and Smurf memorabilia. It's all a steal — so get to it before the movie set dec people do.
3712 Main St., 604-874-2144

Motherland

Look for Emily Carr grad Kristin Nelson "Love Sucks" T-shirts with a mosquito emblem (a hit on Valentine's Day) and knitted book covers with a vintage Harlequin romance inside. Naughty knickers by local designers, and great sportswear, sunglasses, etc. for guys and gals alike.
2539 Main St., 604-876-3426, motherlandclothing.com

Narcissist Design Co.

Great-fitting T-shirts and cute '50s-style dresses at the adorable new boutique for one of Vancouver's best independent labels.
3659 Main St., 604-877-1555, narcissist.com

Simple

Photo: Solo

A tiny storefront with a studio behind it is where owner Kelly Deck (a recent graduate of Emily Carr Instutute of Art and Design) makes gorgeous silk pillows to complement the well-designed, inexpensive, mainly white housewares she stocks. Find little gifts for your design-conscious friends, like a stainless steel yoyo or business card case.
3638 Main St., 604-877-0323

YALETOWN

Though many of the showrooms have moved to the new **Fashion Exchange** building on Kingsway, Yaletown is the city's original fashion district. Dominated by converted warehouses, late-night restaurants, and recently vacated dot-com offices, new stores and spas open up regularly to cater to the young, affluent folks who live in Concord Pacific condo towers and the lofts above the shops. Like most fashion districts, don't expect much to be open before noon. Better to go late afternoon, then ease into happy hour at one of the great patios that spread onto the cobblestone loading docks.

Dadabase

This so-called "technology boutique" has several claims to fame. It throws great parties for its art exhibits (the microscopic **Xeno** gallery is in the back hall); its new line of Government clothing from the Ministry of Style is made from real army fatigues; and it's home to what must be the city's smallest change rooms.
183 E. Broadway, 604-709-9934, dadabase.ca

Forbie Active Wear

Vancouver is notoriously short on spots to get great bathing suits, but this new store will make one for you from scratch (or a tear sheet from a fashion magazine). Get them to replicate the famous '60s bikini with knife belt from *Dr. No*, or choose from their own great designs (some of them inspired by the ones in the Victoria's Secret catalogue). The owners ran a large sporting goods company back in Iran and know what they are doing. Bikinis start at $58 and one-piece suits at $45.
2678 W. 4th Ave., 604-731-4242, forbie.ca

Now + Then

This curious second-hand store owned by a DJ from Manila manages to make a display of Lady Di memorabilia look edgy. A selection of old celebrity biographies, movie posters, and pirated movies, as well as unique knick-knacks, make it a great place for a quirky, romantic gift.
1936 W. 4th Ave., 604-572-4574

Paperhaus

This is a great spot for design junkies who like nothing better than honing their gorgeous leather portfolios and meticulously filling in their designer agenda books with fine-tipped black pens. Architects, photographers, graphic designers, and stylists beware: you will want everything.
3057 Granville St., 604-737-2225, paperhaus.com

The Perfume Shoppe

Although the majority of its sales are online, this tiny little store in a small downtown mall sells 700 types of rare and discontinued perfume — including Etro's "Messe De Minuit" that smells like the inside of a church.
757 W. Hastings St., 604-299-8463, theperfumeshop.com

Phtalo Boutique

Photo: Solo

Atomic Model

Of-the-moment tops and jeans from upper-end L.A. and New York lines. Labels Joie, Nolita, Mon Petit Oiseau, and Ella Moss jump off the racks. If you're a model, most of your wardrobe is probably from here.
1036 Mainland St., 604-688-9989, atomicmodel.ca

Fine Finds

A stylish young woman named Jane travels around Asia filling containers with teak furniture and great fashion accessories. It's hard to leave without buying something. How she gets chicken feather purses through Customs we will never know.
1014 Mainland St., 604-669-8325, fine-finds.com

Photo: Solo

Honeycomb Interiors

A new husband/wife venture stocks hefty furniture from India that would look great in a minimalist interior. Large dark wood coffee tables – one of the hardest things to find anywhere – are a steal at less than $400. It's part of the store's philosophy not to gouge customers with mark-ups, and profits are funneled back to the makers in India, not to middlemen.
104-1111 Homer St., 604-648-2844, honeycombinteriors.com

Photo: Solo

Intra-Venus

A stylish little shoe store for people who work on their feet but wouldn't be caught dead at Rockport: skaters, actors, bartenders, shop girls – even hip young doctors.
1072 Mainland St., 604-685-9696, intra-venus.com

Karma Active Wear

An instant hit when it opened in late 2002, the yoga clothing store has expanded to L.A. A serene white-and-glass interior designed by Darren Onyskiw (also credited with Jacqueline Conoir's impressive studio-store) is a perfect backdrop to the colourful, stretchy clothes that come tiny enough for Bikram's yoga and comfy enough for walks on the seawall.
1146 Pacific Blvd., 604-685-2762, karmaactivewear.com

LightForm

All manner of fashionable, Italian lighting is on offer at this new store. Check out the tube-shaped floor lamp: for $3,500, you can have your room change from red, to pink, to purple, at your whim.
1060 Homer St., 604-688-7022, light-form.com

Looking for the finer things in life? That's this new Yaletown store's *raison d'être*, with offerings for those with more dollars than sense. Consider the antique silver egg cup for a trifling $1,500. Or $40 truffles from the chocolatier to the French royalty, sold exclusively here in North America. Should the dazzling chandeliers be not baroque enough for your digs, venture upstairs to the store's art gallery.
1067 Hamilton St., 604-689-2789

Propellor
A group of graduates from the nearby Emily Carr Institute banded together to create this innovative little studio that's a welcome break from the hand-weaving and hippie pottery on Granville Island. Closer to industrial design than artwork, find cool chalkboards for your kitchen, refurbished vintage chairs, hand-made cards, and modern chandeliers.
4-494 Old Bridge St., Granville Island, 604-682-6665, propellor.ca

The Spy Store
Does a booming business in nanny cams and electronic gadgets for peeping toms. But now that all those Yaletown condos are so close to each other, who needs a telescope to spy on the neighbours?
1804 W. Broadway, 604-731-6662

T.H.E. Store

An acronym for Total Home Environment, this store is a microbe-a-phobe's dream come true. One can sleep soundly knowing that one's mattress and pillow are made from 100 percent organic materials, such as wool from free-range sheep. No fire-retardant sprays or chemical anti-mold treatments to keep you up at night. Shop for all manner of environmentally conscious furniture (reclaimed wood), greeting cards (recycled paper), natural cleaning products, and biodegradable golf balls. A home reno centre, adorable children's clothing, and organic cosmetics will ensure clean living for the whole family. There are even organic cotton Q-tips and thong underwear. *2662 Granville St., 604-738-0692; 2453 Marine Dr., West Vancouver, 604-922-4665, t-h-e-store.com*

Wilkinson's Automobilia

Wheely, wheely great stuff. Just off Broadway, this automotive lovers' store sells vintage miniatures, diecast cars, Fomula 1, and Indy models — just about anything vehicular. *2531 Ontario St., 604-873-6242, wilkinsonsauto.com*

Photo: Solo

Lola

Co-owned by a noted fashion journalist from London and a talented young fashion designer from Vancouver, it's a formula for international chic. If you like one thing here, chances are you love it all: vintage china sets, pink silk dresses, House Inc. bedding, and the beautiful children's line, Lola bis. *1076 Hamilton St., 604-633-5017*

Mavi

Photo: Solo

The jeans shop that is the Turkish equivalent of the Gap has opened its first Canadian store. When denim is creeping up above $250 in nearby shops, it's refreshing to see stylish jeans teens can still afford. *580 Industrial Ave., 604-708-2373, mavi.com*

Twentyfour

Flanked on one side by its art gallery (**Made**) this shop houses a very exclusive selection of sportswear. Visitors from Japan and New York snap it up, since back home it's already gone. Collectible figurines, an in-house magazine, and a menu that features post-pot smoking "munchie" food like grilled cheese on Wonderbread and Doritos, contribute to the unique little subculture on this corner. *1003 Hamilton St., 604-608-2444, twenty04.com*

spoiled brats

Start cultivating their expensive tastes now.

Photo: Solo

Hip Baby

Though it used to be the butt of many jokes when it was called Absolutely Diapers, the owners have wisely changed the name, while still offering high-quality, environmentally-friendly gear for new moms.
2110 W. 4th Ave., 604-737-0603, hipbaby.com

Junior Home Store

About as far from Toys "R" Us as you can get. Nary a plastic or battery-operated item in the place. 80 percent of the children's furniture and toys are Canadian-made.
1188 Hamilton St., 604-699-0102, juniorhomestore.com

Isola Bella

Tiny clothes by big designers, such as Juicy Couture and Dolce & Gabbana, The $140 shoes will make little Madison the envy of the nursery.
5692 Yew St., 604-266-8808

Little India

Fraser and Main Streets above 49th Avenue comprise Vancouver's Punjabi Village (look for the name on the street signs on these blocks). Other than three-for-a-dollar samosas and eyebrow threading for five dollars, some of the finds here include stainless steel spice containers with glass tops ($15), pashmina shawls (about $110), and beaded slippers that look great with jeans ($5-$25). Remember – bargaining is part of the shopping culture. Check out the **Frontier Cloth House** *(6695 Main St. 604-325-4424)* for pashminas, **Rokko Sarees and Fabric** *(6201 Fraser St., 604-327-3033)* for sarees, and **Ashlina's Jewellers** *(6502 Main St., 604-325-2249)* for accessories.

Naughty but Nice

Art of Loving

This sex shop got in a tiff with police recently for attempting to mount a play in the store that included actual oral sex. One expert concluded that although it might not be illegal to perform the play at the store, they could tape it and sell the video. The police eventually backed off and let the event take place. To a full house, of course.
1819 W. 5th Ave., 604-742-9988, theartofloving.ca

Gay Mart

While not strictly a sex shop, it sells all kinds of Pride paraphernalia in the West End (also known as the Gaybourhood). As the name suggests, it's pretty much one big, happy rainbow.
1148 Davie St., 1-877-429-6278, gaymart.com

Honey

A pretty little store that also sells tasteful (if crotchless) lingerie and instructional books. Open late beside the Park Theatre, browse before or after a flick.
3448 Cambie St., 604-708-8065, honeygifts.com

Love Nest

This 20-year-old "romantic accessories" store started the Love Air Flights out of its Whistler location that had hopeful parents making babies high above the glaciers. It was a hit with the Japanese (conception at high altitudes is thought to be very good) but, alas, the service was cost-prohibitive.

119 E. 1st Ave., North Vancouver, 604-987-1175, lovenest.ca

Photo: Solo

Rubber Rainbow Condom Company

Condoms in every colour, size, flavour, shape, and texture.

953 Denman St., 604-683-3423, rubberrainbow.com

Photo: Solo

Womyn's Ware

The womyn behind this store were pioneers of selling dildos to women in a non-threatening environment. A huge (ahem) selection.

869 Commercial Dr., 604-254-2543, womynsware.com

Asia west

Number 3 Road in Richmond is home to a strip of Asian malls that popped up around 1999 when Hong Kong was repatriated to China and the area experienced a significant Asian immigration wave. The new Chinatown, or "Asia West" as *Vancouver* magazine dubbed it, is certainly the most unique Asian shopping district on the continent. All the signs, cantopop music, and loudspeaker announcements are in Asian languages. It's a unique cultural experience – plus, there are some great fashion and houseware deals to be found. Culture dictates that the marked price is usually double what you are expected to pay, so feel free to bargain. Most stores will not let you try on clothes, and sizes tend to run very small. The best for fashion is **Parker Place** *(4380 No. 3 Rd., Richmond)*. Check out **KOKO** *(604-278-2728)* for funky Japanese shoes – it's not yet illegal for girls to drive in platform shoes, like it is in Japan, so load up on them here, and visit **Sheido** *(604-232-9555)* for European clothing. **Yaohan Centre** *(3700 No. 3 Richmond Rd.)* is the spot to go for Asian groceries and housewares.

Aberdeen Centre
4151 Hazelbridge Way, Richmond, 604-270-1234, aberdeencentre.com

Central Square
4231 Hazelbridge Way, Richmond, 604-278-9399

Fairchild Square
4400 Hazelbridge Way, Richmond, 604-273-1234, aberdeencentre.com

Parker Place
4380 No. 3 Rd., Richmond, 604-273-0276, parkerplace.com

President Plaza
8181 Cambie Rd., Richmond, 604-299-9000 (ext 8181)

Yaohan Centre
3700 No. 3 Rd., Richmond, 299-9000 (ext 8282),yaohancentre.com

A random check on July 11, 2003 turned up 11 feature films, 13 TV series, and five TV-movies shooting simultaneously in Vancouver. A total of 197 movie and television productions were shot here in 2001 (compared to 11 in 1981). The same year, the American magazine *MovieMaker* named Vancouver the number one independent film city in North America. But Vancouver is more than just "Hollywood North." Read on to discover why there was a working phone on *The Urban Peasant* set, what Ozzy Osbourne eats when it's not bat heads, where the last 35 mm porn theatre in North America is, and how Ben Affleck got jumped.

The Case of
the Mystery Phone

He's one of Vancouver's best-known TV personalities with a cooking show – based on the principles of simple, healthy food, prepared fresh and quickly – broadcast in countries around the world. James Barber's grey beard, slight limp, and friendly, bumbling ways made **The Urban Peasant** *(james-barber.com)* a Canadian TV staple. The original set for the show, built in a Gastown loft, resembled a kitchen (ostensibly his) complete with stove, sink, windows, and a telephone, as anyone's kitchen might. As he demonstrated the preparation of the shows' meals – say, an Asian noodle dish, or fresh berry tart – occasionally the phone would ring, and Barber would answer. Since shows like this are usually filmed live-to-tape, with no cuts, this was perhaps a little unusual. The calls would always be short, involving quick answers and, "Yes, Thursday's fine"-type comments. As the film continued to roll, Barber would turn to the camera and explain that it was some tradesman or other calling to arrange an appointment to clean the windows or fix the dishwasher, or sometimes it was his "girlfriend" calling. Was this a producer's ruse to simulate a real life home? As it turns out, the phone was a prop placed there by the producer so that she could call Barber up to tell him that he'd forgotten to put the peaches in the peach cobbler, or that he'd neglected to take something out of the oven.

Welcome to TTV – Oops, VTV

Vancouver Television was launched with much fanfare in September 1997, at the end of a fierce battle for the license between several strong bidders. In the end, the license went to Ivan Fecan's then-Baton Broadcasting, and he arrived in Vancouver to spin his spiel to the local media and to a packed-to-the rafters crowd at downtown nightclub BaBalu (since burned down). As VTV went to air, billed as a local, independent station that celebrated the ethnic diversity of Vancouver, it quickly became apparent that this was not to be a Vancouver station – reporters imported from Toronto quickly bungled the local vernacular, mispronouncing names of local celebrities and landmarks. In one particularly memorable segment about a live concert, the reporter flubbed both the name of the nightclub (ironically, BaBalu), the name of the singer (local mega-talent Michael Bublé whom he called Michael Bubbles), and uttered the phrase that is the trademark of the interloper: "We're here in Downtown Van." You see, there's East Van and West Van, but it's downtown Vancouver to locals. When, after four years, the station reverted to a local affiliate of the national CTV network rather than its own distinct brand, few were surprised – and many wondered if that had been the plan all along.

Kinky People

Leave it to Vancouver to inspire a documentary TV series that follows sadomasochists about their daily agendas. The Paperny Films series *Kink* (seen on the Life Network) gives the viewer insight into the intimate lives of several memorable Vancouver characters, such as the bald-headed, leather-clad tattoo artist who likes to play sex games with a consenting girlfriend on a torture rack, the burly, bearded gay "bear" obsessed with tracking his family tree, and the cross-dressing hairdresser who liked to sing in drag clubs. Stephen Baldwin showed up at the Vancouver Film School launch party for the series, which has since been spun off in Toronto. Next: *Kink Winnipeg?*

TV Times

A few of the TV series filmed in Vancouver and environs:

The New Addams Family
Andromeda
The Beachcombers
The Chris Isaak Show

Cold Squad
Da Vinci's Inquest
Dark Angel

Vancouver is a great place to film movies and TV shows because:

a. the Canadian dollar is so cheap;
b. we're a two-hour plane ride from Hollywood;
c. the mild climate offers opportunities to film year round;
d. the Lower Mainland can double for virtually any big American city, from New York (*Rumble in the Bronx*) and Chicago (*Double Jeopardy*), to L.A. (*Pasadena*) and Seattle (*Dark Angel*).

But where exactly do the movies get shot? In a number of favourite locations.

Sci-fi projects like *I-Robot* and *X-Men* love the concrete behemoth that is the Point Mann Power Station, a 50-year-old backup power plant under the Surrey side of the Port Mann Bridge that was virtually never used.

Versatile Shipyards in North Vancouver was used in the TV series *Dark Angel* and *Highlander*, and in the film *Deep Rising*. The Terminal City Iron Works in East Vancouver was also used for *Dark Angel*, as well *Dead Man's Gun* and *The Dead Zone*.

The interior of the PNE Forum became Mars for several months during the filming of *Mission to Mars*. And *The Chris Isaak Show's* club scenes are usually shot at the WISE Hall at Adanac and Victoria.

Shaughnessy mansions are always popular, especially homes on the Crescent. *Double Jeopardy*, *Little Women*, and *Get Carter* were partly filmed at Hycroft, while *Secret Agent Man* filmed at the Rosemary, which is also known as the Nunnery.

Other popular locations include the Seymour Demonstration Forest in North Van, Bowen Island, Queen's Park in New West, the Boundary Bay Airport, Steveston, Ballantyne Pier, Woodlands, and Riverview.

The Dead Zone

Edgemont
Glory Days
Highlander
Jeremiah
Little Romeo
Madison
Millennium
Poltergeist: The Legacy
Smallville
Stargate SG-1

Wiseguy
The X-Files
21 Jump Street

How to Profit from Hollywood North

We've all heard the stories about people who build houses specifically to rent them out for movie shoots, or neighbours who fire up their lawn mowers beside film sets with the hopes of getting hush money. But there are other, easier ways to profit from the film biz here:

1. Register your house with the **BC Film Commission** (601 W. Cordova St., 604-660-2732, bcfilmcommission.com). Pick up a pamphlet at the office, follow the strict photography instructions, and have your file registered for location scouts to peruse, for free. Feature films pay up to $2,000 a day to rent your house, while you get a cushy hotel room.

2. Got a unique set of wheels that you hardly drive? Register it at **Reel Cars** (305-272 E.4th Ave., 604-222-8558, reelcarsltd.net) and see Ben Affleck drive it instead.

3. Pet iguana not earning his keep? Put him to work through the **Cinema Zoo Animal Agency** (13591 King George Hwy., Surrey, 604-299-6963, cinemazoo.com) and soon he'll be heating his own terrarium.

The Basement Tapes

Deep beneath the CBC building in downtown Vancouver lies one of the city's unheralded cultural treasures: the **CBC Archives**. Thousands upon thousands of old films and tapes documenting the city are hidden away in a couple of back rooms.

Among the gems: former Prime Minister Kim Campbell, nine years old and called Avril, hosting a CBC kids show named *Junior Television Club*; a mind-altering array of video clips of Vancouver's psychedelic bands in the late 1960s; and a 1907 silent movie of downtown, shot by William Harbeck, who mounted a camera on a streetcar and filmed the city as the streetcar travelled Granville, Hastings, Cordova, Robson, and Davie Streets.

Alas, not all important cultural artifacts survived. A CBC crew shot the Beatles' concert live at Empire Stadium in 1964, but somebody accidentally erased the tapes the next day. Footage of Elvis Presley's show at Empire Stadium in 1957 has also disappeared.

What did survive was often because of luck. In the 1960s, tapes of local shows would be erased for reuse, so the original colour versions of many local shows are

BREAST-FEST TELEVISION

It's a sophomoric joke if ever there was one, but it seems guests (and the male hosts) of CityTV's popular daily morning show, *BreakfastTelevision*, can't seem to get their tongues around the show's name. On more occasions than would seem warranted by mere accident, it gets called Breast-Fest Television. It could be the 5 a.m. call times, or perhaps the fact that tall co-host Fiona Forbes' very ample bosom is right at eye level.

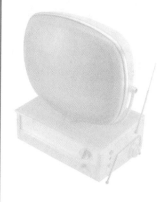

long-gone. But because the CBC had stations in the B.C. interior like CHBC, CJDC, and CFJC, it sent black-and-white 16-mm film copies to broadcast up-country. Many survived, and are now a treasured part of CBC's 155,000 film clips, documentaries, news shows, music specials, variety shows, comedies, and dramas.

GETTING BACK AT BULLIES

Reid Fleming is the World's Toughest Milkman, and Vancouver's top underground comic. The anti-hero created by artist David Boswell is forever threatening little old ladies, beating up punks, and makin' bacon with the ladies. His dark secret? The real Reid Fleming was the bully in Boswell's kindergarten class in Dundas, Ontario.

Bootleg Master

Photo: VPL 79272A

Jack Cullen's *Owl Prowl* radio show was a staple of late-night radio in Vancouver for over five decades. His record collection was renowned, and reportedly grew to more than 300,000 78s, 45s, LPs, radio broadcast transcriptions, and tapes – at one time, reputedly the largest private record collection in the world.

Just before he died in April 2002, the bulk of it was sold for a mere $15,000, and then dispersed around the world via eBay auctions. Lord knows what it fetched – 78s that were bought for a dime apiece were selling online for $5 or $6.

Cullen (in the driver's seat, above) didn't actually own his collection for many years. It was purchased by CKNW in the early 1970s, after CJOR tried to entice Cullen away. To get him to stay, NW gave him a raise, and bought his record collection for $150,000. When CKNW let Cullen go in 1999, the station – now owned by Toronto's Chorus Entertainment – drew a lot of flack. So some corporate genius decided to quietly get rid of the collection, and sold it off to some record collectors.

But they didn't get everything; Cullen had kept thousands of tapes and transcriptions at his home studio, including a legendary bootleg he made of a Frank Sinatra show at the PNE Gardens in 1957. After spreading some "liquid sunshine" among the ushers who saw what he was up to, Cullen hid under the stage with a tape recorder. The results became one of the classic bootleg performances of all time.

The Sinatra tape got Cullen in trouble with the American Federation of Musicians, not to mention Sinatra himself – Frank was one of the few stars Cullen failed to interview in his heyday.

Louis Armstrong was more easy-going. When he discovered the high quality of a bootleg tape Cullen had made of a Vancouver performance, he let Cullen release it as an LP. Cullen also did a famous bootleg of the Beatles show at Empire Stadium in 1964, and released it on his own Dogwood label. The illegal album was quickly killed by Capitol Records, but has since become a collector's item.

Sputnik Surprise

The beaux arts **Sun Tower** *(100 West Pender St.)* is one of Vancouver's oldest and most beloved landmarks. It was built in 1912 by Vancouver's longest serving mayor, Louis D. Taylor as the home for his *Vancouver World* newspaper. No stranger to hype, Taylor claimed the 17-storey, 276-feet-high structure was the tallest building in the British Empire – a claim that had been made two years earlier by the owners of the 13-storey, 147-foot-high Dominion Trust building, and would also be made in 1930 by the 22-storey, 321-foot-high Marine Building.

In any event, the World Tower became the Sun Tower when the papers merged in the 1920s. For many years, its distinctive green copper roof featured one of Vancouver's best neon signs: red lettering that spelled *The Sun*, with flashing lightning bolts coming out of either side.

There are many stories from the Sun Tower, but the best might be the night photographer Dan Scott got a world-wide exclusive of the Russian Sputnik spacecraft orbiting the earth in 1961. Apparently *Sun* publisher Don Cromie was at a cocktail party, where he was buttonholed by a drunk for being a complete idiot, because the greatest technical achievement in the history of mankind (Sputnik) had been launched that day and the *Sun* didn't have any good stories about it.

The publisher went back to the Sun Tower and grabbed the editor, Hal Straight, and accused *him* of being a complete idiot, because the greatest technical achievement in the history of mankind (Sputnik) had been launched that day and the *Sun* didn't have any good stories about it.

CULTURE-JAMMING CAPITAL

Ever wonder where world-famous culture-jamming magazine *Adbusters* would be housed? Not in a corporate tower, of course, but in the lower level of an inconspicuous townhouse in the residential Fairview Slopes neighbourhood (*1248 West 7th Ave.*). There's no sign, but you'll know it by a simple white arrow pointing down the stairs and all the staff's bikes parked out front. The high-concept, high-production-value ***Adbusters*** (adbusters.com) was founded by Kalle Lasn, who coined the term "culture-jamming" and purchased billboards in Times Square and full-page ads in the *New York Times* to spread the magazine's anti-consumerist, anti-American gospel. Tim Robbins and Sean Penn are subscribers, and someone bought a gift subscription for Bruce Springsteen. The magazine fields all kinds of calls from activists with pet causes, including Marilyn Manson, Rage Against the Machine, and actress Mia Kirshner.

So the editor went to the photo department, and told them to go to the airport. They then rented the biggest plane available (a passenger jet) and took off into the wide blue yonder, looking for Sputnik. They flew around the skies over B.C. for a couple of hours, but couldn't spot the Russian spacecraft. Figuring it might be going faster than the eye could see, Scott pressed his camera to the window and shot a roll of film. When he developed it back at the office, he was astonished to find a brilliant flash of white in the dark night sky. Sputnik! The *Sun* ran his photo as a world exclusive on the front page, and sold the shot to other papers around the world.

A couple of days later, Scott and the *Sun* photographers came to the conclusion that the flash of white was in fact the flash from his camera on the window.

Vancouver Landmarks Gone Wrong in Print

There was, of course, the time when former *Mother Jones* and *Vancouver Sun* editor David Beers was called upon by some hapless researcher at *Utne Reader* and asked to offer up a description of Commercial Drive for the magazine's "best neighbourhoods" issue. The California native, now based in Vancouver, described the strip as, among other things, having lots of great tapas bars. When the issue came out, the Drive was described as having lots of "topless bars." No wonder it's so popular. In another case of miscommunication, Douglas Coupland's entertaining words-and-picture book about Vancouver called *City of Glass* has a lengthy section on one of Coupland's favourite topics, the Lions Gate Bridge. We can only presume that he dictated much of it, given that the entry to the bridge is described as being guarded by two "cement lines." Er, that would be lions. There's no way sloppy fact-checking or accumulated earwax was responsible for the following, however. When architect Moshe Safdie's controversial downtown Vancouver Public Library *(350 W. Georgia St.)* was unveiled on May 25, 1995, someone got into the *Vancouver Sun*'s computer system just as the paper was going to press and removed the L from Public in the story's headline, which read: "Ghost of free, democratic institution haunts halls of new pubic library."

GENERATION V

Douglas Coupland launched himself into stardom with *Generation X*, a novel that became media shorthand for the generation of disaffected youth. Lest we forget, the novel grew out of a story in *Vancouver* magazine. There is also a long-standing rumour that it was loosely based on the youthful adventures of his friends Don Prior and Cam Watt at the now defunct nightclub Luv-a-fair. Watt went on to found Canadian Springs drinking water and provided the start-up funds for his former wife Wendy Williams to launch Liberty Design Emporium, a Vancouver furnishings shop.

Looking at the *Georgia Straight* today, it's hard to imagine that it got its start as a wild hippie paper in the 1960s. And when we say wild, we mean *wild*: in its formative years, the *Straight* was in constant battle with the authorities over its liberal use of the F-word, graphic photos, and open advocacy of an "alternative lifestyle."

The story that best illustrates just how "out there" some *Straight* staffers were is the tale of how then-music editor Al Sorenson met Charles Manson and decided to start his own cult.

In the late '60s and early '70s, record companies were confused by the youthquake and were signing all sorts of bizarre acts and concepts. Sorenson was reputed to be one of the most brilliant people to work at the *Straight* in its wild years, and came up with an idea to record underground happenings. He went down to A&M Records in L.A. to try and get a deal. While there, he met Charles Manson, and thought he was pretty cool.

Upon his return to Vancouver, Al started his own cult. Former *Straight* editor Ken Lester, who had been sharing a house with him, thought Al was becoming a bit strange and moved out. Two nurses moved in with Sorenson and his girlfriend, and soon he was bedding all three women and walking around naked in their abode (so he could be ever-ready for action). One of the nurses even had her pet rat castrated, because she wanted the only man in the house to be Al. He eventually left Vancouver for a Christian camp in Hedley. When last heard from, he was working at a computer warehouse in Toronto.

Al never did get a record deal, but one of the tapes from the happenings project was released in 1990 as *Phil Ochs, There and Now, Live in Vancouver 1968* (Rhino Records). The Ochs tape came from a benefit concert Ochs and poet Allen Ginsberg gave on March 15, 1969 at the PNE Gardens, for a defense fund for the *Georgia Straight*, which was having legal troubles at the time.

Mad for Mags

Check out these small budget, local magazines on the newsstand.

Banana
For young Asian Vancouverites who are "yellow on the outside, white on the inside."
bananamag.com

Butter
Edgy fashion and lifestyle, with an emphasis on art over words.
mmmbutter.com

Capilano Review
One of the few truly avant-garde literary magazines in Canada, published out of Capilano College.
capcollege.bc.ca/about/publications/capilano-review/tcr/index.html

Geist
The magazine of Canadian arts and culture that has won best overall magazine in Western Canada twice.
geist.com

Hobo
An ultra-stylish travel mag for the young, beautiful, and intrepid.
hobomagazine.com

Ion

A cute little club 'zine, with bite.

ionmagazine.ca

I-style

A chic fashion glossy aimed at the Indo-Canadian population in Vancouver.

mahiram.com

Modern Dog

A stylish magazine for urban dog owners. Could be called *Dogue*.

moderndog.com

PRISM international

Western Canada's oldest literary magazine, they've been publishing award-winning fiction, poetry, and drama since 1958.

prism.arts.ubc.ca

Ricepaper

A quirky lifestyle and arts magazine aimed at young Asians.

ricepaperonline.com

sub-TERRAIN

An edgy, unapologetic literary mag whose motto is "Strong Words for a Polite Nation." Fiction, poetry, visual art, and reviews.

subterrain.ca

guerrilla media, Vancouver-style

Ken Hegan

Occupation: Prankster, subversive filmmaker, award-winning humourist.

Resumé highlights: The short films *William Shatner Lent Me His Hairpiece (An Untrue Story)* and *Farley Mowatt Ate My Brother*.

Famous credits: Got the mayor to write a grumpy letter to *Vancouver* magazine in response to his hilarious article, "Where is Philip Owen?" about his failed attempts to contact him.

Signature look: bald head.

Biggest coup: Getting thousands of dollars' worth of donations of goods and services for his 2003 wedding via a series of facetious articles in *Vancouver* magazine called "My Big Fat (Insert Your Logo Here) Wedding" and television pleas.

Follow the antics at: voiceoftreason.net

Nardwuar the Human Serviette

Occupation: Guerrilla interviewer/celebrity stalker with an annoying, high-pitched voice.

Resumé highlights: From UBC's alternative radio station CiTR to MuchMusic, in just 15 years.

His Name: Calls himself The Serviette not because many people would want to wipe their hands of him, but because it is the Canadian term for what Americans call napkins.

Signature look: plaid golfing outfits.

Famous coups: Asked Mikhail Gorbachev which world leader wears the biggest pants and televangelist Ernest Angeley if he had the cure for the summertime blues. He was, most famously, the one who got Prime Minister Jean Chrétien to say, "For me, pepper, I put it on my plate!" in the wake of the infamous pepper-spraying of APEC protesters at UBC.

Follow the antics at: nardwuar.com

Photo: K. C. Armstrong

Vancouver and B.C. have had their fair share of homegrown stars (Yvonne de Carlo, Michael J. Fox, Pamela Anderson), but most of them wound up moving south. But one of the biggest (literally and figuratively) chose to come home when he kicked the bucket.

Raymond Burr (aka Perry Mason and Ironside) was born May 21, 1917 in New Westminster, and after he died September 12, 1993, he was buried at Fraser Cemetery in New West. The city honoured its most favourite son by renaming the historic Columbia Theatre (530 Columbia St.) the **Raymond Burr Centre for the Performing Arts**.

The Columbia was the centerpiece of New West's theatre row when it opened in 1927 as a combination vaudeville/movie theatre. It is one of Canada's few remaining "atmospheric" theatres, meaning that the auditorium was painted in a fantasy theme, giving theatre-goers the feeling they were entering an enchanted land.

"An atmospheric theatre is one that visually transports you to another place and time," says the theatre's historian, Jim Wolf. "It was in vogue at the time. In the case of the Columbia, it was the fantasy of a Moorish garden. You stepped into a walled garden city, and walked down an old street in a Moorish town."

The Columbia's wall mural depicts a rolling landscape of trees and classical buildings, alongside a golden shield, crown, and scroll. Winding its way up a beam is a faux-painting of a trellis with wild roses and wisteria; the ceiling is a deep blue night sky, complete with sparkling silver leaf stars. Unfortunately, most of the mural is buried under six layers of paint, drywall, and plaster. Conservator Cheryle Harrison is painstakingly uncovering the mural, layer by layer, as part of a $7 million restoration of the theatre.

The theatre has another little-known fact – underneath the auditorium is an old ravine, and the building is

Not Your Average Newsstands

Big News

It's actually a coffee shop, but they buy hundreds of magazines every month for patrons to read — for free. *2447 Granville St, 604-739-7320*

Chapters/Indigo

Now that the ground floor has been taken over by bargain books and tacky giftware, you've got to leg it upstairs for the magazines — but it's worth the trek for hard-to-find titles like Spanish *People*, British bar magazine *Class*, and *Bus Fayre*, for those oft-overlooked fans of public transit. *788 Robson St., 604-682-4066; 2505 Granville St., 604-731-7822; 8171 Ackroyd Rd. Richmond, 604-303-7392; other locations; chapters.ca*

Does Your Mother Know?

It's true that it has hosted a Canadian *Playboy* model magazine signing, but don't let its name convince you that it specializes in smut — you will, however, find a magazine called *Modern Ferret*. *2139 W. 4th Ave., 604-730-1110*

actually built on piles, as if it were a pier. Before 1927, the ravine was used a garbage dump, and all sorts of relics have been found, including pottery and remnants of the original theatre façade.

"We haven't even done a dig yet, this is all just lying on the surface down there," says Wolf. "It's quite incredible. Inside it's a historic garbage dump of New Westminster going back to the 1860s."

The Crying Room

It's a Vancouver institution with its share of lore: a glassed-in area of **The Ridge** movie theatre *(3131 Arbutus St., 604-738-6311, ridgetheatre.com)* called "The Crying Room" with a view of the screen from the balcony. Intended for mothers with babes-in-arms rather than people who turn into a sobbing mess at movies, the sound is piped in via a squawk box. While wailing infants have priority in the room, it's not unheard of for couples to sneak in for a quickie, or directors and actors to cloister themselves in the room, away from the unwashed masses of the Vancouver International Film Festival (which was, in fact, launched by the theatre). It was long rumoured that Katharine Hepburn had watched a screening of *Vincent* from the room, but a former manager told *The Westender* newspaper that she had in fact been ushered into the regular theatre once the lights were dimmed. Perhaps knowing their clientele too well, the only time the room is off-limits is during the annual *Spike and Mike's Sick and Twisted Festival of Animation*.

film festival fever

Cinemuerte

Horror of horrors, it's another film fest. Affiliated with **Black Dog Video** *(3451 Cambie St.)* and screened at **Pacific Cinémathèque** *(1131 Howe St.)* over a week in July, it's a scream-fest of scary movies. The criteria for entry is that the film must be "dark."
Cinemuerte.com, koroner@hotmail.com

DOXA: Documentary Film and Video Festival

Now in its second biannual year, this budding little doc festival is held over four days in May at **Pacific Cinémathèque** *(1131 Howe St.). vcn.bc.ca/doxa*

New Forms Festival

This edgy four-day festival at the end of July is concerned with emerging forms of multimedia, such as video installation, electronic visuals, animation, gaming art, and digital film.
604-648-2752, newformsfestival.com

Out on Screen

Two weeks, six venues, both genders, and then some at this annual gay and lesbian film festival in August. 2003 highlights included lesbian comedy shorts and a sing-along screening of the *Wizard of Oz.*
mid-August, 604-844-1615, outonscreen.com

The Newsroom
Although Oprah's *O* magazine is the inevitable bestseller at this Kerrisdale newsstand, there's also good reading for the lock 'n' load set in titles such as *Big Buck* and *Fur-Fish-Game.*
2256 W. 41st Ave., 604-263-0588

People's News and Magazines
Find 3,000-plus titles and a loaded fashion rack. They tend to be grumpy about browsers.
2883 W. Broadway, 604-731-5180

Soma
Glossies double as artwork at this minimalist coffee shop/newsstand. The titles are few but choice, with a tendency toward high-end design and architecture.
2528 Main St., 604-873-1750

Urban Fare
The selection at this Yaletown supermarket is strong on food and wine mags. You've got to wonder, though, whether all those well-groomed singles browsing through the racks are less in search of culinary inspiration than they are of someone to cook dinner for.
177 Davie St., 604-975-7550, urbanfare.com

Vancouver International Film Festival

Beginning the last week of September and running two weeks, catch more than 300 films from 50 countries with 150,000 other film lovers. The annual galas at the Law Courts Building and the Vancouver Aquarium are the year's hottest tickets.
viff.org

Vancouver International Mountain Film Festival

Held in February for the past six years at venues around Vancouver, this film festival celebrates all things rocky and dangerous, from mountain biking to rock climbing to mountaineering.
vimff.org

ONCE KISSED

You may have noticed that Vancouver director Lynne Stopkewich has been keeping a low profile lately. Here's why: the producer of a documentary about Lilith Fair, she's best known for her acclaimed first feature *Kissed* (1997), about a female necrophiliac. Now it seems she's being sued by her former common-law husband, director John Pozer, who claims she forged his name to prevent him from receiving profits from *Kissed*.

film competitions

ReelFast: 48-Hour Film Festival

Over an August weekend, about 125 teams of 10 compete to make the best 10-minute film, based on an "inspiration package," which includes a location idea, a sound byte, a photograph, and a surprise. The skateboard/shopping cart dolly shots are classic. The 10 best entries are screened at the Commodore Ballroom *(868 Granville St.)*.
reelfastfilms.com

24 Hour Film Contest

The faster, dirtier, more underground little brother to the 48-hour film festival. Starts and ends on Commercial Drive.
604-640-4749, the24hourfilmcontest.com

cinephile hangouts

If you're into the film scene, keep up to date with *ReelWest* magazine *(reelwest.com)* and hang out here:

Alibi Room

This Gastown restaurant, in a former taxi cab driver's club, has a view of the trains rolling in cinematic clips past the barred windows. There's a film script library to peruse, or just be entertained by the late-night antics of *90210* actor Jason Priestley (a co-owner of the restaurant, along with, among others, actress Gillian Anderson), who sometimes stops by.
157 Alexander St., 604-623-3383, alibiroom.com

Alibi Unplugged Script Reading Series

This monthly public reading series of film scripts-in-development takes place on the last Sunday of the month at 7 p.m at the Arts Club Review Theatre on Granville Island. It's a chance to see some of the city's top film actors up close and intimate for just $5.
alibiunplugged.com

The Anza Club

The Cold Readings Series of new film scripts is held on Thursday nights *(coldreadingseries.com)*. The Australia-New Zealand Club also serves up plentiful pints, screenings, and workshops scripts in development with local actors (and not just Crocodile Dundee).
3 W. 8th Ave., 604-730-8090 or 604-876-7128, anzaclub.org

Red Light Lounge

This monthly guest-list-only event means that only those legitimately in the film and TV industry are awarded entry. Actors Ben Ratner and Peter Stebbings are regulars, and Luke Perry, David Duchovny, Uma Thurman, and Ethan Hawke have stopped in recently. Last Thursday of the month at Balthazar *(1215 Bidwell St., 604-689-8822, balthazarvancouver.com)*.

Video In

This self-serve, artist-run Main Street space is a haunt for indie filmmakers (like Bruce la Bruce) looking to rent equipment or share funding sob stories. Parties and screenings also happen here.
1965 Main St., 604-872-8337, videoin.ca

THE SCREEN SIRENS

This collective of young female film producers working out of South Main offices has made a big name for itself on the film fest circuit. Leah Mallen's short *Shoes Off* won Best Short Film at the Cannes Film Festival in 1999 and Trish Dolman's *Flower & Garnet* won several awards at the Vancouver International Film Festival in 2002. Mallen has since gone on to produce the Chad Lowe-directed short *The Space Between* in Vancouver, filmed while Lowe's wife, Hilary Swank, shot in Vancouver in the summer of 2001. Both Swank and Lowe appear in the film, which has since gone on to the Tribeca Film Festival and critical acclaim. In fact, it could very well have launched Lowe's career as a director: it was good enough to get him a gig directing an episode of *Law & Order*.

best places to get discovered

Local model scouts have been known to scour suburban malls (there are more teenagers in the suburbs), but in Vancouver, **The Cactus Club Cafe** *(1530 W. Broadway, at Granville St.)* or the seats at the entrance to **Pacific Centre**'s atrium *(550-700 W. Georgia St.)* are the places they scout new talent.

Speaker's Corner

Photo: Solo

The CityTV video soapboxes cost one dollar and are open 24/7. Though they are usually used for drunken rants, occasionally a band shows up and sings and gets discovered (as the Barenaked Ladies famously did in Toronto). The best clips get broadcast on CityTV – such as R.E.M. front man Michael Stipe's recent video love letter to Vancouver recently. The Vancouver locations are:

CityTV building, *180 West 2nd Ave.*
Marketplace IGA, *909 Burrard St.*

Second Avenue Studios

Almost all open casting calls take place here. It's also where major movies hold their local castings.
225 W. 2nd Ave., 604-877-7705, second-ave.com

Shoreline Studios

Another prominent casting studio.
33 E. 7th Ave., 604 874-9979

WIN SOME, LOSE SOME

As a film distribution company, the North Shore's Lions Gate Entertainment has to make some tough choices. They scored a hit when they took up *Monster's Ball,* for which Halle Berry won her Best Actress Oscar. But how silly they must have felt after they passed on the distribution of *My Big Fat Greek Wedding,* the smash box office hit of 2002.

just passing through

Johnny Come Lately

Actor Johnny Depp made the leap from telephone pen salesman to international celebrity by way of a two-year stint in Vancouver filming the teen TV drama *21 Jump Street.* The series was mostly shot at Carson Graham Secondary in North Vancouver (where he tried repeatedly and unsuccessfully to pick up one of the female students). The then-nerdy, skinny Depp could often be seen cruising Robson Street in his famous Dayton boots (he wears the same pair, purchased in Vancouver, to this day).

Eastwood comes Westward

Leading man Clint Eastwood makes regular trips to North Vancouver, where his daughter Francesca Eastwood lives with his former girlfriend, actress Frances Fisher (*Titanic*), who filmed the TV series *Glory Days* here. On Christmas Day 2001, the 8-year-old Francesca narrowly escaped when the rented house on the 2000 block of Kirkstone Road caught fire. Her mother escaped with burns to her hands when the house was ablaze at 4:30 a.m. while Francesca jumped from the garage roof into the arms of a neighbour and was treated for minor smoke inhalation at Lions Gate Hospital. Her father jumped in his private plane upon hearing of the fire that destroyed the house and arrived in time to pick up his daughter from hospital and personally thank the neighbours who rescued her. Eastwood's subsequent visits have been less dramatic, such as a quiet chicken dinner a few weeks later at Leandro's Restaurant *(408-16033-108th Ave., Surrey)* on his way to the airport. He stuck around for 2 hours, signed autographs, and left a US$50 tip.

Acting Up: Born and Bred Talent

Simon Baker
Hails from: Langley
Big break: In the Vancouver-filmed drug drama *On The Corner.*
Now playing: The above performance inspired director Ron Howard to cast the 17-year-old sight unseen to co-star in *The Missing* with Cate Blanchett, due for a January 2004 release.

Cameron Bancroft
Hails from: North Vancouver
Big break: A season on *Beverly Hills, 90210* as the virgin Christian quarterback "Joe" took him stateside.
Now playing: A talent for ice hockey (he plays on an American celebrity team) has led to comedic roles in the Vancouver shot Disney flick *Most Vertical Primate* about the ice-skating chimp, and *Mystery, Alaska.*

Richard Gere's Down

Remember when Richard Gere and '80s supermodel Cindy Crawford were married? During that time in 1993 they rented a West Vancouver house while Gere filmed *Intersection*. Known for his politics and Buddhism (he and 4,000 others met the Dalai Lama in Vancouver that year), Gere later told interviewers that Chinese residents in Vancouver thanked him for the comments he made about Tibet at that year's Academy Awards show for which he was severely chastised.

Robin's Hood

Comedian Robin Williams and Vancouver have intersected numerous times, mostly because Williams refuses to play the pampered star cloistered in a trailer when he's here. Instead, he shops, goes to restaurants, and actually talks to people. His most famous impromptu stand-up performance happened as a result of an invitation he received walking down the street in Kitsilano when he was here to shoot *Insomnia* with Al Pacino. A passerby told him there was a comedy club nearby, and the pair headed to the Urban Well *(1516 Yew St.)* where Williams got on stage and regaled the crowd with improvised jokes about the weather and imitations of Prime Minister Jean Chrétien. In 2003, when in town to shoot the futuristic thriller *Final Cut*, he entertained patrons of Cin Cin restaurant *(1154 Robson St.)* and the Gerard lounge in the Sutton Place Hotel *(845 Burrard St.)*, going from table to table telling impromptu jokes. It's all out of the kindness of his own heart, apparently. He was reportedly angry that tipped-off press showed up at Vancouver's Canuck Place *(canuckplace.org)* where he was entertaining terminally ill children – he wants his good deeds to be done quietly.

Gil Bellows

Hails from: Vancouver

Big break: as Billy, Ally's love interest on *Ally McBeal.*

Now playing: a doctor in the Val Kilmer thriller *Blind Horizon.*

Joely Collins

Hails from: Vancouver

Big break: Being adopted as a baby by the singer Phil Collins (her mother was once married to him) was a lucky break. But she won her Gemini for her role on the Vancouver-shot TV series *Madison.*

Now playing: stars in the TV series *Cold Squad.*

Hayden Christensen

Hails from: Vancouver

Big break: Anakin Skywalker in *Star Wars: Episode II, Attack of the Clones*

Now playing: Anakin Skywalker in *Star Wars: Episode III* (due in 2005)

Uma Ma

In town to shoot *Paycheck* in the summer of 2003, Thurman was spotted wheeling baby Roan down Burrard Street with another woman (and no body guards to be seen) and ordering up steak at Gotham Steakhouse *(615 Seymour St.)*.

The Kiss of Ozzy

One woman was so smitten at spotting Ozzy Osbourne gnawing on a T-bone at Gotham Steakhouse (he was in Vancouver for a June 2003 concert) she grabbed the flowers from the restaurant lobby and presented them to him. He, in turn, made some new friends when he spotted a group of women celebrating at a table and old bat-breath kissed the birthday girl on the cheek.

The Bennifer Summer

During the summer of 2003, the affianced pair Ben Affleck and J.Lo, who rented a waterfront house in Deep Cove, were seen trotting about everywhere, from a personal training gym called Executive Lifestyles *(101-555 8th Ave.)* to Glowbal Grill & Satay Bar *(1079 Mainland St.)* in Yaletown. J.Lo was seen trudging through the Urban Fare grocery store *(177 Davie St.)* in ball cap and sweats, and shot an *Esquire* cover in a South Main photo studio while on hiatus from shooting in Winnipeg (henceforth dubbed J.Peg). Affleck, meanwhile, followed the *Paycheck* set around downtown Vancouver, amidst rumours that he was attacked by a bystander on set (an old gambling debt, perhaps?). According to the film biz mole, someone jumped a fence between two of the buildings at Vancouver Film Studios where *Paycheck* was shooting and went for Affleck. The attacker was immediately jumped by Affleck's bodyguards, beaten to a pulp, and had to be airlifted to Vancouver General Hospital. Affleck went back to work that afternoon unharmed. The lesson? Don't mess with Daredevil.

Martin Cummins

Hails from: Delta

Big break: While acting in the Vancouver shot TV series *Poltergeist,* he proved his chops by producing the acclaimed semi-autobiographical film *We All Fall Down.*

Now playing: He's developing *Tie The Knot,* a comedy set in his South Main neighbourhood.

Daniella Evangelista

Hails from: Vancouver

Big break: starring in the horror films *Disturbing Behavior, Ripper,* and *Mangler 2.*

Now playing: Stars in the Vancouver-shot teen series *Edgemont,* has a lead in the film *Scorched* , and is featured in a new Nickelback video, Liv Tyler-style.

Michael J. Fox

Hails from: Burnaby

Big break: As the smart aleck, right-wing Alex in the TV series *Family Ties.*

Now playing: Works as an advocate for Parkinson's disease while chilling at fishing lodges around Vancouver Island.

Jane McGregor

Hails from: Vancouver

Big break: Her role as Flower in the Vancouver-produced indie hit *Flower and Garnet* in 2003 propelled her into American teen blockbusters such as *Slap Her, She's French.*

Now playing: Slap Her, She's French.

Joshua Jackson

Hails from: Vancouver

Big break: Those Tourism B.C. commercials were an illustrious start that eventually led to the role of Pacey on TV teen drama *Dawson's Creek.*

Now playing: Stars alongside Glenn Close in the 2003 film *The Safety of Objects* and with Christina Ricci in *The Laramie Project.*

Where the Movie Stars Stay

Photo: Rob Melnychuk

The billion-dollar local film biz makes for great celebrity watching. And the best place to spot celebrities is on Robson Street downtown.

Many movie stars stay at either the **Sutton Place Hotel** *(845 Burrard St., 604-682-5511)* or the **Pacific Palisades Hotel** *(1277 Robson St., 604-688-0461)*. As a result, Robson between Burrard and Jervis is Celebrity Central. Stars just have to walk around the corner from their hotel and they've got the best shopping in the city. Newly popular among celebrities is the **Opus Hotel** (pictured above, *322 Davie St., 604-642-6787*) in Yaletown, best-known for their cinema-ispired suites and voyeuristic lobby washrooms.

The Sutton Place's Gerrard Lounge is a favourite celebrity watering hole. And a main shopping stop would seem to be the Roots store at Robson and Burrard. The Roots guest book has been signed by Ashley Judd, Wesley Snipes, Antonio Banderas, Melanie Griffiths, Bridget Fonda, Rob Lowe, Vanessa Williams, Janine Turner, Dennis Miller, Linda Hamilton, Corbin Bernsen, Terence Stamp, Max Von Sydow, Lou Gossett Jr., and Tom Arnold, among others. Why Roots? Maybe it's because of the stylish clothes. More likely it's because of the Roots celebrity discount.

Extra Stoned

If you notice some glazed expressions and muffled laughter in the crowd scenes of locally shot movies, it's not due to the exhaustion of long hours spent toiling on set. In the hurry-up-and-wait movie industry, a good proportion of Vancouver extras quell the boredom by getting stoned. Perhaps that explains the unlimited amount of candy and junk food available 24/7 at the craft service tables. The extra wranglers turn a blind eye, so long as the extras do what they're told. Extras get paid $10-plus per hour and get really good at hacky sack.

Up in Smoke

Vancouver has developed a reputation as a marijuana mecca thanks to the internationally-renowned potency of B.C. bud, the proliferation of pot cafés near Hastings and Cambie, and the promotional zeal of pot advocate Marc Emery. But pot has long roots in the city. Hey, **Cheech and Chong**'s stoned pothead schtick started in Vancouver.

The duo first got together at the old Shanghai Junk nightclub in Chinatown, and Vancouver references remained in their act long after they transplanted it to Hollywood: the cop forever trying to bust them was based on a member of the Vancouver narcotics squad.

The Vancouver connection was Tommy Chong, who moved west from Alberta in the late '50s. Chong was originally a musician (he co-wrote the '60s R&B hit *Does Your Mother Know About Me* by Bobby Taylor and the Vancouvers), but switched to comedy when he took over the Shanghai Junk strip club and turned it into an improvisational comedy venue. The catch was, he left the signs for the strip club up outside, so the customers didn't know what was going on.

"It was very funny," says Chong. "Especially when we'd start the show off with a mime artist. That was pure theatre. All these bikers and loggers and miners who have been in the bush and want to see some women and all of a sudden a mime artist comes on picking a flower out of the air."

Chong, who was recently a co-star on the TV series *That 70s Show*, still retains a residence in West Vancouver.

Kristin Kreuk
Hails from: Vancouver
Big break: Her high school acting teacher sent her to an open audition for a role in the Vancouver-shot TV series *Edgemont*, which she won.
Now playing: Stars as Lana Lang (Superman's crush) in the series *Smallville*, also shot in Vancouver.

Carrie-Anne Moss
Hails from: Burnaby
Big break: As Carrie Spencer on the TV series *Models Inc.* (1994).
Now playing: After *The Matrix Reloaded* and *The Matrix Revolutions* (both 2003), she moved on to *Suspect Zero* (2004).

Molly Parker

Hails from: Maple Ridge

Big break: The Lynne Stopkewich film *Kissed.*

Now playing: Stars in a film about a struggling actress called *Break a Leg.*

Jason Priestley

Hails from: Burnaby

Big break: Starred as Brandon in *Beverly Hills, 90210.*

Now playing: A racecar accident has had him laying low for some time, though he still owns a condo and co-owns a restaurant in Vancouver.

Photo: Solo

What were 400 hip young men and women doing lined up outside the **Fox Cinema** *(2321 Main St, 604-874-3116)* on a Saturday night in June 2000? It was a double screening of 1972 porn classics *Behind the Green Door* and *Deep Throat,* billed as "Return to Porno Chic" (the term used by the *New York Times* to describe the mainstream porn trend caused by the films' original release). A tireless promoter named Dimitri runs the ongoing "Porno Chic" series at the Fox, which, according to his research, is the last porn theatre in North America still screening 35 mm adult feature films. He vows to preserve it as one of the last few "genuine cultural slums." A group calling themselves "Criminal Cinema" banded together to give the Fox a much needed scrubbing up, which included new carpets and the removal of the notorious raised seats in the back that had become something approaching a health hazard. 35 mm porn films are no longer made, so the theatre relies on its archive of vintage films, most of which are from the late '70s and early '80s. The theatre's history mirrors that of B.C. film censorship laws. Formerly called the Savoy, it was converted into a porn theatre in 1983 when laws were finally relaxed. B.C. was known for its stringent censorship policies (B.C. chief censor Ray Macdonald was credited with inventing the cougar symbol for restricted movies) and Vancouverites had previously gone on porn road-trips to Washington state to see uncut films. Since 2000, the Fox has been owned by a couple from mainland China, and it still screens porn films from 11:30 a.m. to midnight, 7 days a week. Recent Porno Chic events have included a screening of vintage porn trailers called "Coming Attractions" (get it?) for Valentine's Day, which included cheap beer and porn trivia with the audience. Porn legend Ron Jeremy has also made guest appearances. For "Return to Porno Chic" events, see *therealboogienights.com.*

The local film industry has gone crazy over the last few years, exploding into a billion dollar business. One of the most successful studios was, until recently, located in a nondescript warehouse at 1624 Franklin in East Vancouver.

Founded in 1997, **Sweet Entertainment** has become a major player in the Internet pornography industry with videos such as *The Dirty Old Man*, *Sweetloads*, and *Sadoslaves*. It has hosted several webmaster porn conferences, and staged an "adult talent expo" for aspiring porn stars.

Members of the Vancouver vice squad, however, weren't impressed. In December 2002, the studio was raided and 100 computers seized. Sweet Entertainment's four owners were charged with manufacturing and distributing obscene videos.

art house cinemas

Hollywood Theatre

The Grand Dame of second run, double-bill theatres. The picks are mainstream, but the price is right: $5. *3123 W. Broadway, 604-738-3211, hollywoodtheatre.ca*

Pacific Cinémathèque

Often a venue for offbeat film festivals, obscure Japanese cult films, forgotten European gems, and local indie premieres. *1131 Howe St., 604-688-3456, cinematheque.bc.ca*

Photo: Solo

Ryan Reynolds
Hails from: Vancouver
Big break: Starred as Berg in the TV series *Two Guys, a Girl and a Pizza Place*.
Now playing: With singer Alanis Morissette, several years his senior. Seen in the 2003 comedy remake *The In-Laws* with Michael Douglas.

Rachel Roberts
Hails from: Vancouver
Big break: Already a well-established Victoria's Secret model and cover girl in New York, her transition into acting came when she was the woman secretly cast to play the "perfect" synthetic woman in the 2002 movie *Simone*. She had to sign a confidentiality agreement and go to set with the pseudonym Anne Green.
Now playing: a model.

Park Theatre

A tendency toward feel-good foreign hits such as *Billy Elliot, Monsoon Wedding*, and *Bend It Like Beckham.*
3440 Cambie St., 604-876-2747

Cinemark Tinseltown

Photo: Solo

The only viable business in a moribund mall on the edge of Chinatown, find low prices, stadium seating, reclining seats, free parking, empty theatres, and great foreign films.
88 W. Pender St., 604-806-0799, cinemark.com

Vaneast Cinema

Though it was once briefly a Chinese theatre, it now caters to the bohemian folks on the Drive with marginal, banned, and political films.
2290 Commercial Dr., 604-251-1313, vaneast.com

Varsity Theatre

The owner of this independent, second-run cinema usually runs mainstream flicks, but has lately started supporting the local filmmaking scene with the Kick Start screenings.
4375 W. 10th Ave., 604-222-2235

Nettwerking It

Vancouver's most famous record label and music management company, **Nettwerk Records**, is housed in the gallery district of South Granville. It was from these offices that promotion genius **Terry McBride** is credited with taking relative unknowns and cracking the U.S. market (Diana Krall and Sarah McLachlan being famous examples). A tricky technique they reportedly used to get radio time for the Barenaked Ladies was dropping off fake "bootlegged" tapes of the band (already well-established in Canada) at U.S. college campuses. The theory was that the underground buzz would trickle up to the campus radio stations, and break out from there. Worked like a charm.

Rock's Heavy Metal

Fall, 1987. The name **Bob Rock** is synonymous with success in the Canadian music industry. For nearly a decade, he's fronted a pair of Canada's most successful and critically acclaimed bands, the Payola$ and Rock and Hyde. As a recording engineer, he's worked with some of rock's biggest stars, including Bon Jovi, Aerosmith, and Loverboy. But Bob Rock is broke, with "not a penny to my name."

So he puts his performing career on ice and hunkers down in the studio, this time as a producer. One of his first projects is a Led Zeppelin-style band called Kingdom Come, which becomes the hard-rock success story of 1988. Soon, rock's heaviest dudes are beating a path to Vancouver's Little Mountain Sound: Mötley Crüe, David Lee Roth, the Cult, Little Caesar, Blue Murder, and Bon Jovi; Rock's production resumé is a veritable Top-10 of headbangers.

But it's his production of Metallica in 1991 that really makes his rep. Rock takes the thrash-metal pioneers into bold new sonic realms without compromising the band's dark, ultra-heavy sound. As a result, Metallica makes a quantum leap from a sizable cult act to being one of the biggest bands in the world. And Bob Rock becomes the producer of the moment.

Music Makers

Sarah McLachlan

Known as: The instigator of the travelling festival of songstresses called Lilith Fair and singer of numerous international hits, such as "Surfacing."
Little known fact: Paparazzi camped out for days at the bottom of her West Van driveway after the 2003 birth of daughter India, but she refused to come out.

Bif Naked

Known as: The tiny alt-rock princess whose famous tattooed Goth look has given way to pretty-in-pink of late. *Little known fact:* She lives in the residential tower at the Pacific Palisades Hotel where she spends time painting pictures of her dogs.

Michael Bublé

Known as: The young crooner who has performed at the Super Bowl and at ex-prime minister Brian Mulroney's daughter's wedding and appeared on *Larry King Live* and *The Tonight Show with Jay Leno*. *Little kown fact:* Only one song on his latest album was deemed Canadian content by the CRTC, even though he's from Burnaby.

It's Miller Time

Vancouver has had international success with several high-profile recording studios, such as Little Mountain Sound (Bon Jovi, Aerosmith, Mötley Crüe, Loverboy), the Warehouse (AC/DC, Bryan Adams, R.E.M.), and Mushroom (Terry Jacks, Heart, Chilliwack). But one of the coolest studios is tucked away in a nondescript building in the Downtown Eastside party zone: the **Miller Block**.

The Miller Block draws its name from Miller Jewelers, which used to be located there. © (Copyright) built the studio there in the mid-'90s to record their album *Love Story*, and it was subsequently used by a who's who of local alternative rockers, including the New Pornographers, Neko Case, Zumpano, Kevin Kane, and others, even though it was underground, technically illegal, with no city permits.

The studio was located on the top floor of the two-storey building. One day some musicians went exploring in the abandoned downstairs, and discovered a bizarre mezzanine floor where some addicts and prostitutes had been living. Photographer Karin Bubas shot the remains, and turned it into an affecting exhibit, *Leon's Palace*, which featured pages from one of the prostitutes' diaries.

The best story from the Miller Block is about the musician who was jaywalking across the street to get to the studio, which is near Save on Meats on West Hastings. A cop stopped him and gave him a ticket. The astonished musician pointed to a nearby drug user who was smoking up. "That guy is smoking crack right there!"

The cop looked at him and said, "That's a health issue."

In 1976, a hippie music teacher in Langley recorded an 80-voice elementary school choir singing an inspired, if somewhat bizarre, assortment of pop-rock songs, including *Space Oddity* by David Bowie, *Good Vibrations* by the Beach Boys, and *Calling Occupants of Interplanetary Craft* by Klaatu. Three hundred records were pressed and sold to the students and their parents, and the album was forgotten.

A quarter of a century later, a music fan in Victoria found a copy of the album in a thrift store. He sent *Space Oddity* to a disc jockey named Irwin Chusid in Jersey City, N.J., who played it on his Internet radio show and received a massive positive response.

Intrigued, Chusid started searching for the teacher, Hans Fenger. After some Net sleuthing and several phone calls, he located Fenger, who was still teaching music at Cunningham elementary school in Vancouver. Fenger then sent Chusid a second album he had done in Langley in 1977.

Chusid was the driving force behind a trio of wildly successful albums by the Mexican king of "space-age bachelor pad music," Esquivel. He convinced the Dutch Basta label to reissue the two Langley albums on compact disc in Europe, and got Bar-None records to license it for North America.

The results became the left-field hit of the decade. The album drew raves from the *New York Times*, the *Washington Post*, and *Rolling Stone* magazine. Songwriter Bowie was also impressed. "The backing arrangement is astounding," he said of the CD reissue, which is called *Innocence and Despair*. "Coupled with the earnest if lugubrious vocal performance you have a piece of art that I couldn't have conceived of, even with half of Columbia's finest exports in me."

The masses agreed. About 100,000 copies of *Innocence and Despair* were sold around the world after it was rereleased.

Swollen Members

Known as: The local hip hop band who've been pulling in just about every Canadian award out there, with hits like "Breath" and "Fuel Injected."

Little known fact: The reason front man Madchild (a.k.a. Shane Bunting) always wear a ball cap? He's balding.

Veda Hille

Known as: A popular singer/songwriter with several albums to her credit.

Little known fact: She almost became the only female member of the Barenaked Ladies in 1995 when they asked her to become their keyboardist.

The Fuck Band That Could

Photo: Chris Buck

The **New Pornographers** are the biggest band to come out of the Vancouver underground in several years. They are also the most successful Vancouver fuck band ever. Fuck bands are made up of musicians who start a side project for fun with their friends. Sometimes the friends aren't even musicians, like Blaine Thurier of the Pornographers, who is better known as a filmmaker than a keyboard player.

In the Pornographers' case, Carl Newman (from Zumpano) and Dan Bejar (Destroyer) teamed up with Thurier, John Collins (Evaporators), and Fisher Rose (Citroen), then added singer Neko Case. Rose quit and was replaced by Kurt Dahle (Age of Electric, Limblifter), who recruited Todd Fancie (Limblifter, Taste of Joy). The band only played a handful of gigs before their album became a surprise hit — and the band members wound up making the Pornographers their main focus.

It's a heartening story for anyone who ever rocked to classic fuck bands like the Melody Pumps, Rude Norton, or Ogre. Such bands are known for their colourful names, such as East Van Halen, the Christ Killers (a Jewish Christmas act), and Skinny Yuppie (a take on Skinny Puppy). And who could ever forget the immortal Power Clone, an Iron Maiden cover band who wear clown outfits on stage?

Elvis is in the Building

Loud rock 'n' roll manager **Bruce Allen** (Bryan Adams, BTO, Loverboy) has lived in palatial houses in Point Grey and on the Fraser River flats. But he's never felt more at home than in his current digs, a 2,700-square-foot penthouse on the north shore of False Creek.

The two-storey pad is Bruce Allen to the max. Everywhere you look, there's a piece of Elvis or Coca-Cola memorabilia (his two obsessions). There's a pool table, a bar, and five TVs strategically placed throughout the apartment, which he likes to turn on all at once, so he can walk from room to room and not miss anything.

The heart of the downstairs living area is the games room, which features a blue felt pool table, an incredible 1930s Coca-Cola icebox, and Elvis Presley's personal barber chair, which he bought for US$18,000 at a Las Vegas auction.

Elvis has been Allen's idol since his youth. Vintage posters for Elvis movies like *G.I. Blues*, *King Creole*, *Viva Las Vegas*, *Blue Hawaii*, and *Speedway* adorn the walls and an Elvis statuette phone sits atop the well-stocked bar. Instead of ringing, Elvis' hips begin to swivel and the phone starts playing "Hound Dog."

The pad is packed with groovy music memorabilia, like Roy Orbison's Gibson guitar, autographed by the Big O himself (a gift from record producer Mutt Lange and music executive Clive Calder) and a 1945 Wurlizer jukebox, stocked with 78s. His favourite item, though, might be in the bathroom: a copy of a gruelling 1974 tour schedule that had the King playing 21 shows in 17 days, all in different cities, with no days off. It is framed alongside a letter, from Elvis' manager Col. Tom Parker, about the tour, and a scrunched up piece of hotel stationery, on which a depressed Elvis writes a note to God asking to be taken to a place "where there are no worries."

Sunny Payday

The Poppy Family was the first Vancouver musical act to strike it big internationally: their single *Which Way You Goin', Billy* hit No. 2 on the U.S. charts in 1970.

After the group folded, songwriter Terry Jacks hit the jackpot in 1973 as a solo artist with his version of a Jacques Brel song, *Seasons in the Sun*. *Seasons* sold 14

Sid Sick (Rabid) — Sid Hourniet.

Jon Doe (Rabid, Scramblers) — John Williams.

Gary Middleclass (Generators, Payola$, e?) — Gary Bourgeois.

Dave Schmorg (Schmorgs) — David Mitchell.

David M. (No Fun) — David Matychuk.

Zippy Pinhead (Dils, Los Popularos) — Bill Chobataur.

Buck Cherry (Active Dog, Los Popularos, Modernettes) — John Armstrong.

Mary-Jo Kopechne (Modernettes) — Mary Wiltshire.

Dash Ham (Active Dog, Pointed Sticks) — Gord Nicholls.

Andy Graffiti (various bands) — Andy McMaster.

Herald Nix — John Wood.

Bob Rock (Payola$) — Bob Rock.

Music Stores

Bassix

The original vinyl shop for the party scene, co-founded by the legendary House DJ T-Bone.
217 W. Hasting St., 604-689-7734.

Black Swan Records

Classical lovers who get down to Dvorak head here.
301-207 W. Hastings St., 604-734-2828, blackswan.bc.ca

Red Cat Records

An indie rock destination with lots of local talent and street cred. The female co-owner is in the band Clover Honey.
4307 Main St., 604-708-9422, redcat.ca

Scratch Records

Where DJs shop for vinyl.
726 Richards St., 604-687-6355, scratchrecords.com

million records, and became one of the top-10-bestselling singles of all time.

But Jacks is notoriously self-conscious about his voice, and initially didn't want to record it. He produced a version of *Seasons in the Sun* for the Beach Boys, but they decided not to release it. So he reluctantly put out his version, and it turned out to be his biggest hit.

But he had to share the jackpot with his ex-wife, Susan. Still unsure about his version of *Seasons*, Terry offered to split the proceeds from his single if she gave him half the royalties from her own single. Susan's 45 stiffed, Terry's went through the stratosphere, and there was enough to make them both rich.

Susan wound up moving to Nashville with former football star Ted Dushinski, where she operates a business. Terry lives on the Sunshine Coast, where he's active in environmental causes and fishes a lot.

One former Poppy Family member, though, still has a thriving musical career. Tabla player Singh is now regarded as one of the world's foremost tabla musicians and makes his living teaching and performing concerts with Indian orchestras. Singh, who lives in Surrey, apparently spends eight hours a day practising his instrument.

Where the Rock Stars Stay

Rock stars tend to stay at different hotels than movie people. Billy Joel digs the Bayshore, R.E.M. favours the Opus and the Wedgewood, and Bryan Adams often stays at the Fairmont Waterfront Hotel rather than going home to his pad in West Van. The Rolling Stones usually stay at the Four Seasons. Moby likes Pacific Palisades

Former Van Halen singer David Lee Roth was the most enterprising hotel guest: when he was recording an album at Little Mountain Sound in the '90s, he passed on the high-end hotel circuit to stay at the budget-priced Nelson Place Hotel at Nelson and Granville. Roth liked staying in a seedy area of town, and liked being able to personalize his room: he took over a whole floor, and extensively remodelled it by taking out walls.

Photo: Solo

just passing through

Moist Interesting

Though David Usher now lives in Montreal with his wife, the former Moist front man and now solo artist did time in Vancouver. In the mid-'90s, he sold button-downs and chinos at the Robson Street Club Monaco store, spending his coffee breaks chatting up the shop girls at nearby Aritzia. But those hard-earned wages went to help cobble together Moist's debut indie album, *Silver*. The record won them a recording contract with EMI, and Moist went on to tour internationally with the likes of Green Day and Hole. Usher has since gone on to record *Little Songs* in 1998 and beat out Leonard Cohen for best pop album of 2002 at the Juno Awards with his *Morning Orbit*.

Michael Stipe for Mayor

It was a big deal when it was announced in the spring of 2003 that R.E.M. was arriving in town to record an album. The band booked out some rooms at Yaletown's Opus Hotel *(322 Davie St.)* and apparently liked Vancouver so much, they as good as moved in. All the group's members showed up in costume at the hotel's summer pajama party and they were spotted regularly at the hotel's French brasserie, Elixir. As the band left on tour, lead singer Michael Stipe posted the following on a fan website: "Thanks to the crew there in VanBC who set it all up and thanks to the folks in LA who put it together. I miss the studio and everyone there [katie! kirk! scott! plus] and I really miss VanBC [West Van – yes – ! Burnaby! Vij's! House of Venus! Yelltown – uh huh that's right – ! Granville!].... You see now why we never do dedications on records, I'm a cheeseball. Vancouver, I have to say it's a great city filled with great people and great food and great vistas and great contradictions...." Vancouver loves ya right back, Mike.

Teenage Rampage Records

Around the side of a building on the camping store stretch of Broadway, it's got a cult following.
19 E. Broadway, jononation.com

Photo: Solo

Virgin Megastore

The only one in Canada.
788 Burrard St., 604-669-2289, virginmegamagazine.com

Zulu Records

Even in the new, bigger location, the goal isn't to move 100,000 units of Britney Spears. Instead, find that obscure Latvian version of "Hotel California," themed listening stations (punk, alt country, down tempo), quality used CDs, a ticket counter, magazines, and smart staff.
1972 W. 4th Ave., 604-738-3232, zulurecords.com

Photo: Solo

ALSO CHECK OUT:

Boomtown Import Records & CD's

102-1252 Burrard St., 604-893-8696, boomtownrecords.com

Beat Street New & Used Records

3-712 Robson St., beatstreet.ca

Scrape Records

17 W. Broadway, 604-877-1676, scraperecords.com

Noize Sound

540 Seymour St., 604-681-7007

Neptoon Records & CD's

3561 Main St., 604-324-1229, neptoon.com

Mint Records Inc.

604-669-6468, mintrecs.com

Boompa Records

604-879-2666

Billy Joel's Free Concert

When Billy Joel last swung through town for a concert, an unsuspecting crowd watching a busker at Granville Island got a big surprise. As a somewhat amateurish street performer plonked away on his electic keyboard in the drizzle, a big black van pulled up. Out jumped Billy Joel and four bodyguards all dressed in black. Joel, with an unmistakeable grin on his face, circled the crowd, who probably hoped he would jump in and put this poor man out of his misery. Alas, it was not to happen. Joel jumped back into the van with his entourage and sped off. But it must have got the wheels turning: after his concert that night, he returned to his hotel (the Four Seasons) and entertained the crowd on the bar piano until the wee hours.

Stan, My Vancouver Man

Vancouver actor Devon Sawa (born 1978) may have more than a dozen movie credits to his name (including *Casper* and *Slackers*) but it was his appearance as the crazed fan called Stan in Eminem's video of the same name that was his real star turn. Sawa won the role after Macaulay Culkin turned it down; it was Sawa's performance in the thriller *Final Destination* that convinced the producers that he'd do well as the psycho fan Stan. Since then, Sawa has gone on to appear in *Extreme Dating* and has reportedly done a very convincing impromptu performance of a really drunk guy in first class with a dog on a recent flight from L.A. to Vancouver.

Cameron Diaz's Lover Boy

Described variously as glam rock, cock rock, or just plain rock, the '80s band Loverboy and its front man Mike Reno just won't go away. Still living on the North Shore and now hitched to a private yoga instructor, Reno's experiencing a second coming with his 1981 hit "Working for the Weekend" showing up on the soundtrack of *Charlie's Angels Full Throttle*. Even better, the movie posters, which showed Cameron Diaz making the peace sign behind her leather-clad butt, pays homage to the cover for Loverboy's *Get Lucky* album cover.

Nightlife

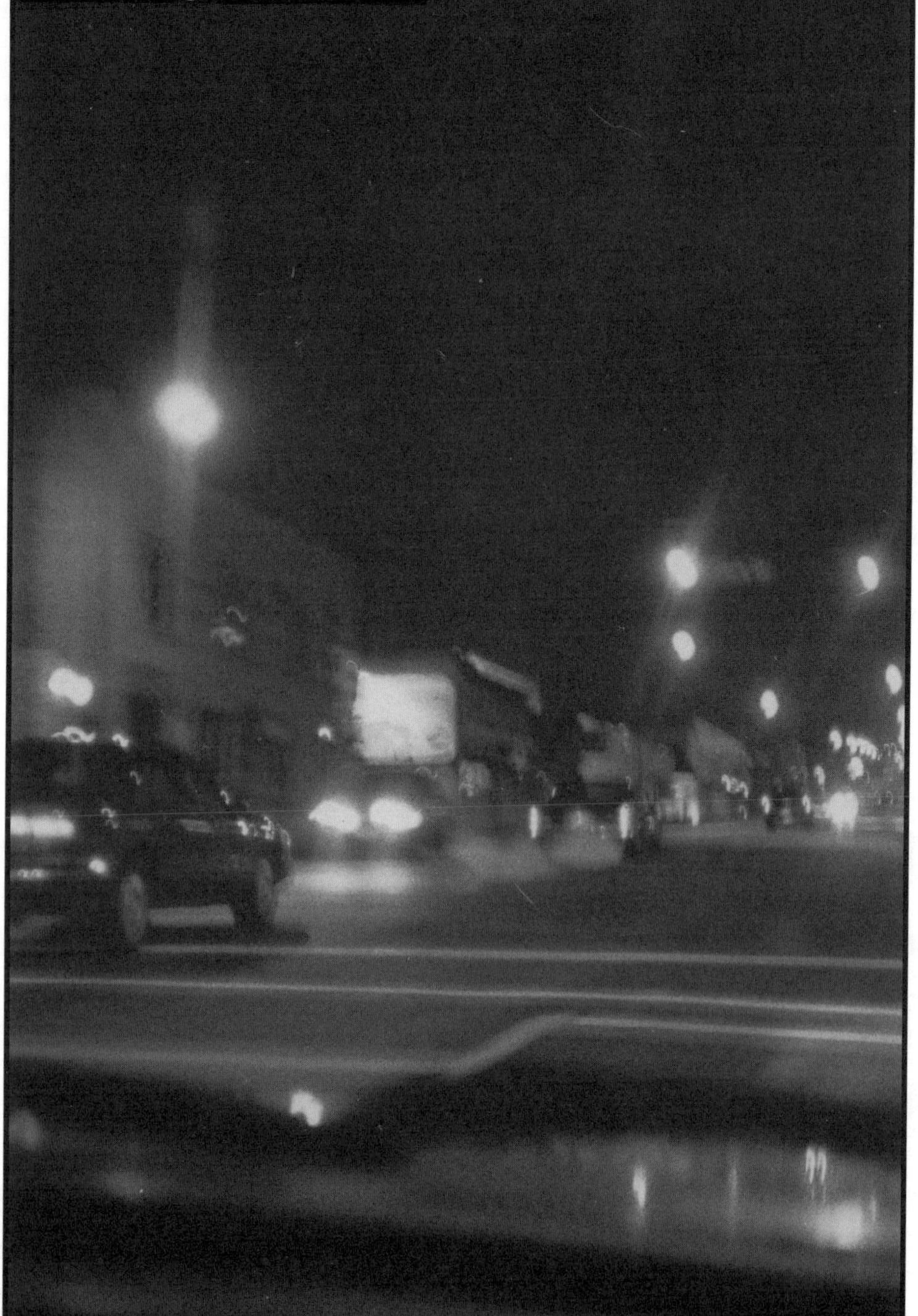

Photo: Mandelbrot

Vancouver's nightlife scene is full of contradictions: is it "No Fun City" or "Sin City of the North"? We'll help you decide, and also tell you about punk karaoke, a cop clubhouse, a bar dubbed the Gun Club, where to smoke a hookah, and your friendly neighbourhood pub ghost.

A Whiskey Bar on
Blood Alley – and,
Boo! A Ghost!

Photo: Solo

Shebeen is Gaelic for an illegal moonshine den, but the **Shebeen Whiskey House** is fully legit, and stocks the largest selection of whiskey in B.C., including 30-year-old Glenfiddich and the rotating Chivas Revolve – perfect for a game of spin the bottle. Located behind the Irish Heather gastropub, this little 2-level whiskey bar is tucked away in a former coach house, and has been visited by the likes of Bob Geldof and the Chieftains. It's located at the intersection of Blood Alley (so named because it used to house a row of butcher shops) and Gaoler's Mews, the site of Vancouver's first jail, first fire station and customs house, and, legend has it, the site of the city's last public execution.

A tip: If you happen to knock your glass off the table and it smashes on the floor, just blame it on the mischievous ghost. Owner Sean Heather says it happens all the time, usually after the bar is closed and empty.
7 Gaoler's Mews, 604-915-7338

One by one, the great nightclubs of Vancouver's past have fallen by the wayside. The Cave, the Palomar, the Marco Polo, Isy's, the Arctic Club, the Smilin' Buddha, the Living Room, the Kublai Khan, Oil Can Harry's – they're all long gone and fading into memory.

But one club has managed to ride out the trends and remain standing through the booms and busts in the downtown real-estate market. The **Penthouse Cabaret** *(1033 Seymour St., 604-683-2111)* has been a city fixture since 1945. It started out as an after-hours speakeasy, became a legal cabaret in 1950, achieved infamy as a hooker hangout in the '60s and '70s, and has been one of Vancouver's most notorious strip clubs for the past two decades.

The Penthouse was the brainchild of Joe Philliponi (whose name was spelled wrong by an immigration officer when he arrived in Canada from Italy) and his younger brother Ross Fillipone.

Joe started off as a bicycle courier in the Depression and branched out into the taxi and trucking business. At the end of the Second World War, Joe and Ross decided to start their own nightclub. For years the Penthouse operated as a "bottle club," where customers would sneak in their own liquor and hide it under the table.

"It was an unlicensed after-hours club," says Ross Fillipone. "There was no liquor licence in those days. It was strictly all bottle clubs. In those days, you had to brown-bag it."

HAVE A CRIMINALLY GOOD TIME

The **Crime Lab** restaurant near Stanley Park is located in the former studio of a photographer who shot crime scenes and mug shots and did fingerprints for the Vancouver police in the 1940s and 1950s. The restaurant carried on the lab tradition with drinks served in glass beakers, but alas, the patrons kept stealing them. But beware of getting robbed yourself: a single glass of white wine can cost $15.

1280 Pender St., 604-732-7463, thecrimelab.ca

GAMBLING, HIDDEN HOOCH, AND AN OPIUM DEN

The restaurant **Lucy Mae Brown** used to be a gentleman's gaming house and opium den in the 1950s, run by a New Orleans widow of the same name. The downstairs bar, now called the **Opium Den**, has a huge steel door leading to a concrete room that is thought to be where they stored illicit hooch. The tradition continues at this cavernous hideaway where the party sometimes continues well into the wee hours.

862 Richards St., 604-899-9199

The 120-seat Penthouse quickly became a late-night hotspot – and a target of the police. In 1947, a 20-man police squad raided the club, seizing 49 bottles of liquor and 467 bottles of beer ("the largest liquor seizure in a decade," said the *Vancouver Sun*). The Filippones were charged with selling liquor, but the charges were thrown out.

In 1950, the Penthouse went legit, sort of, when it became a licensed cabaret. Finally, it could advertise that it was a nightclub and dining establishment. The only problem was, it still couldn't legally sell liquor, so it remained a bottle club.

"You talk about the Keystone Cops," says Ross. "There used to be about a dozen cabarets in the city, places that were prominent like the Commodore, the Palomar, the Cave Supper Club. These places were not licensed. These places you had to bring your own bottle in illegally. And we were one of them. But we were on a smaller scale at the Penthouse.

"It was known as an after-hours club. People used to come to our place after they went to these other places. We'd be open until six, seven in the morning. There were no hours or regulations. You just stayed open as long as you had people."

The Penthouse remained a favourite target of the city "dry squad" in the '50s. "The police would come in 20 or 30 strong two or three times a week," says Filippone. "'We used to have spotters on the roof. You couldn't miss five or six police cars coming down the street. We'd press a buzzer and tell the waiters, who'd tell the customers [to put their bottles on the floor]. It was a joke."

Over time it became a celebrity hangout for people like Bing Crosby, Bob Hope, and Victor Borge. Errol Flynn dropped in the night before he died. Harry Belafonte once popped an obnoxious drunk on the nose, a one-punch knockout. At the end of a 1957 show, Frank Sinatra announced from the Orpheum stage that he would "see you all at the Penthouse," and the line to get in snaked all the way down Seymour to Nelson and up to Granville. (Unfortunately, the masses didn't get to see Frank, who booked a private V.I.P. room for his entourage.)

"They never gave us a liquor licence, but we didn't give a damn," says Filippone. "We had them lined up down the street. We couldn't make any more money if we had a licence. We were getting admission of $5.95

at the door and selling [soft drink] mix at 50 cents at a bottle – $600 [of mix] only cost [us] $50. You don't make that with booze!"

But times changed and so did the Penthouse. In 1965, Filippone brought in go-go girls, an attraction that evolved into the exotic dancers of today. In 1968, the Penthouse finally got a liquor licence, which forced it to close at 2 a.m.

Prostitutes also started frequenting the club. In 1975, Ross and Joe were charged with living off the avails of prostitution. The brothers were initially convicted and faced fines of $50,000 each and 60 days in jail. They were cleared of all charges on appeal, but not before they had spent three years in the courts, plus $1 million in lawyer's fees and lost income (the club was closed throughout the trial).

Joe was killed during a robbery at the club in 1983. The Fillipone family continues to own and operate the club, with Ross's son Danny now in charge.

Sex, Booze, More Secret Tunnels, and Another Ghost!

Balthazar restaurant has been many things, including a 1920s beauty school and boarding house for girls known as Maxine's, named for its enterprising Parisian proprietor. In the 1930s, it was used as a hideout for two of America's most wanted fugitives (one of whom was captured here by J. Edgar Hoover himself). When times got tough, Madame Maxine used the lower floor of the school as a brothel, hence Balthazar's "Bordello" room. There is also a filled-in tunnel (once used for rum-running during U.S. prohibition) connecting the building to boathouses at English Bay. A second, lesser-known tunnel connected the brothel to what was then called the Rogers Mansion, now **Romano's Macaroni Grill** (1523 Davie St., 604-689-4334, macaronigrill.com); the Rogers Sugar magnate liked to have his own secret point of access and egress to the brothel. You can still see where the tunnels were filled on the basement floor. But be wary if you venture down. The restaurant's manager says he has received internal pages from the basement phone late at night even though he's the only one there. 1215 Bidwell St., 604-689-8822

Unknown Music Venues

The Ironworks

By day it's a Railtown photography studio (once an ironworks shop) shared by some of the city's preeminent talents. By night, the tables and chairs are rearranged café-style and a tiny stage in the corner is host to local talent.
235 Alexander St., 604-681-5033

L'Espace Dubreuil

This unlisted special events venue is tucked under the Granville Bridge between Beach and Pacific Avenues. The absence of residential buildings in the area makes it a great place for late night music events. Keep your ear to the ground (especially amongst the city's francophone community) for events, which have recently included jazz and flamenco nights.
1435 Granville St.
(no listed number).

Star Pics

Kimberly Conrad Hefner

Kimberly Hefner

PLAYBOY

A JAZZY PAST

Just off Broadway and Main, the basement of a building that now houses a T-shirt shop and 99-cent pizza joint was once **The Original Jazz Cellar**, the centre of the Vancouver bebop scene in the '50s, which attracted U.S. jazz musicians to Canada for the first time. Rare recordings still exist of some of the performances, which included Charles Mingus and the Ornette Coleman Quartet. The venue, sadly, now sits empty. To see where it all went down, go around the south side of the hot pink-painted fashion shop called Kiss at the edge of the parking lot. You'll see an old wrought-iron canopy frame and double wooden doors that lead to the basement.

The fact that so many famous *Playboy* playmates hail from Vancouver can be traced to one man: photographer-turned-*Playboy* scout Ken Honey. He discovered Heidi Sorenson (Miss July 1981) at a bikini contest sponsored by CFUN radio where she worked as a clerk; Kimberly Conrad (Playmate of the Year, 1989), who married and had two sons with publisher Hugh Hefner; Kelly Tough (Miss October 1981); and Dorothy Stratten, the 20-year-old 1980 Playmate of the Year who was later murdered by her estranged husband before he turned the gun on himself. Pamela Anderson (Miss February 1990) was also discovered by Honey at a B.C. Lions football game in Vancouver. (Anderson recently bought property on Vancouver Island when she brought then-boyfriend Kid Rock home to meet her parents.) The *Playboy* tradition continues with Playboy Special Editions photographer Waldy Martens based here *(waldymartens.com)* and a recently opened Playboy Enterprises branch in Vancouver. Think you've got what it takes to be the next Miss March? Head to *Playboy's* scouting nights, often held at **Au Bar** *(674 Seymour St., 604-648-2227)* nightclub.

A Bloody Good Time

Photo: Solo

Vancouver's hippest underground party, dubbed "The Gathering," used to take place Saturday nights at **Unit 20 Army and Navy Air Force Veteran's Club**, once dubbed The Bucket of Blood for its tough reputation. For almost a year in 2003, young revelers drank $1.50 beers, played shuffleboard, and danced to a DJ spinning punk and electronic music. The legion's older clientele didn't mind the youthquake: Membership was down, and Gathering attendees became members to get a break at the door. Generations clashed, however, over the Legion's rule that you must remove your baseball hat inside in respect for the Queen. We wonder, though, if the cops who busted it recently took off their hats before taking away the legion's liquor license for being over-capacity.
300 W. Pender St., 604-685-4026

COPS AND IRONIC YOUTH (NO BULL)

The Army, Navy and Air Force Veterans Club Unit 298 is called the Taurus Unit because it's a Bull Club (i.e., for retired cops). Located in the hip South Main neighbourhood, ironic youth mix with the fuzz over cheap beer, darts, and pool.
3917 Main St., 604-879-1020

Meat Draws and Elvis: That's Entertainment

Haven't got the coin to join the Vancouver Club? Membership at **Royal Canadian Legion Branch 176** is $43, and you don't even have to be a war veteran. Also known as "The Billy Bishop," this legion and military museum hosts Sunday meat draws and operates like a regular neighbourhood pub. Special events include Elvis and Tom Jones tribute nights.
1407 Laburnum St., 604-738-4142

Photo: Hamid Attie

A ROOM WITH A VIEW

When all the English Bay beachfront patios are packed, head upstairs to the little-known circular bar called the **Bayside Lounge** (1755 Davie St., 604-682-1831) with a spectacular view of the bay. It's like stepping back into the '80s, where the waitresses have teased hair, the white wine spritzers keep flowing, and the J. Geils Band rocks steady over the speakers.

The pioneering Sugar brothers, Jason and Damon, were left with a sour taste in their mouths when the police and city officials busted a birthday party at their first **Sugarandsugar** studio in November 2002, shutting it down like a prohibition-era gin joint. The pioneering brothers had run this former after-hours space (unofficially called "Sugar's" for years) and had now gone pseudo-legit by applying for nightly special events licenses. With its coat check in a former bank vault, its white baby grand piano, its checkerboard floor, and sleek, modern furniture, Sugarandsugar studio not only attracted the city's cutting edge party scene, but it also came to symbolize the fight against what the media had dubbed "no fun city." When the jig was up, the club also became the movement's sacrificial lamb. In March 2003, the brothers resurfaced like a phoenix from the flames clutching a press release announcing, "We've gone legit!" A fully licensed event venue and cocktail lounge in an even larger space, the new **Sugarandsugar** (99 Powell St., 604-609-9939, sugarandsugar.com) has the same, big city urban feel as the original, and is open for cocktails and snacks during the week. Its circular bar upstairs, and slick chill room down, are two of the most happening bars in town. In homage to the original concept, it is reserved for private parties of up to 200 most nights.

bar stories

Bar None

Photo: Solo

Photo: Solo

When your bar gets the nickname "the Gun Club," it's time to start thinking of hiring a PR representative. The deadly shooting of Hell's Angel Donald Roming, 43, in front of this club a few years ago put a serious dent in its reputation, though it continues to limp along. Some of its owners were involved in the nearby restaurant that collapsed under the weight of its owners' egos and alleged other habits. The joke was on them when they installed a trick mirror in the women's washroom one night that allowed women to spy on the men primping and preening next door. One girl just couldn't keep her mouth shut and an angry guy called the police who shut the place down for the night.

1222 Hamilton St., 604-689-7000

The (Sugar Refinery)

There's something about the word sugar in a venue's name (see Sugarandsugar) that makes it slightly illicit in this city. Located along a strip of porn shops, on the second level at the top of a narrow staircase, "The Sug" operated for years as an informal after-hours venue, with live music, spoken word, and inexpensive pitchers of beer and perogies. The waitresses lit the candles with blowtorches, and everyone had a good time. Because of new regulations, it is now legitimately open till 4 a.m. for more of the same. Around Vancouver Jazz Festival time in late June, watch for its concurrent "Anti-Matter" jazz festival. *upstairs 1155 Granville St., 604-331-1184, sugarrefinery.com*

Photo: Solo

Cobalt Hotel

The Cobalt bills itself as "Vancouver's Hardcore Bar" and that's no understatement. It specializes in punk and death metal and bands with names like "In as Sin" and "Trash Train." Watch for hardcore movie screenings and the riotous Sunday night

"Scaryoke" punk karaoke nights where beer bottles have been known to fly.
917 Main St., 604-255-2088, thecobalt.net

Columbia 303

Bands play weekends, and you can grab a round for less than $10.
303 Columbia St., 604-683-3757

Fairview Pub

This is a no-frills kind of place where you can catch jazz or blues on a Sunday night over a cheap pint.
898 W. Broadway, 604-872-1262

The Ivanhoe

Don't mind the cockroaches crawling up the curtains – you're here for the cheap beer. But there are other deals to be had, too. Fancy a brick of cheddar? Some sushi? A raw steak? No, not from the bar, but from shady patrons who sell stolen groceries out of their raincoats *Sesame Street*-style: "Psssst, wanna buy some cheese?" (It's why the cheese case at the 24-hour Super-Valu at 1255 Davie Street is kept locked at night.) And if your bike is ever stolen in Vancouver, head here straight away. There's a good chance it's being fenced out front.
1038 Main St., 604-681-9118

Section (3)

Some bars and restaurants have always just gone ahead and held regular after-hours parties using special event licenses. This is one of them. You see, the folks here know a thing or two about fighting the system. The name Section (3) refers to the section of the Criminal Code they used to try to fight to keep the restaurant's original name, "De Niro's." Seems old Bobby wasn't too chuffed at having one of the city's most fun restaurants named after him. He's memorialized with a neon sign above the bar, made with letters from the original De Niro's sign, only now it spells "Nerd."
1039 Mainland St., 604-682-2777

singles Vancouver

To paraphrase D.H. Lawrence in *Lady Chatterley's Lover*, there are a lot of fish in the ocean, but most of them are sardines. According to the 2001 census, 52 percent of women over 15 in Vancouver are unmarried (that's 252,169) and the numbers are similar for men. While most of the speed dating organizations are now defunct, here are some singles hangouts that are worth a gamble.

Campoverde

This dating café formalizes the meet market by selling $200 memberships to screened singles who want to meet someone with the same "refined" tastes. Various dating advice books are sprinkled around the tables, as well as member profiles, and the room is swathed in velvet. Luckily, the neighbourhood's penthouses are replete with well-heeled divorcées.
1660 Cypress St., 604-734-1660, campoverde.ca

Dog Parks

Haven't got a dog? Borrow one for the day and take it to one of the two dog parks at the foot of the Cambie Bridge in Yaletown around 5:30 p.m. on weekdays and 10 a.m. on weekends. Let Spunky off his leash and see who he fetches.

The Roxy

There's been a line-up here since 1980. The club tends to get filled with lawyers and stockbrokers on serious after-work benders. There's a house band playing top-40 covers and it's been a regular post-game stop for the Canucks, who often jump behind the bar and start serving up drinks.
932 Granville St., 604-331-7999, roxyvan.com

Voda

The 30-something dating crowd who still have a few years before they are officially called cougars hook up here for drinks and dancing. There's a cool water wall, bathroom stalls that glaze over when you close the door, and a sushi bar catered by Vancouver's top sushi restaurant, Tojo's.
783 Homer St., 604-684-3003

Photo: Solo

Serotonin

A graffittied staircase leads up to a sleek, white room at this new, legal after-hours club. Seratonin is a mood-enhancing neurotransmitter released after dropping Ecstasy, so the fact that there is no alcohol here is not too much of a problem with this crowd. Open Thursday to Saturday, midnight to 7 a.m. Over 19 only.
695 Smithe St., 604-688-8151

The World

Vancouver's longest running after-hours club, it's located, appropriately, underground beside the Capitol 6 movie theatres. Open from 2 a.m. till dawn, it's a cozy little space with two chill rooms and a dance floor where people have been known to dance topless to deep, funky, and tech house.
816 Granville St., no listed phone number, 816.ca

aphrodisiac bars

When you want to spice up a date, head here for some appies – then home for "dessert."

Afterglow

A glowing cube of hot pink from the street, the sleek design is by Vancouver's hottest restaurant design firm, Evoke International. Check out the sexy silhouettes on the walls and windows and the lightweight furniture by local Bombast and ask for the late-night "Aphrodisiac Menu." The bar's name stems from the adjoining restaurant Glowbal Grill & Satay Bar, but could just as easily describe the look on your face after you get home. *1082 Hamilton St., 604-602-0835 glowbalvillage.com*

Tantra Waterfront Lounge and Grill

A restaurant and bar with a tantric sex theme, it offers seductive dishes that just won't stop, like spicy prawns and Tantric Pleasure martinis. Events held at the lounge have included tattoo contests. Wander over to aromatherapy chain **Saje** *(604-988-9688)*, also in the Quay, to pick up items from their Tantric Lovers line to take home – where the party will really get started. *123 Carrie Cates Court, Lonsdale Quay, North Vancouver, 604-986-6111*

CHAMPAGNE ALL AROUND

The new ice-topped champagne bar attached to fine dining restaurant the **Bear Foot Bistro** *(4121 Village Green, Whistler, 604-932-3433)* claims it has the best champagne selection in B.C. You rest your flute in circular cut-outs in the ice, and fibre optic lighting flashes down the bar turning your glass from pink to blue to green. However, in order to fit into these little ice-fishing holes, the champagne flutes are all stem and no base, so if you set it down on the bar – whoops, you'll be wearing your Dom.

lounge lizards

Vancouver's grooviest hotel lounges.

Best Bathroom Peep Show

Photo: Solo

You and your date head down the stairs to the side-by-side bathrooms. The woman you see in silhouette on the other side of the curtain putting on lipstick at the mirror is your date. Wait a second, she's now flashing you, and that's certainly not your date. Then you notice the live video feed on a monitor from the bar upstairs – there's your date, back upstairs, getting it on with your best friend! This scenario and many versions of it play themselves out nightly at the adjoined men's and women's bathrooms at the bar of the chic new **Opus Hotel**. Hotel staff worried men might get out of hand because of the sheer curtain separating the bathrooms, but as it happens it's the women who can't keep their clothes on.
322 Davie St., 604-642-6787

The Peep Show That's No More

The **Tiki Lounge** at the **Waldorf Hotel** is one of a few remaining in a Canadian chain from the '50s at the height of post-Pearl Harbor Polynesian-chic. Though many underground cabaret nights with burlesque girls, swing dance contests, and lounge acts like Michael Bublé were held there in the mid-'90s, fire regulations and other red tape issues kept getting in the way of all the fun. It's been a bit of a pattern, in fact. If you venture down into the largest of the three rooms that make up the lounge, take note of the paintings of Polynesian dancing girls on the walls near the bathrooms. When they were delivered to the lounge originally, the girls were topless. The bikini tops were added later, when the paintings were deemed indecent by local authorities.
1489 E. Hastings St., 604-253-7141

Lobby Lounges

The Fairmont Hotel Vancouver
Although wide open and in the middle of the lobby, the bar is often strangely empty, making it the perfect place for a clandestine meeting.
900 W. Georgia St., 604-669-9378, fairmonthotels.com

The Four Seasons Hotel Bar
The hotel's sleek '60s bones make for a cool lobby, but the bar renovation, sadly, went straight for the mid-'90s, with dark leather and lush pile. Still, the bar is usually empty and can be a convenient place to sink into a big club chair after a long day of shopping at the mall.
791 W. Georgia St., 604-689-9333

The Sylvia Hotel
Built in 1912, this former apartment building's top-floor restaurant Dine in the Sky was the toast of the town in the '50s, where patrons danced to organ music. In 1954, the Sylvia was the first hotel in Vancouver to get a liquor license. When the area got built up, the restaurant moved down, ending up in its current main floor location with a view of English Bay after a 1985 renovation. It has yet

unknown sports bars

The Green Room

to experience a retro revival, but it's a slice of Vancouver history worth checking out.
1154 Gilford St., 604-681-9321

Zin at the Pacific Palisades Hotel

This retro-chic bar is on the wrong end of Robson, but it's worth venturing to for a chance sighting of the stars who work out of the hotel and its residential tower — Bif Naked and Matthew Good, for example. The U-shaped couch in front of the fire is fun for a large group, and check out the groovy chandelier made entirely of zap straps.
1277 Robson St., 604-408-1700, zin-restaurant.com

Bacchus at the Wedgewood Hotel

It fills up with stock-jokers by about 4, then continues to get busier as the after-work and pre-theatre crowd floats in, followed by media types and local personalities not ready to call it a night. The fireplace, uniformed bartenders, and lounge pianist lend the place a bit of old-school class.
845 Hornby St., 604-689-7777, wedgewoodhotel.com

Photo: Solo

Formerly called the Media Club, this gathering place for CBC lifers lost a lot of its big drinking clientele when it got spiffed up a few years back under new management. But local personalities have been known to wander over after taping in the CBC studios across the street. During the hockey playoffs, the bar mounts a huge TV screen and serves cheap beer, with chairs enough for everyone. Pity the poor suckers crammed into the Shark Club sports bar just around the corner getting a better view of someone's armpit than the hockey game.
695 Cambie St., 604-608-2871

The Meriloma Clubhouse

A 1923 heritage-award-winning wooden clubhouse on the edge of Connaught Park in Kitsilano is the home of the Meriloma Sporting Club, known best for its rugby players. The beer is cold, the fire is warm, and the men are big and burly. If they get cocky, remind them that their club (originally for swimmers) used to be called The Mermaids. Members only.
2390 W. 10th Ave., 604-733-4366

Morton's of Chicago, The Steakhouse

Vancouverites have yet to discover what might be the best little bar in town: the one at the front of Morton's Steakhouse. Not only is the service snappy, but wait staff circulate with platters of complimentary mini-hamburgers — a little taste of the same kind of stellar beef served in the swanky restaurant for $45 and more a slab. Plus, there's a great view of the TV from the bar. At least there was.
750 W. Cordova St., 604-915-510

best places to go club hopping
without leaving the building

Lick Some Honey

The **Lotus Hotel** (formerly the Heritage House Hotel) is now owned by men's clothing retailer-cum-brew pub millionaire Mark James (née Mark Jamblowski). It's on the fringes of skid row, but James has managed to gradually gentrify it. He's renamed the original nightclub the Lotus Sound Lounge (known for its fetish nights) and remodelled the sleek **Lick** and dark **Honey** lounge (formerly gay haunts Chuck's Pub and Uncle Charlie's Lounge). Now connected with backroom passageways, the lesbian Lick has an urban feel, while Honey is warm and velvety, and still attracts lots of drag queens. If Abbott street is lined with Vespas, you'll know it's the monthly Mod Club at Honey, with 54-40's Matt Johnson on the decks.
455 Abbott St., 604-685-7777

A Side of Jazz

This two-in-one club called **The Purple Onion** has an intimate jazz lounge on one side, and a hopping nightclub on the other. But don't try to carry your drink across the hall to the other venue: just one more crazy Vancouver liquor law.
15 Water St., 604-602-9442, purpleonion.com

Everybody Dance Now

Atlantis
As Graceland, it was one of the hottest '80s clubs, playing new wave, ska, and early break beats. It's since been bought by a local bigwig in the urbanwear scene who has given it the facelift it was begging for. Nelly Furtado agrees.
1320 Richards St., 604-662-7707, atlantisclub.net

Caprice
This former movie theatre is still long and narrow, but now the show plays out on the massive dance floor. Hip-hop to it.
967 Granville St., 604-685-3288, capricenightclub.com

Photo: Solo

Shine

It's like walking down into an underground cave, only to find you are in a spaceship. The chill room at the back has a different vibe (check the Nowhere Fast nights), but portal windows keep you abreast of what's happening on the main dance floor. The crowd can be a bit like Keanu Reeves: young, dumb, and full of cum.

364 Water St., 604-408-4321

Sonar

Vancouver's leading electronic venue is responsible for nurturing much of the city's early DJ talent. Erstwhile London music magazine *Ministry* called it one of the best electronic venues in the world, and it continues to pull in hot international acts and DJs. Though it's not looking as fresh as when it first opened, you're there to dance old skool, right?

66 Water St., 604-683-6695, sonar.bc.ca

off-beat entertainers

Some of Vancouver's most notorious people of the night.

The Fluffgirls Burlesque Society

Led by pioneer Fluffgirl Cecilia Bravo, this troupe of accomplished stripteasers is often hired entertainment at events and clubs. With stage names like Mia More, Misty Vine, and Betty Bijou, they perform 1940s burlesque – which means they'll get down to sparkly G-strings and pasties, but no less.

Little Miss Naughty

A performance artist, she shows up in a vinyl teddy and administers spankings with a wooden paddle to unsuspecting (and suspecting) crowd members.

Dave Briker

He got his start on the scene in the late '90s with a magic act called "El Ballistico, The Man who Knows" at **The Penthouse** nightclub. He then gained a following for his retro '80s DJ act, "My Older Brother's Bedroom," that came complete with an Atari video game, rock posters, and a bed with old *Playboys* stuffed under it. His latest venture is a fashion design company called Some Product, and a new '80s DJ act called "The Rec Room" at **Honey** lounge *(455 Abbott St., 604-685-7777)*.

Cass King

A former cigarette girl at the Waldorf Hotel, King's own brand of "überlesque" and beat poetry has her in demand. See *cassking.com*

Christine "Tiny" Taylor

She's famous as the girl with the chainsaw-tossing act that she once performed at a birthday party for Madonna. Look for posters for the Happyland cabaret nights, held at the post-WWII dance hall called the

Grandview Auditorium (2205 Commercial Dr.), where she once performed with a guy billed as "The Only Male Hunchback Burlesque Dancer in the World." We'll give it to him.

Watermelon

Described as looking like she "fell out of a 1960s *Playboy,*" the curvy comedienne and pot promoter has been a fixture at comedy festivals, in the gossip columns, and at Wreck Beach, where she vends, you guessed it, watermelon. Her tag line: "I'm not here to judge, I'm here to jiggle." See *melongirl.ca*

gay & lesbian

A lot of the famous gay clubs in Vancouver such as **Playpen South**, the **Gandydancer**, and **Ms Ts** (which burned in a massive fire in July 2003) are no longer around, while the gay scene has moved into the pubs and restaurants (and organic grocery stores) around Davie and Denman Streets. Look to annual events such as Wiggle at **Sonar** and Red8 at **Video In** for cutting edge drag and gay performance art. But what you are more likely to find in Vancouver these days is events that mix both gay and straight crowds.

Tonic

It used to be the Paradise Theatre and before that it was the Eve, a soft-core porn theatre. A massive mirror ball makes the university crowd glitter over three levels.
919 Granville St., 604-669-0469, thetonicclub.com

The Stone Temple Cabaret

If you like top-40 as much as Ben Affleck, here's where you'll find it, and him, when he's in town.
1082 Granville St., 604-488-1333

The Dufferin Hotel

Known as The Duff, gay clientele from around the world check into the rooms while locals call it Suffrin' at the Dufferin. Don't miss the nightly karaoke, when the place becomes a Cage aux Folles of big hair, falsetto voices, and Diana Ross tunes. Be kind and spare the crowd another rendition of "It's Raining Men" or "I Will Survive."
900 Seymour St., 604-683-4251, dufferinhotel.com

House of Venus

An event production company, not a club, it's responsible for a lot of the gay-oriented club nights and parties in the city. Michael Venus, also known as Cotton, is the city's foremost drag artist who can morph into any number of lovely ladies. See *venushouse.com*

The Lotus Sound Lounge

It was known as a lesbian bar when it was called the Lotus Cabaret. Some of that crowd still shows up on fetish nights that take place the last Saturday of the month. Don't be fooled like Tom Cruise: there is no password.
455 Abbott St., 604-685-7777

Numbers

One of the oldtimers; retro-chic in that it hasn't changed much in decades.
1042 Davie St., 604-685-4077

The Oasis Pub

Piano bar/lounge that's (surprisingly) located atop a Denny's restaurant.
upstairs, 1240 Thurlow St., 604-685-1724

The Odyssey

The city's biggest gay dance club best known for attracting a young and buff crowd. Get wet on Shower Power Thursdays.
1251 Howe St., 604-689-5256

PumpJack Pub

Where the leather boys are.
1167 Davie St., 604-685-3417

Shine

The gay crowd on "Nice" Sundays means straight girls flock here to get down-and-dirty on the dance floor with guys who couldn't care less.
364 Water St., 604-408-4321

Sleaze Balls

It's a mixed crowd at **The Penthouse** nightclub's infamous Sleaze Balls, where fashion meets burlesque meets drag meets whatever else they've dreamed up.
1019 Seymour St., 604-683-2111

CLUBBING HIGH ABOVE YOU

The owners of the new three-level **Skybar** *(670 Smithe St., 604-697-9199)* with a rooftop patio were used to operating clubs in Calgary where the business-friendly climate fast-tracked their openings. How sorely surprised were they when it took them several months more than anticipated to open their Vancouver club in the summer of 2003. But now that it's here, you can dance on levels one and two or ride the glass elevator up to the roof where you'll encounter $80,000 worth of palm trees, a VIP room, three fireplaces, and a retractable roof should raindrops start falling. Hey, maybe these guys do know a thing or two about Vancouver.

strip city

The first place many American male tourists want to go when they arrive at YVR? A Vancouver strip club. Vancouver peelers have a world-wide reputation, not least for the fact that, unlike in the U.S., their G-strings actually hit the floor. It may not be everyone's cup of tea, but here's a tour:

Brandi's Exotic Nightclub

The strippers are female, but so is the owner and a quarter of the clientele. Why? Some have theories about post-feminist empowerment, though we suspect the real pull is celebrity ogling. Jason Priestley and Bif Naked are regulars; Judd Nelson, Goldie Hawn, the Backstreet Boys, Sylvester Stallone, Chad Lowe, Jean-Claude Van Damme, Christian Slater and Ben Affleck (we could go on) have all stopped in; Affleck's alleged (and denied) canoodling here was the subject of much tabloid fodder in the summer of 2003. While it is not as down and dirty as most strip clubs, its high-end reputation comes from its penthouse location more than anything else. The talent, however, would be considered accomplished gymnasts, with or without their g-strings on. According to local legend, some of the money to fund the club came from the lottery winnings of a Horseshoe Bay fish and chip restaurateur, but Brandy Sarionder (not her given name), a Turkish-born single mother, is the front woman. Our own Heidi Fleiss, Sarionder also runs the Swedish Touch Massage Parlour one floor down. One of the club's services is $10 shoulder massages, on offer for the men in "gynecology row." There is also a street person who waits outside the club at closing time and walks the dancers to their cars. Though there's a regular dance floor, we have yet to see anyone on it. There are seven private rooms for rent (with cameras monitored from the DJ booth) and 12 private booths. Reservations recommended. No cover for women or celebrities. *595 Hornby St., 604-684-2000, brandislounge.com*

Billiards Parlours

Photo: Soho

Photo: Soho

Automotive Billiards Club
New location, same old game.
1095 Homer St., 604-682-0040

Guys and Dolls Billiards
16 billiards and snooker tables, cheap prices.
2434 Main St., 604-879-4433

The Office
"Honey, I'll be at the office late tonight." Not a word of a lie.
1409 W. Broadway, 604-734-9914

Soho Café and Billiards
Licensed Yaletown restaurant that's a popular place for web designers to blow off steam.
1144 Homer St., 604-688-1180

Sing for Your Supper

And you thought karaoke was for the Japanese. The 10,000 Korean students who live in Vancouver are the ones keeping these places in business with glassed-in private karaoke rooms that seat parties of 10 or so. Look for them underground or above other businesses. But don't make the same mistake as Tony Blair's wife, whose karaoke rendition of "When I'm Sixty-Four" was bootlegged and made into club mixes in Ibeza. The two best downtown spots are:

Photo: Solo

Fantacity
downstairs, 745 Thurlow St.,
604-899-0006

Karaoke Box
upstairs, 1238 Robson St.,
604-688-0611

The Cecil Exotic Show Lounge

A *Party of Five* star was spotted here having a party of many, and people in the neighbouring apartments have seen live jaguars being ushered through the back door. *1336 Granville St., 604-683-8505*

No. 5 Orange

Photo: Solo

This strip club in a grimy part of the Downtown Eastside has two claims to fame: it was where Courtney Love got her start as a stripper, and where Bon Jovi saw the sign that became the name of their album "Slippery When Wet." *205 Main St., 604-687-3483*

Retro Porn and Cocktails

The pink courtesy phone at **Ginger Sixty-Two** is rumoured to be a link to this swanky lounge's previous identity as the Austin Hotel strip club. What is for sure is that famous sexpots named Ginger adorn the walls (peeler Ginger Lynn, and *Gilligan's Island's* flame-tressed vixen, for example). A private "Red Room" and fancy billiards table with transparent balls aren't the night's only entertainment: At the back of the main lounge, there's a mini-theatre screening vintage porn. There's no sound though, so grab a new friend and create your own dialogue. *1219 Granville St., 604-688-5494*

where to light up

Smoking rooms and hot boxes.

Bacchus at the Wedgewood Hotel
While this high-rolling lobby bar attracts the business crowd, the real deals go down later on in the glassed-in smoking lounge at the far end of the restaurant.
845 Hornby St., 604-608-5319

Blunt Bros
In the smoking room at this Gastown pot café, you're allowed to spark up a fatty, but not cigarettes or cigars. That's Vancouver for you.
317 W. Hastings St., 604-682-5868

City Cigar Emporium
After the '90s boom and bust of cigar smoking, this cigar club is still puffing away, thanks to its good prices and friendly staff. There are humidified cedar lockers and a Havana-style smoking lounge for members, who are invited to bring their own bottles. Master Cuban cigar rollers do demonstrations, and check out the Cohiba snowboard on the wall. Free delivery.
888 W. 6th Ave., 604-879-0208, citycigarcompany.com

Diva at the Met
The new heated year-round patio was created with smokers in mind.
645 Howe St., 604-602-7788, metropolitan.com

Havana
A Cuban restaurant could not be without a smoking area – although this one's on the patio, not in the restaurant.
1212 Commercial Dr., 604-253-9119

Photo: Solo

Mona's Lebanese Cuisine
This one-of-a-kind restaurant has belly dancers, fortune tellers, and an open-air patio in the centre. In winter, lounge on large cushions between trips to the smoking room where they can set you up with a hookah. The fortune teller's advice increases in direct proportion to the amount of red wine you buy her.
1328 Hornby St., 604-689-4050

Jazz, Dance, and Entertainment

The Jazz Cellar Café and Restaurant
There are very strict rules about not talking during the performances and you must order food, so consider it more of a civilized jazz dinner than a wild night out. Still, many consider it the city's top venue.
3611 W. Broadway 604-738-1959

Kino Café
Several nights a week the tiny stage in the middle of the café comes alive with young flamenco dancers or tabla players. It feels slightly like a Spanish roadside café, with its board floors and rickety tables. Best of all, it's free.
3456 Cambie St., 604-875-1998

Mainstream
Formerly called the Hot Jazz Club, it's a blast from the past with its big bands, circular raised dance floor, and aging romantics who come to dance.
2120 Main St., 604-873-4131

The Alibi Room
(downstairs bar)

The Zen-like bar in the basement of this hip film biz restaurant goes off. Check the waterfall urinal in the men's room. Call ahead to make sure it's not booked for a movie wrap party — or, just tell them you're the Best Boy and head on in.
157 Alexander St., 604-623-3383

Clove

Late night Indian-spiced snacks and great down-tempo grooves in a modern room.
2054 Commercial Dr., 604-255-5550

Public Lounge

The food is so-so at best, but the DJ spins off a surfboard. Rad, dude.
3289 Main St., 604-873-1944

The Reef

A packed South Main Caribbean restaurant that feels more like a club after 10 on weekends.
4172 Main St., 604-874-5375

The Penthouse
No idea if it is legal, but let's just say if you light up a Marlboro at this strip club, no one's going to stop you.
1019 Seymour St., 604-683-2111

Persian Tea House
What else? It's an authentic Persian tea house, hookahs included.
668 Davie St., 604-681-6672

Tonic
This nightclub has a smoking room on the second level, right beside the bar.
919 Granville St., 604-669-0469

talk of the town

The now defunct Press Club on South Granville started the revival of spoken word nights in the late 90s, and since then, one-off poetry slams having been popping up in nightclubs and restaurants. Don your black turtleneck and head here:

Bukowski's
Named for the most famous beatnik of them all. *The English Patient* author Michael Ondaatje once stopped by, but sadly didn't take the mic.
1447 Commercial Dr., 604-253-4770

Café Deux Soleils
Not to be confused with Café Du Soleil, also on Commercial Drive, this is where to find "Cat Call," an all-female open-mic night on the last Thursday on the month.
2096 Commercial Dr., 604-254-1195

Montmartre Café
Your black beret will look perfect at this little French café. Hope to catch local spoken word legend Paul T. St. Marie here.
4362 Main St., 604-879-8111

Notoriety

If the mark of a world-class city is a *National Enquirer* bureau, then Vancouver has truly arrived. Every year more celebrities visit here, move here, and cause scandals here. We've had mass murderers, terrorists, con-men, and police brutality, and their stories are here, warts and all. Read on if you dare.

Home, Sweet Celebrity Home

Celebrities seem to love Vancouver. The scenery's great, the weather's (usually) nice, and the masses don't hassle them as much as they do in the States. It isn't surprising, then, that many celebs have bought places here.

Goldie Hawn and Kurt Russell (whose son plays junior hockey here) have a place in Shaughnessy, Gillian Anderson (who filmed *The X-Files* here) retains a house in West Van, and Jean-Claude Van Damme has an apartment in the Wall Centre highrise downtown. Local hero Jason Priestley owns an apartment in Gastown, while jazz star Diana Krall has a condo on False Creek. Sarah McLachlan, Bryan Adams, and Tommy Chong have places in West Van, and k.d. lang has a hobby farm in Langley. Christian Slater had purchased a home, but after the *National Enquirer* ran a picture of the house and was rumoured to have it under regular surveillance, decided to find another. "I intend to be a Vancouver resident for at least a while," he told the *Vancouver Sun*. "I love it."

Most of the other celeb housing stories fall in the "unconfirmed rumour" camp. John Travolta supposedly had a place in the West End, basketball stars Shaquille O'Neal and Hakeem Olajuwon have spent lots of time in West Van, and Terence Stamp has a favourite doctor in Vancouver that he often visits for treatment.

The **Georgia Hotel** (now the Crowne Plaza Hotel Georgia, *801 W. Georgia St., 604-682-5566*) is not only a cool building, it's a historic one. Entertainers like Elvis Presley, the Beatles, and Frank Sinatra stayed at the Georgia during their Vancouver appearances. But the most important guest was arguably Nat King Cole.

In the early 1950s, black people were barred from the city's top hotels. Sinatra refused to ever stay at the Hotel Vancouver, because it had once refused a room to Louis Armstrong. Promoter Hugh Pickett thought the black issue was ridiculous, and decided to do something about it. He was bringing Nat King Cole to town, and phoned up his friend Bill Hudson at the Georgia to ask if Cole could stay there. "I said 'Look, why don't you let me put Nat in the hotel and we'll see what happens,'" recalled Pickett. "'If something does, alright, that's it, we won't try any more black people in your hotel.'

"He phoned the next day and said, 'All that happened was all the guests wanted his autograph.' There was no feeling against black people here. There may have been in the States, but there sure wasn't here. So from then on, everybody we had went into the Georgia."

Alas, you can't book the 12th-floor room where Elvis and the Beatles stayed. The top floor is now an elite executive floor, and has an executive lounge in the spot where Elvis did his thing.

SPRUCE UP THE PLACE

Being a homeowner in Vancouver means you're always on the lookout for a bargain. People spend countless hours cruising garage and demolition sales for that cheap stained glass window or kitchen cupboard that will add a certain *je ne sais quoi* to their adobe. The real fanatics are regulars at building material junk dealers. The biggie is **Jack's Used Building Materials** on Still Creek Avenue in Burnaby, where you can find almost anything. Cast iron claw foot bath tubs, fridges, toilets, windows, doors, gas pumps, artificial legs, rickshaws — you name it, it's been through Jack's.

Photo: Gordon Sedawie/Vancouver Sun

David McTaggart was an environmentalist, a businessman, a politician, a sailor, and a bit of a rogue. And he used all of his talents, charm, and tenacity to take **Greenpeace** from a small Vancouver environmental group to a worldwide eco-powerhouse.

As the years go on, though, it's gotten hard to find killer bargains at Jack's — too many people know about it, and pick it clean. The really in-the-know bargain hunters used to have an ace in the hole, a small used building materials shop in Surrey's Bridgeview, that weird zone of used auto parts dealers just west of the Patullo Bridge. This place fit right in: you definitely got a weird vibe there.

The name of the place was P&B Used Building Supplies, which stands for Pickton Brothers. Yes, that Pickton: Robert "Willy" Pickton, the Coquitlam pig farmer who has been charged with the largest mass murder in Canadian history.

Talk about tainted goods? Ugh.

McTaggart was saluted by environmentalists around the world in March 2001, after he was killed in a car crash in Italy, where he had lived for several years. But his reputation was less than sterling with many original Greenpeacers, who think he staged a coup when the organization went international and moved to Amsterdam in 1979, with McTaggart as director.

McTaggart was not one of the founders of Greenpeace, as he often claimed. He grew up in an affluent Vancouver family that owned a home on Southwest Marine Drive. He drove a Jaguar, and was the Canadian singles badminton champion in his late teens. He then moved to the U.S., where he was a developer until he went bankrupt. At the age of 40, with his marriage on the rocks, he set sail for the South Pacific.

McTaggart was recruited to the environmental movement by Greenpeace's Ben Metcalfe, who selected him from about 150 people who had volunteered to sail a boat to protest against the French nuclear testing on the South Pacific island of Mururoa in 1972.

"He had quit his job in Fiji, where he was managing a resort," recalls Metcalfe. "When he arrived in Auckland, he was searched and charged with smuggling watches into New Zealand. And on the eve of our departure they arrested him and put him in the slammer. I had to bail him out. They delivered him to the dock and we took off."

Metcalfe fell out with McTaggart and left the boat. But McTaggart sailed on, and made headlines around the world when his boat was rammed by the French navy. He made another protest voyage the following year, and was beaten up by French commandos. Photos of a bloodied McTaggart were sent around the world, and became part of the legend.

I Do, Big Time

Venture capitalist Jamie King made scads of cash from the boom in Internet stocks. So when he got married to Christie Darbyshire, he decided to spare no expense. Bryan Adams was flown in from London to provide musical entertainment (Billy Joel, Christie's first choice, was unavailable). Roses were flown in from Ecuador and Holland to decorate the ballroom of the Hotel Vancouver. A Yaletown boutique was converted into a disco and casino so guests could boogie till 4 a.m. The blushing bride even requested a unicorn, prompting media to wonder if she knew they didn't really exist. The cost: $500,000 to $1 million.

King and Darbyshire tied the knot in a small ceremony in Cabo San Lucas April 29, flying in local fashion photographer David Fierro, then threw the reception for 400 at the Hotel Vancouver. Adams – who was paid either $250,000 or $750,000, depending on who you talk to – opened an hour-long set with his hit ballad, *Have You Ever Really Loved a Woman*.

The reception took over the Hotel Vancouver's convention floor, and featured a waterfall, sculpted topiaries, and an ice sculpture more than a metre high of a vase with an enormous floral arrangement. How enormous? Thousands of flowers, including 500 lilacs, 500 peonies, 500 lilies of the valley, 500 chartreuse snowball viburnum, and a seemingly endless expanse of smilax, a lush bright green garland from Florida.

The bride was resplendent in a wedding gown from Ron et Normand, Vancouver's elite dressmakers, that was hand-embroidered with 3500 Swarovski crystals. She was also wearing a diamond tiara and necklace that was rumoured to have cost $1 million.

It was borrowed, by the way.

Photo: Mandelbrot

TERROR AVERTED

The **2400 Motel** *(2400 Kingsway, 604-434-2464)* is a 1940s classic, with a great neon sign and 19 immaculate white cottages spread out over a three-and-a-half acre property. It was also the scene of a terrorist plot.

On December 14, 1999, Ahmed Ressam was arrested in Port Angeles, Washington after crossing by ferry from Victoria in a car loaded with bomb-making chemicals. He confessed that his intention had been to plant a bomb at the Los Angeles airport, and detonate it. He had assembled the ingredients for the bomb at the 2400 Motel, where he stayed after moving from Montreal.

Photo: CVA Port. P. 1725, N. 1023

Ressam is an Algerian national who moved to Canada in 1994, using a false French passport to get into the country. Customs officials caught him, but he claimed refugee status and was released. His claim was eventually rejected, but he remained in Canada illegally, stealing from tourists to make a living. He even got caught by the police, but still managed to stay in the country.

After hearing about an Islamic jihad, or holy war, from a friend who had come to Montreal, Ressam went for terrorist training in Afghanistan for six months in 1998. He was part of a plot that was to hit airports around the U.S. on the eve of the new millennium. Some cohorts were arrested in Europe, but Ressam decided to go ahead.

When Ressam was stopped and arrested by U.S. Customs agents in Port Angeles, more than 130 pounds of explosive material was recovered from the wheel well of his car trunk. The cache included high explosives EGDN, RDX, and HMTD, as well as urea fertilizer, which can be modified to create an explosive fuel.

Vancouver journalist Lee Bacchus once nominated **Joe Fortes** as "best dead person" in a spoof of those annoying "best of Vancouver" posters and contests. The legendary black lifeguard of English Bay was known for his kindness towards kids and his dedication to his craft – he is credited with saving 100 people from drowning. He was so well-liked that when the parks board bought up all the land on the beach side of English Bay to convert it to public parkland, it allowed Fortes to move the Beach Avenue cottage where he lived to Alexandra Park at Harwood and Beach. The cottage was torn down after the death of "Old Black Joe" in 1922.

Fortes' cottage hinted at the early days of English Bay, when it was a summer resort for city dwellers who were then centred around Gastown. The last two summer cottages in the West End lasted until 2002, when they were torn down for a condo project.

There is still one tiny waterfront cottage left in the city proper – across from the Hastings Mill Museum on Alma Street, just north of Point Grey Road. But it will probably have to be moved to survive, because it's on a million-dollar view lot.

One of Fortes' old residences still survives as well: Joe is listed in the 1892 directory as living at 216 Carrall Street in Gastown, which is now the Blarney Stone pub. Presumably he lived in the rooms upstairs rather than the bar. Incidentally, a rear wall of the Blarney Stone fell over when a developer was excavating a hole for a condo tower next door in the late '90s. Luckily it wasn't a support wall, otherwise the whole building might have tumbled down.

The End Was Nigh

In Los Angeles, enterprising souls have developed ghoul tours of spots where celebrities met their maker. A Vancouver tour would begin at 1310 Burnaby Street in the West End, where **Errol Flynn** died in the penthouse apartment on October 14, 1959.

The 50-year-old Flynn had come to Vancouver to sell his yacht to West Vancouver stockbroker George Caldough. Always flamboyant, he arrived with a beautiful 17-year-old girl on his arm. Flynn's autobiography is called *My Wicked, Wicked Ways*, and it seems they were finally catching up to him. He arrived looking terrible — he had vomited on the plane from L.A.

This didn't stop him from checking out local nightspots like the Cave, the Panorama Roof, and the Penthouse during his stay. The legal drinking age was 21, but his teenage girlfriend didn't have any problems getting in because she was with a movie star.

Flynn initially stayed at the Hotel Georgia, but later moved into Caldough's home on Eyremont in British Properties. After six days in Vancouver, Flynn was headed to the airport to fly home to L.A. when he developed a back pain.

Caldough, who was driving the couple to the airport, took Flynn to see his friend Dr Grant Gould (the uncle of pianist Glenn Gould) in the West End. In Gould's Burnaby Street penthouse, Flynn went for a lie-down in the doctor's bedroom, saying, "I shall return." But he didn't. His girlfriend went to check on him after a couple of hours, and found him dead.

The cause of death? It could have been one of several ailments he suffered from, or maybe it was a combination of them all. The death certificate said Flynn suffered from myocardial infarction, coronary thrombosis, coronary atherosclerosis, liver degeneration, liver sclerosis, and diverticulosis of the colon.

WHEN GOOD ACTORS ARE BAD

Local hotels make a lot of money off the film industry, but sometimes the stars can present problems. One adventure movie actor is reported to have an insatiable appetite for hookers. He was renting the palatial penthouse at a downtown hotel and had an endless succession of prostitutes drop by to satisfy his urges. But he forgot to tell his wife, who arrived unexpectedly and found him with another woman. They had a battle royale, and totally trashed the suite, resulting in thousands of dollars of damages.

He learned his lesson. When he comes to town now, he parties at massage parlours, where his wife can't find him.

Love Me Not So Tender

HEAD OF STATE

Float planes are a groovy way to fly, but have been known to cause some heart palpitations when they hit air pockets and get bounced around (hence the old Air BC nickname Scare BC). Government officials are among the planes' regular users, which bring us to an old story an NDPer used to tell about a Socred cabinet minister.

It seems he showed up for a flight with his girlfriend one sunny summer afternoon. Both were drunk. He made a big stink about getting a blanket for the flight, but the pilot said there weren't any available. So he stumbled to the back of the plane and plopped down.

After the plane lifted off, the NDPer, who was on the same flight, felt sorry for the Socred and got up to offer her coat to him. She walked to the back of the plane, and was greeted by the sight of the Socred's girlfriend "resting" her head in his lap. A government perk, we suppose.

While **Courtney Love** has been recently quoted in the media as saying she regrets having had liposuction on her bum since it's now gone flat, a Vancouver masseuse, who gave the rock star a massage in her room at the Sutton Place Hotel, reports that the feisty Love has a surprisingly lithe and fit physique. No wonder then, that she's paraded it around Vancouver before, most famously at the Number 5 Orange peeler bar well before her Hole days, and more recently, on a month-long time to film *Trapped* with Charlize Theron and Kevin Bacon. During this time she managed to pull a whole series of stunts. First there was the time at the Alberni Street fashion store Bruce when she marched out of the change room buck-naked with daughter Frances Bean (her child with Kurt Cobain) in tow. Then there was the time she jumped on stage at Richard's on Richards where ex-Lemonheads frontman Evan Dando was performing. According to those in the crowd, she chewed off her "movie fingernails" the better to jam on a borrowed guitar and sing an improvised song about her sex life, among other things. When the show was over, Love eventually convinced the club to let her keep performing by lifting her halter top and flashing the crowd. Back at the aforementioned hotel suite where she was to be massaged, she walked in smoking a cigarette and complaining how people in Vancouver were spineless pushovers. So when she refused to put out the smoke while lying on the massage table, the therapist insisted that she butt it out or there would be no massage. Love did, with no complaints. (So who's spineless now?) Her ire at Vancouver was not assuaged, however, when $10,000 worth of jewellery was stolen from her Pacific Palisades hotel room — including her wedding ring from Kurt Cobain and a $30,000 ring from her ex, actor Edward Norton, as well as some of

NOTORIETY 205

her daughter's toys. A box containing lingerie for gifts for her *Trapped* castmates was emptied, and cigarette butts, empty beer bottles, and other garbage were put in the lingerie's place. If that wasn't enough, Love reportedly suffered a miscarriage while shooting the movie and managed to get sued by a Vancouver homeowner for breach of contract after she failed to pay for the waterfront mansion she'd rented for her stay. All in a month's work.

If These Walls Could Talk

From Hollywood tough guys to real life wise guys, **Il Giardino** *(1382 Hornby St., 604-669-2422)* has hosted them all. One run-in the early '90s between then-bad-boy actor Sean Penn and local mobster Ray Ginetti (pronounce it "ragin' Eddie") was broken up by fellow thespian Robert DeNiro – but not before Ginetti's gun fell out onto the restaurant floor. Genetti was eventually murdered in his West Vancouver home, asphyxiated by his own family jewels.

CLOWNING COPS

Vancouver police are fodder for some of the best comedy out there, but this blunder takes the cake, so to speak. On August 1, 2002, Prime Minister **Jean Chrétien** was cutting the ribbon at the opening of Chinatown's Millennium Gate when police apprehended and detained William Christiansen, 41, for eating a piece of cheesecake. Fearing a repeat of the cream-pie-in-the-face incident endured by the PM in Charlottetown in August of 2000, and having been tipped off that there was a potential pie-tosser in the crowd, they questioned Christiansen about his being in possession of said slice of cake. His defense ("I was hungry") was not accepted by police, who demanded that he immediately eat the cake which he had purchased at a nearby store, or he'd have to follow them. The irked Christensen opted for the latter. Though the police

And the RCMP did, but not before he'd bilked a Vancouver couple out of $150,000 and a Whistler couple out of $16,400. International con man **Christopher Rocancourt** has claimed at various times to be a Rockefeller, Prince de Galizine, the son of Sophia Loren, a diamond smuggler, a Hollywood high roller, a Russian aristocrat, and the nephew of Oscar de la Renta. He was actually the 33-year-old son of an alcoholic French house painter and a prostitute and was already wanted in the U.S., France, and Switzerland when he arrived at the Whistler ski resort in 2001. Accustomed to hanging around rich haunts (he'd already cleaned out the Hamptons, for example), he spent two months in Whistler claiming to be a Formula 1 racecar driver named Michael Van Hover with a $28-million contract with Ferrari and $250 million in assets. He brandished his "wealth" about, offering up $100 tips, staying in a $1,500-a-night suite at the Westin Resort and Spa, and putting a phony $100,000 down payment on an $8.8-million dollar chalet which he visited daily, offering suggestions to the builders. In the autobiography he published after his arrest in Victoria B.C., entitled *The French Hustler*, he claims that Whistler's Bear Foot Bistro was his favourite restaurant (no surprise that it is also known as one of the most expensive in the country). The restaurant's staff say he would arrive a day before the lavish dinners he held there, walking through the wine cellar selecting bottles like a connoisseur. Remarkably, the restaurant says he did pay his bills – but with whose money is another question. Rocancourt told a Vancouver couple holidaying in Whistler, Robert and Norma Baldock, that he would invest $5 million in Robert Baldock's Heartlink Canada, a company that was developing a tool to diagnose mental illness by way of heart rates. As he prepared the deal, he convinced them to cover his expenses, which included a Vancouver apartment. Meantime, he charmed the front desk clerk at the Westin and her boyfriend out of $16,500. When finally arrested in Victoria's tony Oak Bay neighbourhood in April 2001,

presumably had their man, they also apprehended Cameron Ward, another bystander, impounded his car, and demanded to search his trunk for pies. They found nothing. So they strip-searched him back at the station (just how many pies could he have been hiding in there?). Police later admitted it was a case of mistaken identity, but they could not have chosen a worse victim: Ward is a high profile civil-rights activist and lawyer who represented pepper-sprayed APEC protesters subsequent to a previous Chrétien visit. When the apology Ward requested was not forthcoming, he launched a B.C. Supreme Court lawsuit against the Vancouver police and other officials. The judge was quoted as saying that the actions of the officers "at a minimum amount to gross negligence and more likely amount to malicious or willful misconduct."

he was charged and forced to give back the $16,000 in cash he had on him, a $26,000 Rolex watch bought for him by Robert Baldock, and a laptop computer. He was also obliged to pay $112,000 in restitution to his victims. Rocancourt was held in a Port Moody jail cell for 14 months before being extradited to the U.S., where he has a wife (a former *Playboy* Playmate) and son. He was later reported to have said that he does not have remorse for his victims. "They are greedy and poor businessmen," he said. He also believes he is not a criminal because he "steals with his mind." The movie, of course, is in the works.

Guess Who's Busted?

In a legal case that was stranger than an episode of *Law and Order*, a now-infamous North Vancouver resident named Gillian Guess was sentenced June 22, 1998 to 18 months in jail for obstruction of justice. The reason? She'd had an affair with accused murderer/drug lord Peter Gill while she was a juror on his trial. The obstruction of justice case was the first of its kind in the British Commonwealth, and it was also the first and precedent-setting instance of jurors being called upon testify about their deliberations. The trial received

HOLD THE TORTILLAS

Vancouver's richest resident — and indeed one of the wealthiest men in the country, with an estimated net worth of $2.75 billion — has a truckload of lore that follows him.

Jimmy Pattison stories include the oft-told legend that he grabbed under-performing salesmen on his used car lots and cut their neckties off. A teetotaling Christian, his famous non-alcoholic booze cruises around the harbour have no doubt spiked sales in pocket flasks. From hiring the dethroned ex-premier Glen Clark for his neon sign company, to appearing in commercials to bolster Vancouver's

2010 Olympic bid, he's never out of the news for long. But a story he'd likely not want in the news comes by way of a Bowen Island farmer and beekeeper who used to work as a domestic in West Vancouver when she first arrived from her native Mexico. The family she worked for loved her traditional Mexican dishes, like the handmade tortillas she would grill right on the burners of the stove. One night, a visiting Jimmy Pattison was invited to stay for dinner. "As long as it's none of that Mexican crap," the domestic worker remembers him saying. She walked straight out the kitchen door, never to return.

international media attention, criminologists called it "a circus," and book and TV-movie deals were liberally bandied about. Guess was a media frenzy waiting to happen, as someone who had changed her name to Guess in 1990 because it had five letters (she was born May 5, 1955) and thought it sounded "mysterious" was wont to be. She regaled the media with sound bytes such as "after six months of jury duty, even the judge was starting to look good," and with her over-the-top wardrobe of short, tight suits, trademark fake Chanel sunglasses, bubblegum lipstick, and *AbFab* blonde hair. She pulled media stunts such as showing up for a radio interview in a leopard print miniskirt, and her 13-year-old son (who occasionally acted as her spokesperson) was clad in a green metallic shirt and silver pants. She would gasp audibly in court, ask to be addressed as "Gillian" rather than "the accused," and tow a Yorkshire Terrier named George with her to the courtroom. Her amateurish website was filled with glamour shots and articles about herself and her opinions on the case, and she used it to both sell herself and field marriage proposals; the *Washington Post* called it "one of the strangest self-promotion sites on the Internet." No surprise to learn that before the trial she had been studying toward an MA in psychology at Simon Fraser University, where she had attempted to publish "The Guess List," a compendium of all the eligible bachelors in Vancouver. Going into her trial, she was quoted as saying, "If I have to do community service, does that mean I have to go back to dating firemen?" (As opposed to, say, accused murderer/drug lords?) Guess, strangely, has fallen off the public radar of late, though Vancouver's Force Four Productions still has the rights to her story. Her website is down and she reportedly lives in Newfoundland, but the *Law and Order* episode based on her shenanigans remains in rotation. Easy come, easy go.

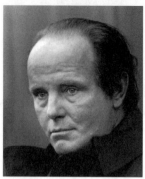

"Michael Moriarty" and "Drunk" equals 365 hits on a Google web search. "Michael Moriarty" and "police" equals 2,230 hits. Actor **Michael Moriarty** played straight-arrow Assistant DA Benjamin Stone on *Law and Order* until he left the show in 1994 and moved to Canada in 1996. After avoiding charges from a 1997 Halifax bar brawl, the self-confessed "functioning alcoholic" went west, and saw some real-life courtrooms in and around Vancouver. First, there was the time he slapped his common-law wife, Margaret Brychka, in a drunken rage at Robson Street's Milestone's restaurant in 2001. The assault charges were stayed so long as he did not drink in her presence. A year later, he was jumped by five men outside the Wolf Pub, his regular watering hole in the suburb of Maple Ridge where he was living. The broken nose, damaged eye, and wrecked shoulder were "the price of fame" he said at the time, adding that, "Because I'm a high profile, blatant drinker and smoker, I'm an easy target...." He also admitted he'd been in three fights in two months. When he's not in bar brawls, the right-wing Moriarty has kept himself busy attacking Canadian gun control laws, socialized health care, and the tax system, while threatening to run for mayor of Maple Ridge (being a U.S. citizen makes him ineligible). Meanwhile, he considers himself a civic booster, putting out a jazz album in 2002 called *Temporary Child* (not Permanent Child?) with a track called "Big Wet Cedar" that he calls "an unabashed tribute to Vancouver." The self-styled political columnist was also given space in the *Vancouver Sun*, for a meandering October 6, 2000 article entitled "Vancouver after Dark" in which he seemed to compare the city to New York ... or something. In 2000, he finished shooting his own original screenplay *Hitler Meets Christ* in Vancouver's Downtown Eastside, in which he plays a man who thinks he is Hitler. In June 2003 he told the *Illinois Leader*, "If I live long enough, which is questionable

THE SECRET DRUG MARKET

You thought Granville Street was the city's most blatant open drug market? Sadly, it's actually on the open-air patio of a city hospital. A doctor visiting several years ago commented that he had never seen anything like it in his work as a physician around the world: the open selling of stolen merchandise and use of illicit, injectable drugs like heroin within the confines of the hospital. A doctor currently working there confirms that the site is so popular as an open drug market that the floor number has worn off the elevator button. The hospital's staff was recently embarrassed by a call from a downtown pawn shop that was in possession of a grand piano that appeared to belong to the hospital. The staff denied they were missing a piano until a quick check confirmed that indeed, the piano had been swiped from right in front of them.

these days, yes, I will run for President of the United States in 2008." Perhaps Moriarty should just take a page from his own "screenplay in development" about the misadventures of a grandiose actor, entitled, "The Has-Been."

THE SMOKING JUDGE

When regular Vancouverites want to go for a smoke at work, they find themselves huddled in the rain outside. When a Vancouver judge wants to smoke at work, well, she just lights up at her desk. Such was the case with Justice **Mary Southin**, dubbed The Smoking Judge, who brazenly and publicly violated Vancouver Bylaw 6.5 (e) by smoking regularly in her chambers and refusing to stop in January 2003. The B.C. government's response? Spend $19,000 of taxpayers' dollars to ventilate her office (which would still violate the bylaw, since a "smoking room" cannot double as an office). The public outcry led the judge to admit that she had offered to pay $12,000 of the fee herself, which the government apparently neglected to take her up on.

Not So Quiet Riots

Photo: Solo

While it is unlikely that the heavy metal band **Guns 'N' Roses** is named for the famous incident of U.S. peaceniks placing flowers down the barrels of the National Guard's guns, they don't seem to attract a peace-loving type of crowd. The band was slated to launch their first North American tour in nine years in Vancouver on November 7, 2002. But when the concert was cancelled at the last moment, outraged fans rammed the security barriers outside GM Place through the stadium's glass doors starting what has since been dubbed the Guns 'N' Roses Riot. After 20 minutes or so, police arrived with dogs, clubs, and pepper spray and roughed up the perps, creating dramatic TV footage of a young tough being kicked to the ground, knocking out his two front teeth. The crowd retaliated by throwing rocks and uttering threats. The riot prompted lead singer Axl Rose (whose plane had been late touching down from L.A.) to give his first interview in 10 years to a U.S. radio station, saying the band had only heard that the concert was cancelled through the stadium's P.A. system, and that it had been the building manager who cancelled the show, not the band. The Vancouver police posted a website to help identify the rioters. At press time, 27 of the 47 riot suspects had been fingered.

Mr Nobody

It was one of the most baffling cases of missing identity in recorded history, centering around a young amnesiac calling himself **Philip Staufen**. He arrived in Vancouver in November 2000 after having checked himself into a Toronto hospital when a mugging left him with a broken nose. He claimed total amnesia, and not knowing his name or country of origin, and having no identifying documents, an international search was launched to help him recover his identity. Experts concluded that his accent was from Yorkshire, England, that he was well-educated (he spoke French and read Latin), and that he was about 26 or 27 and possibly of Germanic origin because of the moniker he had randomly chosen when checking himself into the hospital: Philip Staufen was the name of a medieval German lord. Media appeals in Germany, England, and Australia proved fruitless. Vancouver lawyer Manuel Azevedo took up Staufen's case *pro bono*, attempting to get him a Canadian birth certificate so that he could get a passport to travel to England to discover his roots. Staufen, meanwhile, lived on welfare ($525 per month) in an East Vancouver bedsitting room and spent his time at the downtown branch of the Vancouver Public Library reading sonnets in Latin. In his February 2001 statement to the B.C. Supreme Court, he wrote "My actual situation has left me prey to too many abuses and humiliations. I have found myself having to live in the streets or with violent or vulgar people.... I consider myself a prisoner; therefore I am kindly asking to be set free." Strangely, however, he turned down offers of hypnosis for his amnesia, and stayed in his apartment for days at a time, refusing to talk to media and TV shows who wanted to help publicize his case. The Courts denied him a birth certificate, but he was awarded an 18-month citizenship permit. Then, in January 2002, the case took another bizarre twist when a man from London contacted the European gay porn magazine *Vulcan*, saying he believed Staufen was French porn model Georges Lechit, 27, who had appeared regularly in the magazine but had not been seen for two years – which would explain why Staufen had been deeply suntanned "all over" and had an immaculate manicure and pedicure according to the nurses who examined him at the Toronto hospital. The magazine confirmed the incredible likeness. The case is still open.

A '70S KINDA GUY

"He was a '70s kind of guy in the 1990s" was the phrase the lawyer for Vancouver actor **Adrian Hughes** used to explain his clients bad behaviour. In 2001 he was accused of sexual assault by six Vancouver women, most of them in the film industry, and convicted on one charge of date rape. The tall, dark, and handsome actor had made international tabloid headlines for dating actress Gillian Anderson, co-star of the Vancouver-shot *X-Files* series. The case that finally got this macho man nailed involved an

Tony Robbins: he's a self-help guru worth US$400 million who knows how to help himself – to a 28-year-old blonde named Bonnie Lynch from Langley, who apparently Awakenened His Giant Within. The pair met in 1999 and began to date regularly in 2000, when they were spotted riding mountain bikes together along Robson Street. Since engaged, they have plans to marry once Lynch's divorce from a Langley businessman goes through. Seems that since Robbins has entered the picture, Lynch's estranged husband now has dollar signs in his eyes. He's hired a U.S. lawyer and is suing Robbins for "alienation of affection." Bonnie Lynch told the *Vancouver Sun* she had never even heard of Tony Robbins when she left her husband in 1998, and has said of her husband, "It's obvious that the only reason he's doing this is to gain attention at the cost of my fiancé's reputation in an attempt to extort money." Tony Robbins' lawyer, meanwhile, told the paper he would "vigorously oppose the suit." Robbins' official website (*anthonyrobbins.com*) tells a different story. It claims he is "a dedicated father of four and a loving husband to his wife Sage Robbins." Believe what you will.

actress he met through a telephone dating service. They met at his apartment, had rough sex, and while he was in the bathroom, she took off. It was two years after the incident (when the actress began hearing of other women in the film industry who had problems with Hughes) that she went to police. Their conflicting court testimony about the night in question has her saying she wore a floral "Mother Earth" dress that went to her ankles and him saying she wore a short tube dress and heels. Hughes was sentenced to jail for two years.

just passing through

Tom Jones Was Here

Tom Jones comes through Vancouver often, and when he does he often hooks up with his close friend, Vancouver socialite and Army & Navy department store owner, Jacqui Cohen. You are likely to see them dining post-concert at Umberto Menghi's restaurant Il Giardino, or pal Jean-Claude Ramond's bistro The Smoking Dog, where they have been known to consume copious amounts of Veuve Cliquot champagne and Monte Cristo cigars (Jones' fave) and keep the place open until 7 or 8 in the morning. He once got fellow female diners so excited they started a commentary on the chalkboards in the women's bathroom that started with, "I've got a thing for Tom Jones." Another female added "I've got a thing for Tom Jones' Thing" until Jones himself was obliged to enter the women's room to take it to even more base levels.

Goldie Hawn and Kurt Russell's Missing Car

When Goldie and Kurt moved to Vancouver in late 2002, their every movement was tracked by local tabloids, from the shopping sprees on South Granville to the seafood dinners at Cardero's. Magazines wondered if hockey-mom-chic would return as a fashion statement, as Goldie was tracked to teenage son

Wyatt's practices (it was his hockey ambitions that prompted the move to Vancouver in the first place). The chinzy décor of the pair's Shaughnessy mansion was revealed in a splashy colour spread in the *Vancouver Sun*, and a caller to a local radio show claimed she'd seen Russell run out in the middle of the street in a downpour to save a dog that had escaped from the SPCA. But what finally caught the interest of the

SCAM OF SCAMS

In possibly the most monumental case of telemarketing fraud in history, Vancouver "businessman" **James Blair Down** bilked U.S. seniors out of US$200 million starting in 1986, with a phone-based scheme based on bogus foreign lotteries, sweepstakes, and puzzle contests. With the FBI on his trail, he was indicted and served 180 days' jail time in the U.S. and agreed to pay $12 million in restitution to his victims. Until recently, he was living the high life in the top two floors of Vancouver's Sheraton Wall Centre, in a converted double-decker penthouse. In June 2003, Canadian investigative journalism TV show *W5* aired a one-hour special about his case, including scenes of him fleeing *Vancouver Sun* reporters in an SUV. The very next week after the special aired, a for-sale listing appeared in the *Vancouver Sun*'s real-estate section, for a unique two-storey penthouse in the Wall Centre.

international gossip press (The *New York Observer*'s Page Six, for one) was a car heist that happened right in front of the house. Their Porsche was stolen from its parking spot along the leafy boulevard – though the pair were so preoccupied they didn't notice for days.

Fidel Castro's Snooze

In an unofficial visit, the three planes that carried 76-year-old Cuban leader Fidel Castro's 175-person entourage stopped briefly to refuel at Vancouver International Airport en route from Japan to Cuba on March 4, 2003. Castro checked into the Delta Airport Inn where he had a nap (and forgot to call Prime Minister Jean Chrétien) while his entourage stocked up on American candy bars in the gift shop. Meantime, reporters caught wind of his surprise visit and gathered in the lobby practicing their Spanish. When Castro emerged, he regaled reporters for 10 minutes with views on baseball's World Series, the U.S.-led war on Iraq, and the Olympic Games. Before leaving he turned to the scrum saying, "Take care of your city. And take care of the salmon."

Bill Clinton's Special Diet

When in Vancouver for the 1997 APEC conference, then-U.S.-President Bill Clinton famously toured Vancouver, stopping in at Hill's Indian Crafts to buy a marble bear's head figurine which later turned up in court documents as a gift he gave to Monica Lewinsky. He reportedly stopped in at the now-defunct Raintree restaurant for an impromptu snack of squash soup and a winter vegetable tower that was made according to his special diet and tested by the Secret Service. His entourage took over most of the Waterfront Hotel. But the one West Vancouver institution that didn't need the publicity was the top-rated Capilano Golf and Country Club, which turned down his request for a round of golf based on the size of his entourage, deciding it would be too disruptive for members. Clinton ended up playing with Prime Minister Jean Chrétien in the rain at Shaughnessy Golf and Country Club instead.

JUST NOT PASSING THROUGH

Famed Hollywood madam **Heidi Fleiss** almost came to Vancouver in May 2003, along with '70s porn star Ron Jeremy, to do a commercial for a new brand of "herbal Viagra." But she was stopped at Customs and turned around because she did not have the special visa required to enter the country. Ms Fleiss, as it is well known, spent three years in a California prison for money laundering and tax evasion. The quick-thinking Fleiss returned to L.A., got the visa, and headed straight back to Vancouver, only to be refused entry once more on the basis that she was entering the country for "immoral purposes."

Find out where to get the best pedicures, vintage sweaters, organic food, acting classes, and job training – and that's just the section for dogs. This chapter tells you what you really want to know about Vancouver, like the secret nude beach in West Van, the most popular tourist tattoos, where to go to DJ school or how to find your very own butler.

If These Walls Could Talk

Photo: Solo

If you live at 827 East Georgia Street (pictured left), you are the fortunate occupant of a home once owned by Jimi Hendrix's grandmother, Nora Hendrix, in the '40s and '50s. Of course, you would already know this if you had hired James Johnstone's **Home History Research Services** (604-254-4666, homehistoryresearch.com). For $500 (and up), he'll prepare a house genealogy in the form of a booklet that tells you who lived there, what they did, who built it, how much it cost, and a plethora of other historical details, including maps, news clippings, obituaries, and photos. He'll even uncover court cases and explain the history of street names in your area. Johnstone was recently involved in a project that saved Vancouver's oldest house, the Clark House (built in 1888 at 243 East 5th Avenue), which was rescued from demolition by being relocated to a spot behind 130 West 10th Avenue. The city's property records can be spotty (especially in neighbourhoods where immigrants settled) and home cataloguing by the city ceased in 2002, so Johnstone's service is particularly valuable. And now you have the perfect housewarming gift.

odd hobbies & pastimes

Mothers of Invention

The West Coast is a lunatic fringe: it's where social misfits end up because they can drift no further – just look at B.C.'s premiers, the first of whom renamed himself Amor de Cosmos "lover of the universe." Inventors, like politicians, tend to be iconoclastic, so perhaps this is why Vancouver has the highest rate of inventions per capita in the world. The history of local invention is long and storied, replete with coincidences. These days, the strange-but-true invention that is causing a buzz is a collapsible house that comes complete with working appliances and bathroom, and can be folded into the shape of a standard shipping container. Imagine the possibilities for developing countries or disaster relief. But the curmudgeonly inventor Ramon Kalinowski, a civil engineer, turned down an offer to build the first prototype because it would have been funded by government money. Fifteen years later, he's finally pulled together his own financing and is about to get rich. These all-on-one devices are a recurring theme: the inventor of the Newt Suit, a sort of personal submarine, is an engineer who resides in Deep Cove.

Adult Lego League

The adult Vancouver LEGO club meets once a month to showcase their handiwork, play games, and trade bricks. They also get offers (more than they can handle) to showcase their work publicly. They are one of around 40 adult LEGO leagues in the world; co-founder Alexandria Carstens told the *Vancouver Courier* recently, "It's nice to know you're not alone in your insanity." Indeed: on average every person on earth owns 52 LEGO bricks.
akasa.bc.ca/vlc

Deliverance Us From Effort

When you are too busy to get it yourself, or – let's face it – too lazy to get off the couch, these delivery and concierge services do the dirty work for you.

Churchill's Fine Cigars
Will deliver premium hand-rolled cigars to your door.
1062 Mainland St., 604-66-CIGAR, churchillsfinecigars.com

Dairyland Home Service
Delivers milk, eggs, cheese, juice, and other staple items.
6800 Lougheed Hwy., Burnaby, 604-421-4663, dairyland-ca.com

Dial-a-Bottle
The name says it all. Delivery charge is eight dollars. Cash only!
604-688-0348

Fresh Egg Mart
A dozen to your door.
269 E. Georgia St., 604-685-1925

ORGANIC GROCERIES

Greenearthorganics.com
604-708-2345

Stitch and Bitch

In the modern incarnation of the sewing circle, so-called Stitch and Bitch clubs for women are popping up in bookstores, hair salons, and fashion stores everywhere. Making your own clothes is once again in vogue, and even models can be seen crocheting and knitting backstage. The newest Vancouver group meets at the **Barefoot Contessa Atelier** above the store *(3715 Main St., 604-879-1137, thebarefootcontessa.com)* to get crochet lessons and sip wine on the third Sunday of every month. The meetings at West Vancouver's **32 Books Co.** *(3018 Edgemont Blvd., North Vancouver, 604-980-9032, 32books.com)* have been filled to capacity since they launched. Find fellow stitch-and-bitchers at:

Knitwear Architects
1185 Mainland St., 604-879-7010

The Knit and Stitch Shoppe
2419 Marine Dr., West Vancouver, 604-922-1023, knit-n-stitch.com

A Touch of Wool
4273 Dunbar St., 604-224-9276

Organics Delivery B.C.
604-505-6322, odbc.ca

Small Potatoes Urban Delivery

This is the top organic food delivery service in the city. Or shop direct from the retail store open Saturdays and Sundays only
1660 E. Hastings St., 604-215-7783, spud.ca

Photo: Solo

DIET MEALS

Lowcarbexpress.ca

A low-carbohydrate food delivery service launched by the son of CTV news anchor Bill Good.

The Specialty Gourmet

They deliver three meals and two snacks a day prepared according to the guidelines of whichever fad diet you are on: Atkins, The Zone, or Heart Health. Prepared by caterer The Lazy Gourmet.
604-983-8511, thespecialtygourmet.com

dirt diggers & muck rakers

No, not gossip, gladiolas. Gardening is the number one hobby among Vancouverites. Blessed with a temperate climate and a long growing season, the fact that we use more fresh water per person than anywhere else in the world is perhaps a result. Add that to the fact that the Lower Mainland comprises the largest biomass (living things by weight) in the world, and you'll see there's plenty of inspiration around. Gardening styles range from formal English gardens in Shaugnnessy, to Japanese Zen gardens in Point Grey, to unkempt guerrilla gardens on all the round-abouts in East Van. Of course, Vancouver is also home to internationally-known gardening empressario Thomas Hobbs of Southlands Nursery (no, not the philosopher, that's Thomas Hobbes, though a B.C. judge once wrote a decision regarding First Nations land claims that included the mistake – causing political scientists to complain that the judge was more familiar with his tony neighbourhood florist than with land rights). Farmers' markets are great places to buy plants, and you'd be surprised at the tulips you can grow from Home Depot bulbs, but here are some of the best gardening resources in the city:

Best Florists

Photo: Solo

Artistry in Flowers
Hydrangeas from Australia, tropical flowers from Ecuador, and orchids from Singapore.
851 Hornby St., 604-682-6222, artistryflowers.com

Donna Hutton Flowers
Ever wonder who was responsible for the stunning bouquets on the end of the bar at Lumière? Now you know.
2533 W. Broadway, 604-733-0064

Flower Factory
Staffed by young artists and fashion designers.
3604 Main St., 604-871-1008, flowerfactory.ca

Garlands Florists

Stalks of myrtle in your bunch of tulips and rice-paper wrapping are signature.
2950 W. Broadway, 604-739-6688, garlandsflorists.com

Granville Island Florist

Inside the Granville Island Market, they'll even make your carton of blueberries into a festive gift bouquet.
1689 Johnston St., Granville Island, 604-669-1228

Hilary Miles Flowers Ltd.

The city's top spot. Order your really, really important flowers here.
1-1854 W. 1st Ave., 604-737-2782

Oasis Flowers

Two hip young women doing fashion-forward bouquets.
2793 Arbutus St., 604-730-7992, oasisflowers.ca

Meinhardt Flowers

Like an open-air French flower market, adjoining the specialty grocery store.
3002 Granville St., 604-732-4405, meinhardt.com

Mine: Stylesource

Specializing in event flowers, they've already cornered the market on gay weddings.
177 E. Broadway, 604-875-9435

The Avant Gardener

2235 W. 4th; 1460 Marine Dr., West Vancouver, 604-736-0404, avantgardener.com

Lee Valley Tools

1180 SE Marine Dr., 604-261-2262, Leevalley.com

Photo: Solo

Art Knapp Urban Garden

1401 Hornby St., 604-662-3303

Dig This Garden Shop

10-1535 Johnston St., Granville Island, 604-688-2929, digthiscanada.com

Southlands Nursery

6550 Balaclava St., 604-261-6411, southlandsnursery.com

A Messy Business

Sad but true, it is sometimes better to get someone else to clean Uncle Henry's brains off the ceiling or the closet full of Rover's remains after poochie went missing for three weeks. **Trauma Scene Clean Up Services** does the dirty work – for about $1,500 to $2,000. Neat and discreet, their trucks have no writing on them, so you won't have to worry about nosy neighbours. *604-584-8000.*

Run Free, Fifi, Run Free

Dog owners have a rough time finding space in Vancouver for their pets to mix and mingle. The anti-dog lobby have made almost all parks in the city either dog-free or dog-on-a-leash territory, and city officials are ready to strike with a fine if you dare let Fifi run free. You're even supposed to have your dog on a leash in the UBC Endowment Lands.

But there is one spot right off downtown where you can let your furry friend romp around to his heart's content – the non-park park.

The non-park is called the non-park because the parks board tried to make it into a sports field a decade ago, but were beaten back by the anti-sports lobby. So a 10-acre parcel of land just off Malkin Avenue in southern Strathcona remains a dog-friendly wasteland of scrub trees, gravel, mud, and water, awaiting redevelopment.

Dogs particularly like to run up, down, and around piles of dirt and tree mulch that city crews deposit on the site.

There is no sign to indicate where the non-park park is, but it's fairly easy to find. Take the first right off the Georgia Viaduct on Prior heading east, which is Malkin. Keep to the right as it curves, then stop just before the new city works yard and the row of warehouse buildings on Malkin. The break in the fence is the non-park park. Be warned, though, if it's been rainy, it can be pretty muddy.

Chores and Errands

From laundering your clothes to nanny screening, here's how to make your messy life neater.

Creative Concierge

A personal valet service, like London's *quintessentially.com* that caters to the Royal Family. Be Queen for a day and have these reliable female entrepreneurs organize your child's birthday party, take the dog to the vet, pick up a dozen rolls of toilet paper, or interview nannies while you watch *Oprah*. Discreet and efficient, they'll do anything you ask as long as it is legal (i.e., they'll pick up your Valium prescription but won't score you a gram of blow). $40 per hour. *604-454-1453, creativeconcierge.ca*

LAUNDRY/DRYCLEANING/ALTERATIONS

Kay's Cleaners

They specialize in cleaning wedding gowns, costumes, and fine clothing. *3212 Dunbar St., 604-738-3209*

pet control

Photo: Solo

Kerrisdale Cleaners

They do both pickups and deliveries for large orders but all that really needs to be said is that they got a red wine stain out of white jeans.
2383 W. 4th Ave., 604-738-0626

Sun Chueng

A bit hard to find (in the basement of a building off Broadway and Spruce), but the prices are very reasonable and the service is quick from this husband-and-wife alterations team.
*100-2480 Spruce St.,
604-731-8370*

Robson Shoe Renu

The city's top shoe stores (like John Fluevog) send shoes here for fast, inexpensive repairs.
520 Robson St., 604-685-5413

A word of caution: while being fairly pet-friendly, Vancouver is also full of pet vigilantes. You'll often hear news stories about people's pets being stolen from their cars or from outside the grocery store. Usually, these are cases of pet-napping by animal extremists who take the animals to the pound or to controversial organizations such the unlisted Animal Advocates in West Vancouver. Remember – even though most businesses will not allow you to take a dog inside, dog tethering is technically illegal in Vancouver, so the pound can do nothing about the people who drive around snatching dogs off the street. That said, according to the B.C. SPCA, between a quarter and half of Vancouverites own a pet, and literally hundreds of stores and services have sprung up in recent years to cater to them.

Mobile Groomers

Dirty old dogs get scrubbed up (including ears and nails) by **Happy Dog Mobile Hydro Bath** *(604-729-9105, happydogmobilehydrobath.com)* a dog-grooming trailer that parks in front of your house or apartment. Especially great for big dogs.

Doggy Pedicures

Though geared toward humans, **New Mondo For Hair Mondo Spa** *(857 Hornby St., 604-688-3343)* also offers nail-painting for your pooch. You can take home a bottle of polish (in fetching colours like red and silver) for $14, or you can have the staff apply it for you ($20).

Police Dog Training

At 8 a.m. on Sunday mornings at **Kerrisdale School Annex** *(3250 W. 43rd Ave., 604-713-5488)*, take advantage of free dog training sessions from the man who trains Vancouver's police dogs.

Acting Classes

Think your dog's got Lassie potential? Why not sign him up for one of three levels of acting classes? At **Hollywood North Canine Training and Talent Agency** *(571-916 W. Broadway, 604-738-1568)*, the focus is on developing talent and then ensuring that the animals receive fair treatment once they're working.

Job Training

Dog-play.com is an Internet clearing house for canine training, including Animal-Assisted Therapy, Dog Camps, Education, Eventing, Flygility, Flyball, Flying Disc, Backpacking, Performance Art, Pet-Facilitated Therapy, Skijoring, Socializing and Off-Leash Play, and Weight Pulling. And you thought it was easy being a dog.

Weekend Retreats

Owned by trainer Deborah Wolfe, also seen on Global TV's *Doggin' It*. Doggie weekend retreats at **Camp Good Dog** *(604-515-2267 campgooddog.com)* include hiking on five acres, swimming, training, and a bath, then a Monday morning drop-off.

Pictures Perfect

Kingdom Photo

According to a top local photographer, this inconspicuous lab has the best commercial photo developing equipment in Vancouver, with prices comparable to a one-hour developer. Ask for "sloppy borders" to create instant fine art photography.
3263 W. Broadway, 604-737-6839

Pacific Light Impressions

Located in a basement in Yaletown, many of the city's top fashion photographers use this company's darkroom and lab. Staff have been known to throw in an extra enlarged print for free.
B2-1120 Hamilton St., 604-688-2018, pacificlightimpressions.com

Fine Art Framing

This professional studio caters to artists and offers unconventional as well as standard sizes. Located in the Parker Building of artists' studios, wander around the halls while you're in here — you never know what you'll see in this hub of creativity that has an open house around Christmas time.
322-1000 Parker St., 604-418-6100

Doggy Fat Farm

For the dog that could use a little shaping up, or the show dog that needs to maintain his fine physique, the **Paws Ahead K-9 Sports Centre** *(4025 E. 2nd Ave., Burnaby, 604-298-3647, pawsahead.com)* offers six-week programs that will get your dog running and jumping in a structured and knowledgeable setting. Classes are held in a large indoor warehouse space, and include obstacle courses and games which promote agility and mental fitness as well as physical fitness.

Dog Accessories

Now that your wardrobe has just the right amount of vintage flourishes, why shouldn't your dog's? **Fetch – A Dog's Dog Store** *(5617 West Boulevard, 604-879-3647, fetchstore.ca)* has vintage dog sweaters (made from human sweaters) and custom-made couches for dogs.

DISCOUNT TRAVEL

When you can't stand the drizzle one more second, **Postcard Travel** is the place to call. They can get you an amazing last-minute deal for the very next morning.

2231 Granville St., 604-733-9909

pet health care

Acadia Veterinary Clinic

3142 W. Broadway, 604-738-7321

Kitsilano Animal Clinic

2645 W. 4th Ave., 604-736-8648

Vancouver Animal Emergency Clinic

1590 W. 4th Ave., 604-734-5104, animaler.com

Yaletown Animal Hospital

39 Smithe St., 604-682-7389, yaletownpethospital.com

gourmet dog food

Photo: Solo

Three Dog Bakery

On Sunday mornings, this dog food bakery serves free brunch, which might consist of German shepherd's pie. The dog delicacies in the bakery case look good enough to eat – which the human staff say they do. Get-well gift boxes and dog birthday cakes also available. *2186 W. 4th Ave., 604-737-3647, threedog.com*

Windsor Packing Co.

This meat market makes all-meat dog food from butcher's scraps, frozen into portion-sized blocks. *4110 Main St., 604-872-5635*

Armando's Finest Quality Meats

Lumière chef Rob Feenie has been known to buy at this meat shop, renowned for its special cuts. For Fido, ask for a few pounds of hard-to-find organic beef bones for a dollar or two. They'll even cut them to the size your pooch likes best. *Granville Island Public Market, 1689 Johnston St., 604-685-0359*

Pet Taxidermy

When you just can't bear the thought that old Fluffy has gone to the cat scratch in the sky, have him immortalized by master taxidermist Steve Kulash. *Vancouver* magazine reported that he made a Whistler man's deceased cat into a wine bladder and that he was responsible for a dead ferret that showed up on *Da Vinci's Inquest*. *3977 Kingsway St., 604-437-4656*

Rich Vancouver

If you have the dough, only the best will do. Here are some products and services to fit the big bill:

Personal Chefs

Tired of people badgering you for autographs in restaurants? **Luxe Catering** *(604-618-1414)* has clients like Sarah McLachlan who lap up the fresh soups and signature dishes, like butter-braised lobster with morel mushrooms, in the privacy of their own homes.

Personal Butler

Your very own Jeeves. Available for Vancouver or Whistler, the friendly guy behind **Butler à la Carte** *(1-866-400-1133, butleralacarte.com)* will answer the door, cook, clean, and run errands. Now if only husbands were as willing.

Private Bartending

Don't get stuck behind the bar all night. **VIP Bartending** *(604-839-4739 or 604-839-4739, vipbartending.com)* provides a couple of dapper young men to do the heavy mixing. Your guests will be both shaken and stirred.

kids' Vancouver

Vancouver City Council has been offering festival grants to community groups willing to rid Vancouver of the "no fun" stigma earned by the former council. Expect many more stilt walkers, pie throwers, mimes, and merrymakers to be roaming the streets and parks this year. Here are some of the best festivals for kids:

Festival of Lights at Van Dusen Botanical Garden
Now that gaudy icicle lights have become year-round decor on stores, restaurants, and houses, show the kids what Christmas lights should really look like – on trees. Runs most of December until New Year's Eve.
5251 Oak St., 604-878-9274, city.vancouver.bc.ca/parks/parks&gardens/vandusen

False Creek Lantern Walk
On the winter solstice (December 21), the seawall becomes a lantern parade that wends its way onto Granville Island for fireworks and activities at Performance Works *(1218 Cartwright St.)*. Put on by the Secret Lantern Society *(secretsociety@direct.ca)*.

Illuminares
Annually on the last Saturday in July, this event is produced by Public Dreams, a non-profit society that believes in bringing the art of celebration to the community. The Illuminares Procession, a family event, includes roving performers, drum bands, fire performers and wraps up with a firework finale.
604-879-8611, publicdreams.org

Pet and House Sitting

Run out of favours with friends to take care of your pets? Operating by word of mouth, Andrew Taillon put himself through cooking school with **Being There** *(604-836-9817)*, his house-sitting and pet care service. Now he's a personal chef as well.

Nannies On Call

Many celebrities staying at Vancouver hotels use **Nannies on Call** *(604-734-1776, www.nanniesoncall.com)* – just think, your little one could share a nanny with Angelina Jolie. On second thought....

Nanaimo Bathtub Race

All manner of converted bathtub-boats race from English Bay to Nanaimo on the Sunshine Coast in July. A wacky Vancouver tradition since 1967.
250-753-7223, bathtub.island.net

Parade of Lost Souls

Each Year as Halloween draws near (last Saturday in October), thousands of people meet in Grandview Park to honour the dead, wake the living, and face their fears. The parade, also produced by Public Dreams, weaves its way through the Commercial Drive neighbourhood blending the Mexican "Day of the Dead" celebration with a mix of street theatre, giant puppets, art installations, live music, and pyrotechnics. This unearthly procession provides a scary night of fun for families, spirits, and spooks of all ages.
604-879-8611, publicdreams.org

Soap Box Derby

Dads and kids everywhere. This annual 3-day race down the hill on West 4th Avenue in June is good old-fashioned fun.
604-263-6443

Sunbrite Luna New Year Festival

Every Chinese New Year (late January to mid-February), dragons go on a parade through the streets of Vancouver's Chinatown, which is the second largest in North America (after San Francisco). Don't even think of driving there, as all the roads are blocked off.
604-273-1655, sunbritefestival.com

Vancouver Children's Festival

The world's very first children's festival was started in Vancouver in 1978 and has been visited by all the top performers, like Raffi and Cirque du Soleil. Vanier Park, right on the water near the H.R. MacMillan Space Centre, becomes a wonderland of bright tents, kites, face painters, and roaming performers in May and June.
604-708-5655, childrensfestival.ca

Funky Festivals

Photo: David Blue

Bard on the Beach

Shakespeare is showcased yearly under two huge tents (the biggest seats 525) in Vanier Park. Bring a picnic. June to September.
604-739-0559, bardonthebeach.org

Gay Pride Parade

It's an all-day party when the pride parade rolls down Denman and Pacific Streets over two hours on the August long weeekend. The 25th anniversary parade in 2003 drew 140,000 shiny, happy people.
vanpride.bc.ca

more kids' activities

Granville Island Waterpark

Photo: Mandelbrot

Located beside the False Creek Community Centre, it's the largest free waterpark in North America. Open daily, 10 a.m. to 6 p.m. *1318 Cartwright St., Granville Island, 604-257-8195, granvilleisland.com*

Hair Loft and Little Princess Spa

Young punks will go mad for the blue hair gel and sparkle spray in this hair salon for children. They'll be so distracted by bubbles, toys, and books they won't even realize they're getting a nice, short haircut. On weekends, the new Little Princess Spa gets groups of girls started early on glittery nail polish and hot roller sets done to the pounding beats of Justin Timberlake under a blinking disco ball. If visions of JonBenet Ramsey are coming to mind, no need to be alarmed. They can wash it all off when they get home, and no one is required to sing and dance.
Kids Market, 1496 Cartwright St., Granville Island, 604-684-6177

Kids Market

It used to be called the Kid's Only Market until the shopkeepers noticed the numbers of kids wandering around by themselves with no money. Now, parents are encouraged to come in and shell out for quality toys, most of which don't require batteries or encourage violence. One store is devoted entirely to kites and another to puppets.
1496 Cartwright St., Granville Island, 604-689-8447, kidsmarket.ca

HSBC Celebration of Light

Formerly known as the Festival of Fire, more than a million Vancouverites take advantage of this celebration (spread over several dates) to watch international teams compete in pyrotechnics off English Bay. All the city's beaches are a zoo, so let's hope you've got a friend with a balcony or rooftop, or better yet, a boat. July/August. *celebration-of-light.com*

Vancouver Folk Festival

Drums, dancing, and guitar strumming on seven stages at Jericho Beach Park. July. *604-602-9798, thefestival.bc.ca*

Vancouver Fringe Festival

450 theatre performances in nine venues. But don't be late; it's traditional to lock the doors precisely at showtime. September. *604-257-0350, vancouverfringe.com*

H . R . M a c M i l l a n
S p a c e   C e n t r e

Teach your kids that a planetarium is the machine, not the building that houses it. Little kids like to look at the stars (free on clear, weekend nights), while big kids like the laser light shows, done to music by the Beastie Boys, Radiohead, and Pink Floyd.
1100 Chestnut St., 604-738-7827,
hrmacmillanspacecentre.com

S c i e n c e   W o r l d

The kinetic sculpture outside provides hours of amusement before you even buy your ticket. Located in EXPO 86's silver golfball-like Omnimax (the caulking was done by guys with rock-climbing equipment), you can also catch 3-D films of grizzlies and sharks in the IMAX Theatre. Get there via the **Downtown Historic Railway**, a restored tram service from Granville Island *(604-873-77442, trams.bc.ca/dhr.html)*. Train tickets are only $1 for kids.
1455 Quebec St., 604-443-7440, scienceworld.bc.ca

Vancouver International Jazz Festival

Three days of free outdoor performances at David Lam Park, Gastown, and Granville Island. The new beer garden on top of the Pump Station at David Lam Park is the best vantage point. June.
604-872-5200, coastaljazz.ca

Vancouver International Comedy Festival

On Granville Island, over 12 days, see circus acts, clowning, physical comedy, *commedia del arte*, musical parody, and more. July/August.
604-280-4444, comedyfest.com

Stanley Park Train

There's a Christmas train ride and a spooky Halloween tour on a miniature train that goes through the forest in Stanley Park, where the old Vancouver Zoo used to be. Now, the only animals you're likely to see there are squirrels, skunks, coyotes, geese, and the odd rabbit.
604-257-8531, city.vancouver.bc.ca/parks/ parks&gardens/stanley.htm

Vancouver Aquarium

Photo: Jeff Vinnick

Often used as a party venue for kids and adults alike. Watch whales and sharks from underwater windows or touch gooey and spiny things in the tide pools.
845 Avison Way, Stanley Park, 1-800-931-1186, vanaqua.org

Vancouver Kidsbooks

Photo: Solo

Now that school budgets are next to nil, teachers can't get enough of this store. For the Harry Potter launches, they converted the block-long store into Hogwart's Castle. Look for readings and special events. Gift-wrapping is free.
3083 W. Broadway, 604-738-5335; 3040 Edgemont Blvd., 604-986-6190; kidsbooks.bc.ca

urban oases

Renfrew Ravine Park

The term "park" is only a recent appellation; for the longest time this unloved bit of ravine at Renfrew and 29th Avenue – left over from the days when Still Creek used to flow through here out to Burnaby Lake – was thought of mostly as a convenient spot to dispose of those used refrigerators, paint cans, or stolen Chevies cluttering your backyard. Then locals discovered that the little declivity's thick hedges and trees provided a great sheltering spot for passing birds, and a needed bit of nature on Vancouver's Eastside. Even with the official park designation, the powers-that-be still provide no maintenance, and passersby still dump their junk, but a local citizens' group meets each year to clear out the worst of the debris. Best discovery so far? A 1950s-style Coca-Cola fridge that, when cleaned off, repaired, plugged in, and inspected by an antique dealer, was reported to be the real thing.

Charles Park

Like certain Soviet cities at the height of the Cold War, this little neighbourhood park is so secret that it doesn't appear on any of the maps given out by the city or the Parks Board. So what are they hiding? A delightful little enclave, featuring exotic shrubs with magnificent flowers, a tranquil duck pond, and towering cottonwood trees that seem to block out the noise and bustle of the busy Eastside. Alas, for the casual visitor, trying to locate Charles Park by driving around and

Alternative Video Stores

Photo: Solo

Celluloid Drugstore
The clerk in a lab coat at this video rental store prescribes a cinematic panacea for your pain. Just suffered a bad break-up? Perhaps *The Bridges of Madison County* will bring you back together.
1470 Commercial Dr., 604-251-3305

Black Dog Video
3451 Cambie St. 604-873-6958, blackdogvideo.bc.ca

Cinephile Video
4340 Main St., 604-876-3456

Independent Video
976 Denman St., 604-682-3344

Photo: Solo

Inferno Urban Video
1210 Homer St., 604-646-6655,
iuv.ca

Limelight Video
2505 Alma St., 604-228-1478

Luna Video
2766 W. Fourth Ave.,
604-732-5559

Photo: Solo

Videomatica
1855 W. Fourth Ave.,
604-734-0411, videomatica.bc.ca

asking the locals is a little like wandering the Siberian countryside asking the peasants for directions to Magnetogorsk – they all know it's there, but no one's quite sure where, and anyway, why are you asking? Fortunately, there's an easier way. The next time you take your car for testing at the Boundary Road Air Care station, take a moment and park by the gate. Then get out and wander around. You're there.

Everett Crowley Park

The far southeast corner of Vancouver is an intriguing little realm, seemingly exempt from the laws that govern the rest of the city. In place of the usual comforting grid of streets, this area sports a complicated tangle of cul-de-sacs and curvilinear crescents. And in place of the standard swings and soccer pitch there's Everett Crowley Park (Kerr Road and Marine Way), 13-plus hectares of thick alder woods and grassy meadows, laced here and there with the occasional dark ravine, sunny babbling brook, or cliff top view of Richmond's rural bits. There are paths for strollers, joggers, and mountain bikers, with the only proviso being that Vancouver's quasi-fascist obsession with anti-smoking measures has been given a slightly stronger imperative here: beneath this wilderness playground lie several thousand still-decomposing tons of municipal waste (it was the Kerr Road Dump from 1944 to 1967). The methane seepage is expected to continue for at least another half-century.

unique beaches

Brunswick Point

A very secluded 300-metre clothing-optional beach in Lion's Bay, West Vancouver. Take the Sea to Sky highway 1.6 km north of Lion's Bay. Follow trails to Brunswick Point. Pass the regular clothed beach on the south side of the point. Cross a 1.5-metre rocky outcrop: hidden on the other side is the nude beach.

Urban Beach

Located on the southeast side of the Cambie Street Bridge, above the seawall, a huge tract of imported white sand on concrete is where hundreds of people play beach volleyball on this make-believe beach every day and night of the summer. It was relocated in the summer of 2003 to make room for the huge Cirque du Soleil tents, but is now just across the water. Access it from the staircase halfway across the bridge.

Wreck Beach

Where else in Vancouver can you get a pedicure, play mah jong, drink a cold margarita, have your hair cut, listen to live music, play sand croquet, fly a kite, and score some weed, all without your clothes on? This clothing-optional beach was deemed one of the world's 10 most exclusive on an episode of *Lifestyles of the Rich and Famous*. Part of the reason is its inaccessibility: you must climb down a cliff fitted with a steep staircase at trail marker #6 on Marine Drive at the University of British Columbia. Unlike their predecessors, the current generation of fit cops don't mind doing this, but more often than not, you see them lining up at the empanada stand with everyone else rather than trying to make a bust. The nude volleyball area is a sight to behold, but don't even think of snapping a photo: strict beach etiquette forbids photography and regulars will jump you and confiscate your film within seconds — we've seen it happen. The Wreck Beach Preservation Society, an ad hoc group founded in 1977, runs a website with event and beach information, at *wreckbeach.org*.

Yoga

City Yoga

A large mostly Ashtanga studio handily located across from that Mecca of high-end yoga gear, Lululemon Athletica (2113 W. 4th Ave., lululemon.com).
2-2108 W. 4th Ave.., 604-730-5522, cityyoga.net

Shanti Yoga

Canadian chanteuse Alanis Morissette's twin brother Wade owns this Kits studio.
240-2083 Alma St., 604-739-3248, shantiyoga.org

Vancouver Yoga

Eoin Finn teaches athletic, multi-level classes peppered with humorous commentary. See website for locations (like the Show Boat at Kits Beach in summertime) and classes from other great instructors Tracy and James.
604-734-8932, vancouveryoga.com

body and soul

Vancouver is known as a city of health nuts, where fitness centres stay open later than bars, and children run in marathons. The spiritual philosophy hasn't changed much since the 1970s, only now everything is more expensively packaged, with high-end yoga studios and $20 bowls of granola. In the birthplace of Botox, and the first city in Canada to practice pilates, Vancouverites also love to get toned, primped, and pricked. If you can't beat 'em, join 'em.

UNIQUE FITNESS CENTRES & GYMS

Cocoon
A downtown personal training facility that's been used by Salma Hayek and others. Go for the boxing circuit classes, fencing, or Brazilian jiu-jitsu. Drop-in: $10.
427 Granville St., 604-733-0355, cocoonathletics.com

The Fitness Group
Attention parents: there's a child-care program. Drop-in: $16.
3507 W. 4th Ave., 604-654-1725, fitnessgroup.com

Kitsilano Community Centre
The drop-in rate at this newly renovated gym for community centre members is the best deal in the city. Cardio equipment overlooks Connaught Park, and there's a whirlpool and sauna. Drop-in: $4.
2690 Larch St., 604-257-6976, city.vancouver.bc.ca/parks/recreation/kitsilano/kits.html

Kitsilano Workout
It may be small, but it offers famous Latin funk from "The King" Gustavo Ferman. Drop-in: $10.
1923 W. 4th Ave., 604-734-3481, kitsilanoworkout.supersites.ca

Olympic Athletic Club
Where else can you work out with the B.C. Lions, go to the chiropractor, have a massage, and get your car detailed at the same time? Drop-in: $11.
212 W. 1st Ave., 604-708-9441, olympicgym.ca

ALSO TRY:

Bikram's Yoga Yaletown
1232 Richards St., 604-684-3314, bikramyoga.com

Flow Yoga Studio
101-1409 W. Pender St., 604-682-FLOW, flowyogavancouver.com

Prana Yoga & Zen Centre
1067 Cambie St., 604-682-2121, pranayoga.com

Yogapod
101-260 W. Esplanade, North Vancouver, 604-924-9642, yogapod.com

Yoga West
2662 W. 4th Ave., 604-732-YOGA, yogawest.ca

Ringside Fitness

Canadian Olympic bronze medallist Dale Walters' high-end boxing gym comes complete with towel service, filtered water, and dry sauna. A 14-foot boxing ring is supplemented by speed bags and skipping, crunch, and push-ups stations. Up to 40 percent of private clients are women and there are women-only classes. Circuit drop-in: $15.
Lower Plaza, Four Bentall Centre, 1055 Dunsmuir St., 604-661-5059, ringsidefitness.com

Studeo 55

A boutique personal training studio located in a penthouse downtown. Aimed at executives, it even has indoor basketball and golf.
1114 Alberni St., 5th Floor, 604-684-0544, studeo55.ca

Sutton Place Hotel

It's a little known fact, but you don't have to be staying at this high-end hotel geared towards the film industry to use the gym. Work out beside celebrities and order room service beside the pool, while taking advantage of the towel and robe service and men's steam room. Drop-in: $10.
845 Burrard St., 604-682-5511, suttonplace.com

Sweat Co. Workout Studios

This is the city's top spot for spinning, the sport that has you going nowhere fast on a stationary bike. Call ahead to book a spot (it sells out), then buzz in to the pleasant upstairs studio. Drop-in: $15.
736 Richards St., 604-683-7938, sweatcostudios.com

YWCA

Not just for women anymore, the huge, high-tech facility has over 90 weekly classes, including deep water running and police physical training for civilians. Drop-in: $12.
535 Hornby St., 604-895-5800, ywcahealthandwellness.com

Pilates

Dianne Miller Pilates Center of Vancouver

Pilates is an exercise technique for dancers that uses machines called reformers to exercise the muscles that ballet misses. Even regular folk can develop long, lean muscles and a rock hard core. Dianne Miller is credited with introducing Pilates to Canada in 1985.
719 W. 16th Ave., 604-879-2900

Pilates West Vancouver Workout Centre

1441 Clyde Ave., 604-913-3323, pilateswestvancouver.com

Yaletown Pilates

201-1037 Mainland St., 604-646-0199, yaletownpilates.com

WACKY BEAUTY TREATMENTS

Bored by regular spas? Lucky you. Here are some unique beauty treatments to get you out of your rut.

Bikini Hair Extensions

At **New Mondo Spa** *(857 Hornby St., 604-688-3343)*, there is a salon next door, but some of the most creative hair styling happens on the spa side, where bikini waxes include an option with a glow-in-the-dark tattoo. One expectant mom announced the happy news to her husband with a bikini wax that included a sparkly tattoo that read "Baby!" The latest trend here is bikini hair extensions with bells on them (apparently started in homage to Brad Pitt while he wore bells in his beard). The look works best with a circle skirt and no underwear so he can hear you coming.

Japanese Relaxation Studio

Aimed at stressed-out urbanites, **SoSei Studio** *(501-1540 W. 2nd Ave., 604-731-7291, soseistudio.com)* is a little Japanese relaxation studio in the Arthur Erickson-designed Waterfall building. Over two hours, the deprogramming involves a 30-minute session in a luge-like capsule where you experience light and heat therapy, aromatherapy, massage therapy, and music according to the selected program (stress relief, insomnia, detoxification, etc.). The weight-loss option uses high heat, violet light, and fennel-scented aromas and claims to burn up to 100 calories while you lie still. A one-foot-deep salt water flotation bath follows. Next, a steam shower scented with green tea detoxifies. Your final resting place is a gravity-defying chair in a traditional tatami room where you'll sip cold green tea and look at aura-enhancing paintings and pottery made by monks. The studio claims this circuit will enhance your sleep that night by 40 percent and boost your metabolism for five days. Japanese slippers, disposable underwear, and kimono provided. Don't miss the electronic bidet (called a washlet) and negative ion hair dryer from Japan that counteracts those bad positive ions from your computer.

Photo: Solo

BEAUTY BARGAINS

Like getting a master's degree in hair, licensed hair stylists with at least three years experience come to **Aveda Academy Salon** *(1228 Robson St., 604-689-5484, aveda.com)* for further training from top pros. Clients benefit from reduced prices for colour and cuts.

Turkish Baths

Exotic and spiritual spa experiences that emphasize health and overall well-being over primping and plucking are growing in popularity. Such is the case at **Miraj Hammam Spa** *(1495 W. 6th Ave., 604-733-5151, mirajhammam.com)*, a Middle Eastern-style hammam spa, which is unique in Canada. Its concept is based on the original meaning of "spa" (an acronym for the Latin phrase *salve per aqua*, which means healing through water). Known in Middle Eastern cultures as "the spreader of warmth" and in Europe as "the silent doctor," the hammam comprises a glassed-in steam room where one detoxifies, and a mosaic-tiled room where one experiences gommage, a body exfoliation treatment with loofahs and black Moroccan soap. But be careful who is looking your way: as the hammam is thought to encourage fertility, women in some Islamic cultures have been known to seek suitable wives for their sons there. Moroccan slippers and sarong provided. Make time for the Middle Eastern sweet cakes and Moroccan mint tea in the lushly decorated lounge.

Straightening Perms

Ever wonder why people on TV have such perfect, shiny hair? Well, a lot of them have bio-ionic perms, available at **Zinc Hair Inc** *(768 W. 16th Ave., 604.874-2800)*. The bio-ionic perm is a permanent hair straightening process that works on people with curly, kinky, even straight hair, making it sleek and shiny. It's time-consuming and expensive (about $100 per hour and can take up to 4 hours), and potentially damaging, but for 365 good hair days, it's worth it for some.

Oxygen Bath

The oxygen bar up front at **State of Being Urban Spa Retreat** *(1282 Howe St., 604-633-9557, stateofbeing.ca)* will get you going, but be sure to venture through the labyrinthine corridors to the oxygen bath in the back. A capsule-like device, it uses intensive, oxygen-infused steam to release lactic acid from overworked muscles. Hard-skating Canucks and other athletes use it post-game. A long laundry list of benefits is posted on the wall beside the capsule, and includes intensive calorie burning. Some girls use the treatment pre-beach vacation, claiming it takes inches off their thighs.

Beauty School Drop-In

It's a little-known fact that most beauty schools offer discount spa services to the public so that their students can practice on real clients before unleashing themselves on the world. The prices are about a third of what you'd pay in a spa, so don't expect roses and chocolates at the door. Request a graduating student, leave yourself lots of time, and stick with safe treatments like manicures and pedicures so you'll never risk leaving with just one eyebrow.

Blanche Macdonald Centre
100-555 W. 12th Ave., 604-685-0347 ext.220, blanchemacdonald.com

Dominelli
6453 Bevesford St., Burnaby, 604-431-0777, dominelli.com

Marvel B.C.
668 Seymour St., 604-642-0767, marvelcollege.com

Vancouver Community College
250 W. Pender St., 604-443-8334, vcc.bc.ca

Tooth Jewellery and Eyelash Perms

For would-be rock stars, **New Mondo For Hair/Mondo Spa** *(857 Hornby St., 604-688-3343)* offers tooth jewelry (usually an Austrian crystal) that is applied to the eye tooth with dental glue, lasting up to a year. Eyelash perms curl your lashes for up to two months using a government-approved milk-amino acid formula.

Spray-On Tans

The new Mystic Tan spray-on tanning machine, available at **Sundeck Tanning** *(1915 W. 4th Ave., 604-734-9467, sundecktanning.com)*, is said to be how J.Lo got her glow on at the Oscars. Jump into the booth, don your shower cap, close your eyes, and say a prayer. Sixty seconds later, emerge a bronzed god, and remain that way for a week or so.

Power Drill Pedicures

No, this is not some crazy S&M practice; it's completely safe and painless. Really. At **Saving Face Esthetics** *(219-1628 W. 1st Ave., 604-225-2266)*, Kelly is trained on the Dremel pedicure, as in the Dremel drill that you might just have in your tool box. Specialty bits on a tiny version of the drill developed by a German foot-care company operate like a power sander to blast through calluses in a fraction of the usual time.

Pot Therapy

You can't fault her for not knowing her market when Alberta legend Eveline Charles at **EvelineCharles Salons·Spas** *(1495 W. 11th Ave., 604-678-5666, evelinecharles.com)* added the "Get Stoned" treatment to the menu when she moved her spa/salon empire west with this first Vancouver location. The $320 treatment involves a hemp butter massage, a facial, a pedicure, and a hot rock massage, but no real tokes. If you feel strange in the elevator down, it could be because it has colour therapy lights in it.

Botox-to-Go

You've surely heard about *Botulinum Toxin*, known as Botox for short. It's cosmetic use was pioneered in 1987 by Vancouver's Dr Jean Carruthers, who uses it on herself. We even hear this entrepreneur comes armed with needles to her hairdresser's and administers treatments to him right there in the salon in exchange for her haircut. Or you can visit her clinic, **Dr. Jean Carruthers Aesthetic Facial Ophthalmology** *(740-943 W. Broadway, 604-730-6133, carruthers.net)*.

Manic Manicures

Aestheticians at **Absolute Spa Nails At Holt Renfrew** *(633 Granville St., 604-683-ASPA, absolutespa.com)* are trained in nail art by the celebrity manicurist who scores a perfect 10 with the Olsen twins, Sharon Stone, and Reese Witherspoon in *Legally Blonde*. They can paint tiny daisies on your digits or give you a French manicure with platinum tips.

The Most Expensive Spa in Vancouver

While it may be the most expensive in the city, the **Vida Wellness Spa at the Wall Centre Hotel** *(1088 Burrard St., 604-682-8432, vidawellness.com)* surpasses all others in service and décor. Experienced aestheticians prepare herbal tinctures in a lab-like environment and apply them in plush treatment rooms with natural light. It's owned by one of the tycoons behind the wildly successful dating website, *lavalife.com*.

Mobile Spa

The spa experts behind the **Absolute Spa at the Century** *(604-321-4VIP)* travel to film sets, celebrities' hotel rooms, and corporate retreats. They were recently dispatched to a South Main photography studio to paint J.Lo's nails the perfect shade of red for the cover of *Esquire* magazine.

Secret Stylist

He's unlisted and operates from an unmarked Yaletown loft, but **Leo** *(205-869 Beatty St., 604-331-6991)* is responsible for a great number of the attractive blonde do's downtown. Agents send their new models to Leo to redirect their look while all the other girls you'll see there just want to look cute for the clubs.

Photo: Solo

Smallest Hair Salon

The legendary Judah Down presides over **House of Envy** *(907 Richards. St., 604-687-4247, houseofenvy.ca)*, the tiniest salon in the city, though he's not jealous of the mega-salons as the name would suggest. At just 150 square feet, the salon looks more like a child's playhouse, but he's definitely not kidding around.

DISCOUNT HAIRSTYLING

Apprenticing hairdressers are required to do hundreds of roller sets to develop dexterity in their fingers. Have your hair styled for an evening at the **Future Hair Training Centre** *(2455 Cambie St., 604-709-6055, futurehairtraining.com)*, a busy hair-training studio for just $25. They also offer discounts on other hair services.

Tattoos & Body Piercing

Electro-Lady Lux
All-female tattoo artists.
876 Commercial Dr., 604-488-0284

First on Granville
1149 Granville St.,
604-682-3937 (piercings);
604-689-7789 (tattoos)

Mack's Leathers
A Vancouver institution. Girls can watch guys getting a Prince Albert, otherwise known as a penis piercing.
1043 Granville St., 604-688-6225, macksleathers.com

Next!
1068 Granville St., 604-684-6398, nextbody.com

Sacred Heart Tattoo & Body Piercing
3734 W. 10th Ave.; 725 Nelson St.; 1685 Davie St., 604-224-1149, sacredhearttattoo.ca

Photo: Solo

I used to date a tattoo artist. Turned out he was a real prick. But seriously, Vancouver has a long history of tattoo parlours: in the 1920s and '30s they were concentrated along Cordova and Hastings Street at Main — the area called skid row because they used to skid logged trees down the streets. The oldest tattoo shop in Canada is **West Coast Tattoo Parlour and Museum** (620 Davie St., 604-681-2049, westcoasttattoo.com). Owner Thomas Lockhart has clients who fly in from the U.S., Germany, and New Zealand just for his handiwork, which includes "sleeves" (a tattoo that extends from shoulder to wrist) and entire "body suits" which can take hundreds of hours, up to 10 years to complete, and cost around $50,000 (not to mention the investment in pain). To date, Lockhart has completed 300 sleeves and is working on his 31st bodysuit on a client from Korea. The shop has tattooed actress Christina Ricci with sweet peas on her lower back and gave rocker Tommy Lee a kimono tattoo, but they are sworn to secrecy about what they did for Jodie Foster. Documentary filmmaker Vince Hemingson has just completed a series for National Geographic called *The Vanishing Tattoo* (vanishingtattoo.com) that features artifacts from Westcoast Tattoo's museum, including old tattooing equipment (ouch!). Thomas and Vince say visitors to Vancouver like to get souvenir tattoos: Europeans love Haida designs and little maple leafs.

Now that local chefs keep referring to how they are cooking from the "local larder," why shouldn't you? You'll have to head to the islands or toward Squamish for more unique items such as sea urchins and black chanterelles but the Lower Mainland has its fair share if bounty if you're willing to hike a little. We can't tell you where to get food when conservation is an issue (like Dungeness crabs and snow geese), and we don't recommend walking around East Van picking the fruit from Italian families' homes (though it's very possible), but we're happy to share these treasure troves of local bounty where there's lots for everyone:

Wild blackberries: At Jericho Beach, half-way between the two concession stands, there's a large patch with paths like a Victorian hedge maze. Watch for bunny rabbits.

Wild mushrooms: Uncle George isn't pushing up daisies, he's pushing up edible mushrooms at Mountain View Cemetery at Fraser and 33rd, which is also where Joe Fortes is buried.

Huckleberries: These grow thick in the Brother's Creek trails at the top of the British Properties.

Wild blueberries: Free for the taking along the trails at the base of Hollyburn Mountain in late summer.

Bike Shops

Black Sheep Bikes

This new shop owned by a group of racers specializes in locally made bikes, clothing, and components by Vancouver's Spot Brand (spotbikes.com). Black Sheep is the first Canadian retailer to sell Maverick products (makers of high-end suspension mountain bikes). Check out the very hip Nirve cruiser bikes in the window.

4391 Main St., 604-709-3649, blacksheepbike.com

Our Community Bikes!

Why buy a brand-new bike when you can choose an inexpensive bike out front and let the staff customize it for you with new seat, tires, pedals, brakes, rat trap, kick stand, etc., then

Photo: Solo

test and adjust it to your size – all for around $200.
3283 Main St., 604-879-2453, pedalpower.org

Reckless Bikes

Just off the seawall near Granville Island, this spot happily provides free oil and air for your bike whenever you want it. Tune-ups are inexpensive and they don't try to upsell you on parts.
1810 Fir St., 604-831-2420; 110 Davie St., 604-648-2600, reckless.ca

The most distinctive store in Chinatown isn't Chinese, it's Italian. **Tosi Italian Food Import** *(1624 Main St., 604-681-5740)* is an Italian foods importer and grocery that has occupied the same spot since 1930, and has been in business in the area since 1913.

Stepping into the store is like stepping back in time. The ceiling is high, in the late 19th-century fashion, and shelves are tall and wooden, like those at North Vancouver's late and lamented Payne Hardware.

The fixtures are incredible: old incandescent lights that hang down on chains from the ceiling and are turned on by pulling a string, vintage marble-top counters with wooden bases, and ancient poles that were used to hang and tie string on parcels back in the days before tape.

The heritage look of the place is matched by the heritage look of the owner. Angelo Tosi is a spry septuagenarian who has spent most of his life at the store, literally (he grew up in an apartment above it).

Tosi is from the generation that identifies people by their ethnic background – ask him about his customers, and he'll talk about how the Chinese come for the pasta, the Germans come for the meat, and the French come for the cheese. Every square inch seems to be packed with goods for sale, whether it's olive oil, pasta, or exotic fare like sour cherry nectar from Slovenia. "It's good if you have the gout," he relates. "My doctor buys two dozen bottles at a time, and *he's a doctor.*"

The store dates to a time when Chinatown and Strathcona were half Italian. "The Italian part of Chinatown started from Georgia south," he recalls.

"Georgia, Union, Prior, and Atlantic." Angelo's father, Peter, immigrated to Canada in 1906, and opened P. Tosi & Co at 550 Union in 1913. After moving to its present location, Peter added a new building next door at 618 Main Street and linked the structures by a series of elegant Roman arches.

The outside was given a modest deco façade which makes them look like one building, but 624 Main is much older. It was probably built in 1895, and is the only remaining structure from the original Woodwards.

Most of the Italian community moved east in the 1950s and '60s, but Tosi remained. Peter passed away in 1973, leaving Angelo to run the business. "I promised my dad on his death bed I would never close the front door," he explains. And he hasn't.

cooking schools

Caren's Cooking School

1856 Pandora St., 604-255-5119

Dubrulle International Culinary & Hotel Institute of Canada

1522 W. 8th Ave., 604-738-3155, homechef.ca

Pacific Institute of Culinary Arts

1505 W. 2nd Ave., 604-734-4488, picularts.bc.ca

—

Bike Repairs

When your bike is feeling under the weather, take it to one of the following:

A-1 Cycle
3743 Main St., 604-876-2453

Bike Doctor Bicycle Shop
163 W. Broadway 604-873-2453;
1350 Commercial Dr.,
604-215-7433

Cyclepath
1421 W. Broadway, 604-737-2344

Urban Cycle
3578 E. Hastings St.,
604-294-2453

Photo: Solo

HEY DJ

Why hire a DJ when you can learn to be one yourself? **The Rhythm Institute** (604-696-0769, girlonwax.com) is Vancouver's first and only DJ school, operating out of **Boomtown Records** (1252 Burrard St., 604-893-8696.) Founded by Vancouver's DJ Leanne (catch her spinning at **Lotus Sound Lounge** and **Shine**), a half a dozen pro DJs provide one-on-one instruction in beat matching, pitch control, how to read vinyl grooves, and 10 kinds of scratches. The philosophy is to treat your turntables as an instrument – hence the term "turntablist" starting to replace DJ. Choose from musical styles like Break Beat, Trance, Progressive, and 2Step. They provide the equipment, the soundproof (thank you) room for practicing, and equipment for recording a demo CD. All you have to do is think up a groovy DJ name – sorry, Vinyl Ritchie is already taken. A six-week course is $350.

You Can Whip Their Cream But You Can't Beat Their Milk

When Queen Elizabeth is in Vancouver, there is only one type of milk she will drink: old-fashioned standard milk, where the milk and cream haven't been separated, from **Avalon Dairy** (5805 Wales St., 604-434-2434) in East Vancouver.

Avalon is the perfect place to get old-fashioned milk, because it's an old-fashioned business. The office is in a heritage farmhouse built around 1912, and every day about 300 customers drive in to pick up their dairy products at 5805 Wales.

Avalon still offers milk in glass bottles, and will even arrange for home delivery. It is also doing a booming business in organic milk: a few years ago, they started off with 25 certified organic cows; now they're up to 220.

The dairy was founded in 1906 when Jeremiah Crowley arrived in South Vancouver from Newfoundland. He was a stove-pipe moulder by trade, but he purchased a farm that came with six cows, so he went into the dairy business. (The name Avalon comes from the Avalon Peninsula in Newfoundland.)

The dairy was originally at Wales and Kingsway on land that is now Norquay Park; it moved to its current location in 1909. Once on the edge of nowhere, it's now in the middle of a residential neighbourhood. The dairy was threatened by a park board plan to redevelop a tree nursery next door into housing, but when a new, more sympathetic city council was voted in in 2002, the redevelopment proposal died.

chocolate & sweets

Bain's Chocolates & Candy

An expert chocolatier whose shop resides in a heritage house off Main Street.
151 E. 8th Ave., 604-876-5833

Chocolate Arts

Among other delights, try the dark chocolate medallions designed by First Nations artist Robert Davidson.
2037 W. 4th Ave., 604-739-0475, chocolatearts.com

Le Chocolat Belge Daniel Ltd.

Chocolate delights with an emphasis on freshness.
1105 Robson St. and four other locations, 604-688-9624, danielchocolates.com

Dutch Girl Chocolates

Dutch treats made from world-famous Belgian chocolate.
1002 Commercial Dr., 604-251-3221

Photo: Solo

Party Caterers

Bon Manger Café
Culinary influences span from Bombay to Brittany at this Kitsilano crêperie that travels.
2670 W. Broadway, 604-738-2596

Culinary Capers Catering
The very best in the city — bar none.
1545 W. 3rd Ave., 604-875-0122, culinarycapers.com

Chef's Table
Cordon Bleu-trained personal chef Russell Rootman is a good bet for an haute cocktail party with a healthy budget.
604-709-3044

Fabulous Foods Catering
Les Dames D'Escoffier dame Susan Meister delivers custom-tailored dinner and cocktail soirées from her HQ inside the city's culinary temple, the Gourmet Warehouse.
1856 Pandora St., 604-926-6624/ 604-253-3022

Lesley Stowe Fine Foods
Allow Lesley Stowe to handle larger, more formal dinners or wedding receptions. Skilled pastry hands mean that you can have your wedding cake … and actually eat it too.
1780 W. 3rd Ave., 604-731-3663, lesleystowe.com

Maurya

This Indian restaurant is home to the only portable Tandoori oven in the city.
1643 W. Broadway, 604-742-0622, mauryaindiancuisine.com

Out to Lunch Catering

Satisfied customers include Governor General Adrienne Clarkson (and 400 friends) at a Chan Centre reception.
241 Union St., 604-681-7177, otlcatering.com

Rodney's Oyster House

Let proprietor Stafford Lumley get your next party started with a crab or lobster bake and an oyster shucking station. After all, says Lumley, "Oysters are the original party animal."
1228 Hamilton St., 604-609-0080, letsgofordinner.com

Tamarind Tree Catering

Chef Dora Ho can sometimes be found at swish art openings where her warm, pan-Asian creations are as tastefully turned-out as the crowd.
604-716-5156, dora@chef.net

Vera's Burger Shack

Kids invited? Co-proprietor Gerald Tritt will show up, oversized grill in tow, and serve up the city's best burgers (chicken, beef, buffalo, and veggie) with all the necessary condiments.
1935 Cornwall Ave., 604-228-8372, verasburgershack.com

House of Brussels Chocolate Factory Outlet

Photo: Solo

A great resource for both chocoholics and chocolate buyers, this outlet sells seconds and bulk chocolate at anywhere from 10 to 50 percent off.
208-750 Terminal Ave., 604-713-8052

Purdy's Chocolate Factory Tours

Charlie aside, what child is not deeply fascinated with chocolate factories? Don your hair net and take them on a free tour, then load up on discounted seconds at the factory store ($11 per pound). Here's another little secret: if you've ever walked down 7th Avenue at Spruce, you may have noticed a tiny little park (0.07 hectares) called **Choklit Park**. It was built by the founder of Purdy's for neighbourhood children, right beside the original factory, which is the brick building (now condos) on the east side of the park. Locals used to congregate at the park to drink in the smell of chocolate, before the factory moved to its current 57,000-square-foot location in 1986.
2777 Kingsway Ave., 604-454-2700, purdys.com

Sen5es

Celebrated German pastry chef Thomas Haas has been a guest on *Martha Stewart Living* and appears in the book *The Fourth Star*, about New York's famous Restaurant Daniel where he once worked. He's still winning almost every American dessert award out there since his move to this Vancouver location in the Crowne Plaza Hotel Georgia. What few know, however, is that Haas also works nights at his own North Shore chocolate factory that supplies Sen5es.
801 W. Georgia St., 604-633-0138, senses.ca

patisseries & bakeries

Anna's Cake House

Got an enemy? Give a picture of him to this bakery. They will reproduce the picture on rice paper atop a cake so you can eat him for lunch.
606 E. Broadway, 604-876-ANNA, annas.ca

Artisan Bake Shoppe

The French baguettes made from organic flour are worth the trip alone. Many of the city's top restaurants serve them.
127 Lonsdale Ave, North Vancouver, 604-990-3530

Cupcakes

Cupcakes make the perfect hostess gift, especially if you ask for your order to be placed in the "Pretty in Pink" box that comes with a variety of ribbon colours ($1.50 extra). Tiny versions on a 3-tier stand are great for parties, as are the lopsided Dr Seuss cupcake towers for children's birthdays, or the more refined towers for weddings. Look for black "Puck Cakes" during hockey playoffs and rainbow "Pride Cakes" for the annual gay pride parade. For a fashionista's birthday, a box of the chocolate "Cocoa Chanel" cupcakes would fit just right.
1116 Denman St., 604-974-301, cupcakesonline.com

Fratelli

Real Italian pizza dough that you defrost and roll out is available on request for just $1.50.
1795 Commercial Dr., 604-255-8926, fratellibakery.com

Glacé Frozen Cakery

Ice cream cakes come with your choice of edible, rice paper pictures for the kids.
3073 W. Broadway, 604-733-7889

ICE CREAM

Mario's Gelati
400 flavours, including wacky ones like wasabi, garlic, durian fruit, and a surprisingly popular bright blue version called Viagra.
88 E. 1st Ave., 604-879-9411, mariosgelati.com

Designer Groceries

The Gourmet Warehouse

When your dessert recipe calls for lustre dust, liquid sugar cane, and sheet gelatin, look first at this out-of-the way warehouse.
1856 Pandora St., 604-253-3022, gourmetwarehouse.ca

Mad About Food

The "Over the Top" gift basket here ($250) comes in a hand-woven reed basket. The picnic basket comes with a Frisbee, and there's a bean counter basket for your accountant come tax time.
2836 W. 4th Ave., 604-736-2510, madaboutfood.net

Meinhardt Fine Foods

Italy and France are the primary culinary influences found on the chic metal shelves. One well-heeled customer was seen ordering six of everything from the legendary deli: did her dinner party guests ever know?
3002 Granville St., 604-732-4405, meinhardt.com

La Baguette et L'Echalote Bakery

Dinner party secret: stock your freezer with the par-baked baguettes for crusty, warm bread in 10 minutes.
1680 Johnston St., Granville Island, 604-684-1351, labaguettebakery.com

Liberty Bakery

Specialty breads are made in honour of the baker's eighty-year-old wife, Liberty.
3699 Main St., 604-709-9999

Patisserie Lebeau

Olivier Lebeau uses imported French ovens to achieve that authentic Left Bank taste.
1728 W. 2nd Ave., 604 731 3528

Siegel's Bagels

Chewy, Montreal-style bagels cooked in a wood-fired oven. The Cornwall Avenue location is open twenty-four hours.
1883 Cornwall Ave., 604-737-8151; Granville Island Public Market, seigelsbagels.com

Terra Breads

Kits commuters stop in for their favourite bread sliced and served with preserves and coffee for just $2.25.
2380 W. 4th Ave., 604-736-1838; Granville Island Public Market

Uprising Breads Bakery

A popular spot for seven-grain gourmets.
1697 Venables St., 604-254-5635, uprisingbreads.com

unusual grocery stores

Les Amis du Fromage
Cheese platters from some of the city's most expensive restaurants come from here, so why not go directly to the source? Mother-and-daughter team Alice and Allison will help you select from their 400 cheeses, or just drop off your empty platter and let them arrange it all.
1752 W. 2nd Ave., 604-732-4218, buycheese.com

A. Bosa Foods & Co.
Head to the freezer for hand-made sacchetti pasta, to the deli for cured meats, then to the shelves for staples like Italian coffee, olive oil, and quality tinned tuna.
562 Victoria Dr., 604-253-5578

European Specialty Warehouse
On the edge of Chinatown, enter through the loading bay of this warehouse and find packaged goods from the old country at a sharp discount. Finnish crackers and syrups, Danish biscuits, French cheeses, and German mineral water are the best deals here. There is an entire room devoted exclusively to chocolate. Limited hours.
220 Prior St., 604-688-9528

Photo: Solo

Fujiya
This Japanese supermarket features butterflied shrimp for sushi, black cod marinated in sake, scads of dried seaweed, lots of salty snacks, and fresh sushi and sashimi. An impressive selection of miso paste and nori. Do not be alarmed by the electronic greeting as you go through the doors.
912 Clark Dr. and other locations, 604-251-3711, seanspot.com

ALL THINGS GRAPE AND SMALL

You may have noticed that your local liquor store carries 100 types of bottled Bacardi cocktails but barely any quality B.C. wines. So has **Liberty Wine Merchants** *(4583 W. 10th Ave., 604-224-8050, libertywinemerchants.com).* Brothers Paul and Robert Simpson carry hard-to-find bottles and vintages, especially from small estate wineries who don't produce enough to supply a large chain. Staff at the West 10th Avenue store, as well as the store's other four locations, are extremely well-trained, and unlike government stores, they are actually open at times when you want to buy wine — like Sundays and holidays.

Tea Shops

O-Cha Tea Bar

Exotic Eastern blends like Orchid Oolong, Bombay Spice, or Rose Petal tea.
1116 Homer St., 604-633-3929, o-chatea.com

Tearoom T

This local company's teas are served at Ritz-Carlton Hotels.
1568 W. Broadway, 604-730-8390, tealeaves.com

Herbal Republic

Sleek and modern, check out the designer teapots too.
2680 W. Broadway, 604-732-1732, herbalrepublic.com

INFUZE Tea House

Sells over 50 kinds of tea, including Matcha, a 900-year-old green tea touted to be the healthiest beverage on Earth.
870 W. Cordova St., 604-688-3170, infuzeteahouse.com

Ten Ren Tea & Ginseng Co.

In Chinatown, it offers an infinite variety of green and oolong teas.
550 Main St., 604-684-1566

The Lobster Man

Choose your own lobster, crab, sea urchin, mussels, clams, prawns, scallops, and 10 varieties of oysters. Lobster and crab can be cooked at no extra charge by the staff, who wear hip waders and gumboots.
1807 Mast Tower Rd., Granville Island, 604-687-4531, lobsterman.com

Mitra's Bulk Food and Deli

A destination for pistachios, tiny pickles, basmati rice, dry meat rubs for kebabs, flower-infused cooking waters, and sweet lemons used in Persian cooking.
1451 Clyde Ave., West Vancouver, 604-913-0660

Parthenon Importers

At this Greek market, look for good deals in the deli (nine types of feta, 20 types of olives), and on items such as olive oil soap, tinned Mediterranean legumes, and salt-preserved anchovies.
3080 W. Broadway, 604-733-4191

Punjab Food Centre

Authentic Indian ingredients such as tandoori spices (and stainless steel spice containers), garam masala, naan, and brightly-coloured sugar-coated fennel seeds.
6635 Main St., 604-322-5502

Photo: Solo

T & T Supermarket

Even if chicken ovaries aren't on the top of your shopping list, at this Chinese supermarket chain you'll find live seafood (including, at times, eels and turtles), extremely fresh produce, frozen dim sum, and game birds like duck, quail, and squab.
179 Keefer Place and other locations, 604-899-8836, tnt-supermarket.com

Windsor Packing Co.

With prices half of what you would find on Granville Island and trendy cuts such as lamb shanks, double cut pork chops, and short ribs, you've just discovered yet another reason to visit Main Street.
4110 Main St., 604-872-5635

index

index

index

index

index

index

index

index

JOHN MACKIE has been uncovering the unknown Vancouver for twenty-five years at the *Vancouver Sun*, the *Georgia Straight*, and *Vancouver* magazine, where he has covered rock music, heritage issues, and culture. The highlight of his career was being called a "treasure" in *Frank* magazine.

Born with a last name that would henceforth have her pegged as bookish, SARAH REEDER is one of the rare species known as a fifth-generation Vancouverite. She followed in her grandmother's footsteps by attending both Kitsilano Secondary School and UBC, where she completed an MA in Political Science. She has since worked as associate editor of *Vancouver* magazine and is currently the Western Editor of *Vancouver FASHION Magazine* and its teen version, *FASHION18*. She is the great, great granddaughter of Vancouver's first bookbinder, Gustav Roedde.